Sport Worlds

A Sociological Perspective

Joseph Maguire, PhD
Loughborough University

Grant Jarvie, PhD
University of Stirling

Louise Mansfield, MSc
Canterbury Christ Church College

Joe Bradley, PhD
University of Stirling

Library of Congress Cataloging-in-Publication Data

Sport worlds : a sociological perspective / Joseph Maguire ... [et al.].
   p. cm.
  Includes bibliographical references (p.) and index.
  ISBN 0-88011-972-1
   1. Sports--Sociological aspects. 2. Nationalism and sports. I. Maguire, Joseph A.,
1956-
  GV706.5 .S73885 2002
  306.4'83--dc21

2001051661

ISBN: 0-88011-972-1

Developmental Editor: Myles Schrag; **Assistant Editor:** Jennifer L. Davis; **Copyeditor:** Patricia L. MacDonald; **Proofreader:** Red Inc.; **Indexer:** Marie Rizzo; **Graphic Designer:** Stuart Cartwright; **Graphic Artist:** Tara Welsch; **Photo Manager:** Leslie A. Woodrum; **Cover Designer:** Kristin Darling; **Printer:** United Graphics

Printed in the United States of America   10   9   8   7   6   5   4   3   2   1

Human Kinetics
Web site: www.humankinetics.com

United States: Human Kinetics
P.O. Box 5076, Champaign, IL 61825-5076
800-747-4457
e-mail: humank@hkusa.com

Canada: Human Kinetics
475 Devonshire Road Unit 100, Windsor, ON N8Y 2L5
800-465-7301 (in Canada only)
e-mail: orders@hkcanada.com

Europe: Human Kinetics
Units C2/C3 Wira Business Park, West Park Ring Road, Leeds LS16 6EB, United Kingdom
+44 (0) 113 278 1708
e-mail: hk@hkeurope.com

Australia: Human Kinetics
57A Price Avenue, Lower Mitcham, South Australia 5062
08 8277 1555
e-mail: liahka@senet.com.au

New Zealand: Human Kinetics
P.O. Box 105-231, Auckland Central
09-523-3462
e-mail: hkp@ihug.co.nz

CONTENTS

Preface   ix
Acknowledgements   xi
Introduction: Towards a Sociology of Sport Worlds   xiii

Part I Sport Inside the World   I

Global Systems and Processes

Chapter I   Sport and Globalisation   3

Debating Point: How Do We Make Sense of Global Processes?   6
Studying Global Sport: Issues, Questions and Dimensions   7
Globalisation and the Making of Modern Sport   9
The Sportisation of English Pastimes   10
Case Study: Sport, Gender Relations and the Global Order   13
Gender and the Contemporary Global Sport Order   15
Power, Citizenship and the Governance of Global Sport   17
Debating Point: Who Is Winning the Global Game?   18
Power, Cultural Struggles and Global Diversity   21
Summary   22
Key Terms and Concepts   23
Review Questions   23
Projects   24

Chapter 2   Sport, Labour and Migration   25

Initial Questions   26
Case Study: Men's World Cup Finals, France 1998   29
Debating Point: Why Recruit and Why Move?   32
Disparities in Sports Migration   36
Reactions to and in the Host Culture   37
Debating Point: Is Importing Labour Good or Bad
   for Local Player Development?   39
Summary   43
Key Terms and Concepts   44
Review Questions   44
Projects   44

Chapter 3   Sport, Media and Society   47

Growth and Development of Mediated Sport   48
Towards an Understanding of Media Sport:
   The Media Sport Complex   50
Debating Point: Does Sport Depend on the Media?   52
Power, Control and Ownership in Media Sport   54
Debating Point: Does Media Sport Reflect
   and Reinforce Dominant Social Values?   57
Race and Ethnic Relations in Media Sport   58
Gender Relations in Media Sport   60
Case Study: Formula One Racing
   and Media Marketing Relations   62
Summary   66
Key Terms and Concepts   67
Review Questions   67
Projects   68

Global Issues Across a Changing World

Chapter 4   Sport, Politics and Democracy   69

Debating Point: Should Sport Be Used for Political Purposes?   70
The Changing Politics of Sport   71
Case Study: Swedish Athletes Test the Swedish Tax System   74
The Changing Nature of Democracy   76
Case Study: Danish Sport As the 'Third Way'   76
Sport, Privilege and Democracy   78
Summary   80
Key Terms and Concepts   81
Review Questions   81
Projects   82

Chapter 5   Sport, the Environment and
              'Green' Issues   83

Debating Point: Is Sport a Threat to the Environment?   85
Sport and Sustainable Development   86
Debating Point: How 'Green' Is Sport?   88
Case Study: Environmental Issues
   and the Global Anti-Golf Movement   92
Summary   95
Key Terms and Concepts   96
Review Questions   96
Projects   97

**Chapter 6   Sport, Communitarianism
and Social Capital**   **99**

Communitarianism As Social Theory and Political Practice   101
Debating Point: Is Sport Good for the Community?   104
Mutual Sport in Demutualised Communities   105
Sport and Civil Society   107
Case Study: Sport, Civil Society and Community
    in Denmark   107
Sport and Social Capital   109
Case Study: The Decline of Social Capital
    in the United States   111
Debating Point: Does Sport Promote Social Inclusion
    and Social Capital?   111
Summary   112
Key Terms and Concepts   113
Review Questions   113
Projects   114

Part II Inside the Worlds of Sport   II5

Local and National Communities

Chapter 7   Sport, Place and Space   **II7**

Case Study: The Development of Soccer in Britain   119
The Place of Sport in Nations, States and Society   121
Historical Changes to Sport   122
Debating Point: Has Sport Always Provided
    the Same Functions?   122
Televised Sport in Time and Space   123
Sport As Consumption   125
Debating Point: Has the Media Corrupted Sport?   126
The Context of Culture in Time and Space   127
Summary   129
Key Terms and Concepts   130
Review Questions   130
Projects   131

Chapter 8   Sport, Civic and Ethnic Passions   **I33**

Case Study: The Gaelic Athletic Association
    and Ethnic Identity   135
Sporting Passions   136
Sport and the Imagined Community   137

Debating Point: What Are the Negative Features
    Linking Passion to Sport?   138
Sport and Ethnic Identities   139
Race and Sport   140
Debating Point: Is Sport Symptomatic of Society?   141
Sport and Identity   143
Summary   144
Key Terms and Concepts   145
Review Questions   145
Projects   145

Chapter 9   Sport in the Making of Nations   147

Case Study: Catalans and Basques Attempt
    to Go It Alone in World Sport   149
Nationalism, Sport and the Making of Nations   151
Nations, Nationalism and Identities   154
Debating Point: Should FIFA Bestow Nationhood
    Upon Emerging Nations?   156
Nationalism: What Is It?   156
Debating Point: Do Global Sporting Events
    Promote Nationalism?   158
The Future of Nationalism Through Sport   159
Summary   160
Key Terms and Concepts   160
Review Questions   161
Projects   161

Personal Troubles and Everyday Experiences

Chapter 10   Sporting Subcultures   163

Case Study: Soccer Hooliganism As Subculture   166
Sport As a Social and Cultural Product   168
Socialisation and Sport   169
Debating Point: Are Sporting Subcultures Important?   170
Sporting Journeys of Difference and Distinction   172
Subcultural and Peripheral Activities   173
Debating Point: Are Subcultural Developments Responses
    to Cultural Domination?   174
The Transformation From Subcultural to Cultural   176
Summary   178
Key Terms and Concepts   178
Review Questions   179
Projects   179

Chapter II   Sport, Emotions and Societies   I8I

Debating Point: Are Embodied Emotions Physiologically
    Determined or Socially Constructed?   183
Performing Embodied Emotions
    in the Sporting Pleasure Dome   185
Case Study: Doing Painful Embodied Sport Work   188
Significant Excitement, Sport and Embodied Emotions   190
Debating Point: Are Sporting Pleasures False Needs
    or Genuine Desires?   192
Towards a Sociological Model of Sport and the Emotions   195
Summary   197
Key Terms and Concepts   197
Review Questions   198
Projects   198

Chapter I2   Sport, Gender and Social Relations   2OI

Sport As Male, Manly and Masculine   203
Debating Point: Does Sport Reflect and Reinforce
    Traditional Gender Relations?   205
Shaping Up to Genderhood   206
Sport, Images and Gender Identities   208
Debating Point: Can Sport Challenge
    Traditional Gender Relations?   211
Gender, Women's Rights and Cultural Differences   212
Case Study: Women, Tennis and the Media   214
Summary   216
Key Terms and Concepts   217
Review Questions   217
Projects   217

Conclusion   219
References   221
Index   231
About the Authors   241

PREFACE

Sport worlds are contested arenas, shaped by struggles both on and off the field. Our concern here is to highlight the ways in which such competitions are contoured and shaped more by what happens off-field than on. These off-field struggles focus on questions of what is possible, permissible and pleasurable in sport worlds. Because of the uneven distribution of power resources available to different groups, more dominant definitions tend to push alternative views to the margins of acceptability. As a result, the views and actions of less powerful groups become residual features of sport worlds. Nevertheless, such struggles are never complete, and new, emergent features and views of sport worlds surface.

Established and outsider groups use a variety of means to compete over the character and meaning of sport worlds. These means include economic and political resources, but knowledge is also a power resource. That is, whatever other resources are available to people at any given time or situation, an understanding of how things 'really are' is necessary for grasping their position within sport worlds. This book attempts to paint things as they really are and, as such, acts as a knowledge resource for students. On this basis, they can begin to critically examine the relative merits of dominant, emergent and residual views on what is possible, permissible and pleasureable in sport worlds. And, thus, students can begin to decide 'whose side they are on'! We hope, then, that this book will enable students to take more control of their involvement and experience in sport worlds—as participants, spectators and consumers.

As sociologists examining sport worlds, we seek to understand the co-existence of co-operation and confrontation, power and control. In doing so, we trace the intimate and extensive relationships between sport and other social worlds.

This book is divided into two broad parts. Part I examines sport inside the world. It is divided into two sections that focus on global systems and processes, and global issues across a changing world. We examine a range of global systems, processes and issues that contour and shape sport worlds. The networks, boundaries, conventions and challenges that characterise sport worlds are examined. Attention is given to issues such as migration, the environment and politics. In short, we emphasise how sport is embedded within the world. Part II focuses inside the worlds of sport and involves sub-global issues. It is divided into two sections that examine local and national communities, and personal troubles and everyday experiences. In these mundane or everyday worlds, the significance of sport in the emotional and social lives of people is examined. Attention is paid to questions of gender, place, space and identities. Thus, we emphasise how the worlds of sport are embedded in the lives of people. Through these two distinct but interconnected parts, we see how sport worlds enter our lives from different directions. They are an integral part of the global order, of which societies are a part, as well as part of our local communities, spaces, places and individual identities. Each chapter also contains sets of key terms, review questions and suggested projects. All are designed both to enhance the students' sociological knowledge base and imagination and to allow the tutor to engage students in debate and focused assignments.

Sociologists of sport investigate the values of dominant, emergent and residual cultures and subcultures in sport. They explore how the exercise of power and the stratified nature of societies place limits, and create possibilities, for people's involvement and success in sport as performers, officials, spectators, workers or consumers. They seek not only to contribute to social scientific knowledge, but also to change sport worlds with an eye to a more equitable distribution of power and resources. Research seeks to 'debunk' popular myths about sport, critically appraise the actions of the more powerful groups, and inform social policy towards sport. Sociologists have done this in two broad ways. In relation to established groups, sociologists have sought to influence decision-making by offering expert advice to government agencies on areas such as violence and sport. Yet, they also act as advocates for outsider groups, who argue for athletes' rights and responsibilities, and who challenge inequalities, particularly with respect to access, resources and status within sport worlds. Sociologists also achieve their goals through teaching—hence we suggest that knowledge is a power resource, for citizens in general, and students in particular. We hope that the ideas contained in this book are a resource for other teachers, but also for the students who read it. That is, armed with what they will learn here, students will be better able to challenge the everyday conventions and practices of sport worlds. Through a more informed understanding of sport worlds, humans may yet come together to develop strategies that help make such worlds less wasteful of lives and resources and, in doing so, help build a more humane, and just, set of sport worlds. We shall see.

ACKNOWLEDGEMENTS

We would like to thank our partners, families and friends for their support during the writing of this book. In addition, we would like to acknowledge the resources provided by the universities of Loughborough and Stirling and Canterbury Christ Church University College. We also wish to record our thanks to Rainer Martens, Myles Schrag and Jennifer Davis at Human Kinetics for their commitment to the project. The reviewers also provided valuable insights, but, as always, we are responsible for the final product. We hope we have met some of their concerns. Finally, this book would not have been completed but for the support and technical skills of Barbara Kettlewell—thank you, thank you, thank you.

INTRODUCTION: TOWARDS A SOCIOLOGY OF SPORT WORLDS

Sport As a Social Product

Sport is a social product. There, in beginning this book, we have dared to write these words! In doing so, we are confronting one of the more pervasive taboos that exist: the denial that sport, like art and music, is deeply embedded in cultural processes. This book attempts to show how the production, distribution and reception of sport can best be understood from a sociological perspective. In taking this approach, the book draws its inspiration not just from the sociology of sport, but from the sociology of art as well. Works by Howard Becker (1982/1984), Pierre Bourdieu (1990), Norbert Elias (1991/1994) and Janet Wolff (1981) on the social production of art provide important insights that inform how we view the task of understanding sport worlds. Let us explain.

In her analysis of art as a social product, Wolff confronts 'the romantic and mystical notion of art as the creation of "genius", transcending existence, society and time' (1981). A similar set of mystical notions exists in the sports world. That is, the thrilling performances of athletes, in golf, tennis or soccer for example, are more often than not attributed either to genetic makeup or to some notion of genius that is beyond the range of mere mortals. Emphasis is thus placed on the quality of the performance, which is explained in terms of biomedical properties or uniquely individual creativity. Individualistic and/or behavioural explanations hold sway.

Yet, such explanations provide a very limited grasp of the genesis of performances. And, in addition, they tell us nothing about the stage on which the 'act' is performed, nor the theatre in which the 'play' takes place. As Wolff observes with regard to art:

> All action, including creative or innovative action, arises in the complex conjunction of numerous structural determinants and conditions. Any concept of 'creativity' which denies this is metaphysical, and cannot be sustained. But the corollary of this line of argument is not that human agents are simply programmed

> robots, or that we need not take account of their biographical,
> existential or motivational aspects .... I will try to show how prac-
> tical activity and creativity are in a mutual relation of interdepen-
> dence with social structures. (Wolff 1981)

We needn't deny the creativity of the athlete, but we must take into
account the social structures within which such creativity is expressed.
Thus, like art, in accounting for sport we must emphasise the social and
probe the production, distribution and reception of athletic performances. Let us explain this point further. While the marvellous performances of Tiger Woods or Martina Hingis are very different from that of
Wolfgang Amadeus Mozart, they are all perceived as uniquely gifted
individuals, exceptions who stand outside of general social structures.
However, the products of their brilliance, and the recognition and
reception of their performances, are deeply connected to social processes. The perceived individualism of genius is thus best understood
through a sociological perspective. Writing about Mozart, Elias makes
this point very clear:

> Mozart's individual fate, his destiny as a unique human being and
> thus also a unique artist, was heavily influenced by his social
> situation, the dependence of a musician of his time on the court
> aristocracy. We can see here how difficult it is to elucidate—as a
> biographer, for example, tries to do—the problems individuals
> encounter in their lives, no matter how incomparable an individual's
> personality or achievements may be, unless one has mastered the
> craft of the sociologist. (Elias 1991/1994)

In emphasising the social construction, or cultural making of sport,
we do not seek to destroy the notion of genius, or downplay the
creativity, expressiveness and existential experiences that are part of the
sports world. This is why Elias points us in the direction of developing
a model that emphasises both individual biography and social context
to make sense of the lives and performances of people such as Mozart,
Woods or Hingis.

Being a competent or accomplished social actor and having mastery
over social practices, such as art or sport, involves having a 'feel' for the
task at hand. This feel for the game is developed and maintained by what
Elias and Bourdieu term *habitus*, or what we might more commonly
think of as 'second nature'. In other words, sporting performances are
abilities so well honed through practice that they become habituated
and part of our second nature. We learn to use aspects of them intuitively.
In art and in sport, the quality of performances also swings on a 'hinge'
between the learned and the unlearned (Elias 1987). The saying 'practice
makes perfect' refers to the way in which our unlearned abilities are
fused with our learned attributes. In more able performers, this process

is so well integrated that performances appear 'natural'. Yet, these performances are, in reality, the product of both long-term socialisation processes and the sport worlds that enable or constrain such learning. Addressing this link between the learned and unlearned in producing a feel for the game, and the social game of life, Bourdieu observed:

> The habitus as the feel for the game is the social game embodied and turned into a second nature. Nothing is simultaneously freer and more constrained than the action of a good player. He [sic] quite naturally materialises at just the place the ball is about to fall, as if the ball were in command of him—but by that very fact, he is in command of the ball. The habitus, as society written into the body, into the biological individual, enables the infinite number of acts of the game—written into the game as possibilities and objective demands—to be produced. (Bourdieu 1990)

To reaffirm: Sport is a social product. The athlete's performance involves a blend of the learned and the unlearned. However, the practical activity of the athlete is not limited simply to the level of the individual. The production, distribution and reception of sporting performances are very much social processes. To fully grasp what we mean by these social processes, let us return to the parallels between sport and art. Howard Becker's work on the social production of art draws our attention to the social patterns that lie behind the perceived individualism of artists and their work. Indeed, the title of our book reflects his work, *Art Worlds*, and his insights dovetail well with those of Bourdieu, Elias and Wolff. Let us try to elaborate on the insights Becker provides and then show how these apply to *Sport Worlds*.

Sport As Collective Activity

In examining 'art as collective activity', Becker (1982/1984) highlights how a specific artistic expression is located within a network of suppliers, performers, dealers, agents, managers, critics and consumers. These networks are marked by a series of conventions, taboos, power struggles and commodity chains. Each is essential to the operation of the network and the production of art. Sport performances are no different. Writing of art, Becker could quite easily have been referring to sport:

> Each kind of person who participates in the making of art works, then, has a specific bundle of tasks to do. Though the allocation of tasks to people is, in an important sense, arbitrary—it could have been done differently and is supported only by the agreement of all or most of the other participants—it is not therefore easy to change. The people involved typically regard the division of tasks

as quasi-sacred, as 'natural' and inherent in the equipment and the medium.... Every art, then, rests on an extensive division of labor. (Becker 1982/1984)

Art worlds, then, consist of those people whose activities are necessary to the production of art. In examining how these people interact, Becker refers to the 'co-ordination of activities', the use of 'conventional under-standings embodied in common practice' and the 'established network of co-operative links among participants.'

Becker's idea of networks links very well with how Elias views the set of interdependencies that contour and shape social, and sporting, life. Using dance, a performing art, as his example, Elias writes:

> The image of the mobile figurations of interdependent people on a dance floor perhaps makes it easier to imagine states, cities, families, and also capitalist, communist, and feudal systems as figurations. By using this concept we can eliminate the antithesis, resting finally on different values and ideals, immanent today in the use of words 'individual' and 'society'. One can certainly speak of a dance in general, but no one will imagine a dance as a structure outside the individual or as a mere abstraction. The same dance figurations can certainly be danced by different people; but without a plurality of reciprocally oriented and dependent individuals, there is no dance. (Elias 1939/1978)

The same analysis can be applied to sport. Commenting on this, Elias and Dunning observed:

> In order to play a game, people group themselves in specific ways. As the game runs its course, they continually regroup themselves in a manner similar to the ways in which groups of dancers regroup themselves in the course of a dance. The initial figuration from which the players start changes into other figurations of players in a continuous movement. It is to this continuous movement of the figuration of players to which we refer when we use the term 'game-pattern'. (Elias and Dunning 1986)

Thus, following Becker and Elias, we understand sport worlds as networks, or figurations, of interdependent groups of people. Adding to this understanding is the work of Johan Goudsblom. In his book, *Sociology in the Balance* (1977), Goudsblom identifies four key 'points of departure' that are necessary to guide any sociological enquiry. These points can be used to sensitise us to the networks that contour sport worlds: (1) human beings are interdependent; their lives evolve in, and are significantly shaped by, the social figurations they form with each other; (2) these figurations are continually in flux, undergoing changes of different orders—some quick and ephemeral, others slower but perhaps more lasting; (3) the long-term developments taking place in human social figurations have been and continue to be largely unplanned and unforeseen; and (4) the development of human knowledge takes place within human figurations, and forms one important aspect of overall development.

These points of departure provide some general lines of orientation to make sense of sport worlds, within which Becker's insights into art worlds help us to focus on the specific case of sport. For Becker, art worlds have five distinguishing characteristics, the first of which—as we have already discussed—is the role of networks in their production. Second, the boundaries that surround art worlds are permeable—it is difficult to discern what is art and what is not without reference to other worlds. And what is defined as art is dependent on these other social worlds. Third, while the people involved in art worlds try to distinguish their world from others, they too have 'intimate and extensive relations' with people from those other worlds. Fourth, art worlds are sustained by conventions, but innovations and challenges also occur. Finally, art worlds have degrees of relative autonomy from interference by other groups and social worlds. While Becker overemphasises the co-operative dimension of art worlds (or, conversely, downplays the power struggles that make up such worlds), he effectively questions the extent to which artistic expressions are free and autonomous.

Applying Becker's insights to sport worlds, we see that sport is a form of collective action, involving a host of different people, connected in particular networks, and creating particular forms of sport products and performances. In this book, we seek to highlight the networks, or interdependencies, involved in sport worlds. Attention is paid to the 'conventional understandings' that mark sport subcultures and govern sport practices. And, like Becker, we critically examine the extent to which sport worlds are free from the political and economic context in which they are situated. In the 'established networks' linking sport worlds to other social worlds, we focus both on the process of co-operation and, unlike Becker, on the process of confrontation. Co-operation and confrontation, such as that between allies and foes, characterise the networks that shape sport worlds.

In comparison with art, sport might seem unimportant or mundane. These are value judgements. As in the study of art, sociologists do not seek to make aesthetic judgements. Rather, our concern as social scientists is to discern the significance of sport worlds. In political, economic, cultural and social terms, sport worlds are highly significant. This is not to suggest that the mundane isn't significant (Simmel 1978). Indeed, it is the very everyday ordinariness of sport that makes it so significant, so deeply intertwined with the workings of society. As sociologists examining sport, we are just like our colleagues who examine art, religion, medicine and work—we are all studying how people cope with the problems of interdependence.

An Invitation to the Sociology of Sport

Before moving to an outline of the specific features of the book, we want to say something about the aims of the sociology of sport, and how its exponents seek to intervene in sport worlds. Maguire and Donnelly (2000) have recently outlined several aims for this subdiscipline. Sociologists of sport seek to critically examine the role, function and meaning of sport in the lives of people and the societies they form. In addition, they attempt to describe and explain the emergence and diffusion of sport over time and across different societies. In doing so, they identify the processes of socialisation into, through, and out of modern sport. Sociologists of sport investigate the values and norms of dominant, emergent and residual cultures and subcultures in sport. Additionally, they explore how the exercise of power and the stratified nature of societies place limits, and create possibilities, for people's involvement and success in sport as performers, officials, spectators, workers or consumers. These aims have guided our choice of the subject matter that forms this book.

Sociologists of sport contribute both to the knowledge base of sociology more generally, and also to the formation of policy that seeks to ensure that global sport processes are less wasteful of lives and resources. Sociologists of sport can be found in both mainstream sociology departments and physical education. In the context of sport sciences, sociologists of sport seek to generate knowledge that will contribute to human development as opposed to performance efficiency. That is, they seek to critically examine the costs, benefits, limits and possibilities of modern sport for all those involved, rather than focus solely on the performance efficiency of elite athletes. Those sociologists working within sociology departments examine sport in the same way they would examine religion, law or medicine—to highlight aspects of the general human condition.

Sociology of sport, then, seeks not only to contribute to its parent discipline, but also to change sport worlds. With respect to the latter goal, research seeks to 'debunk' popular myths about sport, critically appraise the actions of the more powerful groups involved in sport, and inform social policy towards sport. As Maguire and Donnelly (2000) argue, sociologists of sport over three decades have sought to intervene in sport worlds in several ways. They have offered expert advice to government agencies, public enquiries and commission reports on areas such as drugs, violence and health education. In addition, sociologists of sport have acted as advocates for athletes' rights and responsibilities. Researchers have sought to provide knowledge for groups who seek to challenge inequalities of gender, class, ethnicity, age and disability, particularly with respect to access, resources and status. More broadly, sociologists of sport have argued for the better use of human and environmental resources to ensure that there is a sporting future for generations to come. These, then, are some of the aims and tasks that sociologists of sport have set themselves. This book shows what has so far been accomplished.

The Structure of Sport Worlds

Sport worlds are contested terrain. Sociologists of sport must examine the co-existence of co-operation and confrontation, power and control, in order to understand the struggles that shape sport worlds and their permeable boundaries. For example, consider the question 'What is sport?' For sociologists, such a question requires understanding the set of social practices adhered to by a set of conventions—akin to how Becker describes art. That is to say, an understanding of what sport 'is' requires an analysis of the sport worlds that produce sport. We must trace the intimate and extensive relations between sport and other social worlds. We must analyse sport worlds with respect to their relative degrees of autonomy from these other worlds, and the different forms of co-operation and confrontation that characterise these connections. For example, sport worlds are interconnected with questions of foreign policy, big business, environmental degradation, the medicalisation of social life, and the socialisation of citizens of different societies. We must look at the conventions that define sport worlds, but also at the innovations and challenges that emerge out of these relations to other social worlds, such as the recent developments of 'extreme' sports and the Gay Games.

We share with Becker a sense that sport worlds are marked by the same type of features as those found in art worlds. Moving beyond these features, we highlight three additional dimensions that shape sport worlds. First, there is a temporal dimension—past and present sport worlds need examination. Second, there is a comparative dimension—global frames of reference are required to make sense of contemporary sport worlds. Third, there is a spatial dimension—subcultures, places and identities need consideration.

This, then, is our invitation to *Sport Worlds*. C. Wright Mills, in outlining what he termed a 'sociological imagination', argued that it was essential to grasp the 'interplay between history, biography and social structures' (Mills 1959). In examining sport worlds, evidence of this interplay becomes only too evident. Each chapter attempts to show how people's sporting lives are connected to history, social structures and global processes. We hope that through the review exercises, specific projects and tasks that we have assigned to each chapter, the 'sociological imagination' will be encouraged and enhanced.

In his *Invitation to Sociology*, Peter Berger suggested that 'sociological thought would have the best chance to develop in historical circumstances marked by severe jolts to the self-conception, especially the official and authoritative and generally accepted self-conception, of a culture' (Berger 1963/1976). Our hope is that this book provides a 'jolt' to the student's self-conception and, in turn, in some small way, to the sport world. Armed with what they will learn here, students will be better able to challenge the everyday conventions and practices of sport worlds. The necessity of understanding sport as a social product not only debunks the myth of the athlete's exceptionalism. More importantly, through a more informed understanding of sport worlds, humans may yet mobilise to make such worlds less wasteful of lives and resources and build a more humane, and just, set of sport worlds. That is our hope.

PART I

SPORT INSIDE THE WORLD

Global Systems and Processes

Chapter 1   Sport and Globalisation
Chapter 2   Sport, Labour and Migration
Chapter 3   Sport, Media and Society

Global Issues Across a Changing World

Chapter 4   Sport, Politics and Democracy
Chapter 5   Sport, the Environment and 'Green' Issues
Chapter 6   Sport, Communitarianism and Social Capital

CHAPTER 1

SPORT AND GLOBALISATION

Objectives

After completing this chapter, you should be able to

- discuss the concept of globalisation;
- discuss how the concepts of interdependency chains and civilisational struggles help explain contemporary sport;
- critically consider different approaches to and perspectives on globalisation;
- describe the main phases in the emergence, diffusion and globalisation of sport;
- explain the concept of global flows and apply this to the study; and
- critically evaluate issues of power, governance and sport in the light of globalisation processes.

Modern sport is bound up in a global network of interdependency chains that are marked by uneven power relations. Consider the popularity of sports events and leisure clothing. People across the globe regularly view satellite broadcasts of English Premier League and European Champions League matches. The best players from Europe, South America and Africa perform in these games. The players use equipment—boots, balls, uniforms, and the like—that is designed in the West, financed by multinational corporations such as Adidas and Nike and hand-stitched, in the case of soccer balls, in Asia using child labour. This equipment is sold, at significant profit, to a mass market in the towns and cities of North America and Europe. Several transnational corporations are involved in the production and consumption phases of global soccer. Some of these corporations own the media companies and also have, as in the case of Sky TV, shareholdings in the soccer clubs they screen as part of what sociologists term the global media sport complex.

The sports/leisurewear industry can also be used to highlight how people's consumption of cultural goods is bound up with global processes. As a fashion item, sports footwear has become an integral feature of city life and consumer culture. One premier brand is Nike. The purchase and display of Nike footwear by soccer players are but the final stages in a dynamic network involving designers, producers, suppliers, distributors and the parent or broker company. Though Nike's headquarters is located in the United States, the range of subcontractors involved straddles the globe. Its suppliers and production companies are located in a host of Southeast Asian countries, including Thailand, Singapore, Korea and China. Its designers provide soccer boots with a worldwide demand that will also appeal to local tastes. Local franchises ensure appropriate distribution backed by global marketing strategies. Here again, Nike uses the media sport production complex by endorsing sports stars such as the Brazilian Rinaldo and sports/leisure festivals such as soccer's World Cup. In addition, Nike advertises within the television schedules that carry these sports and other programmes deemed appropriate. In the 2000–2001 Premier League season, it was reported that Nike was to become the official sponsor of Manchester United with a deal brokered at some £300 million over 15 years. In brief, elite sport now occurs on a worldwide scale and is patterned along what sociologists term **global flows.**

Global flows involve several dimensions: The migrant dimension involves the international movement of people such as tourists, exiles and guest workers; the technology dimension, created by the flow between countries of the machinery and equipment produced by corporations and government agencies; the economic dimension, centred on the rapid flow of money and its equivalents around the world; the media dimension, entailing the flow between countries of information and images that are produced and distributed by newspapers, magazines, radio, film, television, video, satellite, cable and the World Wide Web; and, finally, the ideological dimension, linked to the flow of values centrally associated with state or counterstate ideologies and movements. All five dimensions can be detected in late-20th-century sport development. Thus the global migration of sports personnel has been a pronounced feature of recent decades and appears likely to continue in the future. The flow across the globe of goods, equipment and 'landscapes' such as sports complexes and golf courses has developed into a multibillion dollar business in recent years and represents a transnational development in the sports sphere. Regarding economic issues, clearly the flow of finance in the global sports arena has come to centre not only on the international trade in personnel, prize money and endorsements, but also on the marketing of sport along specific lines. The transformation of sports such as American football, basketball, golf and soccer into global sports is part of this process.

Media-led developments have been closely connected to these global flows. The media sport production complex transmits images of individual sports labour migrants, leisure forms and specific cultural messages to large global audiences—consider the worldwide audience for the 2000 Sydney Olympic Games. The marketing of American track and field stars Marion Jones and Michael Johnson is an example of these processes at work. The power of this media sport complex has forced a range of sports to align themselves to this global model that emphasises spectacle, personality and excitement. At the level of ideology, global sports festivals such as the Olympics have come to serve as vehicles for the expression of ideologies that are transnational in character. Note, for example, how the opening and closing ceremonies of the Sydney Games were designed to project images and messages about Australia both to its own people and to a global audience. Before seeking to trace how this present pattern of modern sport has emerged out of the past, we must consider how sociologists seek to make sense of these global sport processes.

Debating Point:
How Do We Make Sense of Global Processes?

For students examining the global sport process there are three points that need to be grasped. First, it is necessary to examine the intercon-nected political, economic, cultural and social patterns that shape mod-ern sport. Attention also has to be given to how these patterns contain both enabling and constraining dimensions on people's actions—there are winners and losers in this global game. Societies are no longer—and except in very rare cases, never were—sealed off from other societies. Ties of trade, warfare, migration and culture are of long standing in human history. Witness, for instance, the connections made throughout Renaissance Europe. More recent **globalisation** processes have un-leashed new sets of **interdependency chains,** the networks that have (inter)connected people from distant parts of the globe. It is in this context of global **power networks** that the practice and consumption of elite modern sport can best be understood. Second, in order to trace, describe and analyse the global sport process it is wise to adopt a long-term perspective (Maguire 1999). A historical and comparative ap-proach can help us explain how the present pattern of global sport has emerged out of the past and is connected with a range of what Maguire has termed **civilisational struggles.** A model of the emergence, diffu-sion and globalisation of modern Western sport forms, personnel and ideologies will be described later in this chapter.

The third point of significance concerns the concept of globalisation itself, which is a subject of intense debate (Beck 2000; Featherstone 1991, 1995; Featherstone, Lash and Robertson 1995; Held et al. 1999; King 1991; Lechner and Boli 2000; Robertson 1992; Roudometof and Robertson 1995; Sklair 1991; Therborn 2000; Tomlinson 1999; Wallerstein 1974). We will not examine the merits of the arguments here (cf. Jarvie and Maguire 1994; Maguire 1999); it is sufficient to note that the concept refers to the growing network of political, economic, cultural and social interdepen-dencies that bind human beings together—for better and for worse. We can also note that globalisation processes are not of recent origin, nor do they occur evenly across all areas of the globe; they involve an increasing intensification of global interconnectedness and are very long-term in

nature, but during the 20th century the rate of change gathered momentum. Despite the unevenness of these processes, it is more difficult to
understand local or national experiences without reference to these
global flows. In fact, our living conditions, beliefs, knowledge and
actions are intertwined with unfolding globalisation processes, which
include the emergence of a global economy, a transnational cosmopolitan culture and a range of international social movements. A multitude
of transnational or global economic and technological exchanges, communication networks and migratory patterns characterise this interconnected world pattern. As a result, people experience spatial and temporal dimensions differently. There is a 'speeding up' of time and a
'shrinking' of space. Modern technologies enable people, images, ideas
and money to cross the globe with great rapidity. Globalisation leads not
only to a greater degree of interdependence but also to an increased
awareness of the world as a whole. People become more attuned to the
notion that their lives and places of living are part of a single social
space—the globe.

Globalisation processes, then, involve **multidirectional** movements
of people, practices, customs and ideas that involve a series of power
balances, yet have neither the hidden hand of progress nor some all-
pervasive, overarching conspiracy guiding them. Although the globe
can be understood as an interdependent whole, in different areas of
social life the **established** (core) and **outsider** (peripheral) groups and
nation-states are constantly vying with each other for dominant positions. Given this growth in the multiplicity of linkages and networks
that transcend nation-states, it is not surprising that we may be at the
earliest stages of the development of a transnational or global culture, of
which sport is a part. This process entails a shift from ethnic or national
cultures to 'supranational' forms based on either the culture of a super-
power or of cosmopolitan communication and migrant networks. In this
connection, there is considerable debate as to whether global sport is
leading to a form of homogenised body culture—specifically along
Western or American lines. There is some evidence to support this. Yet
global flows are simultaneously increasing the varieties of body cultures
and identities available to people in local cultures. Global sport, then,
seems to be leading to the reduction in contrasts between societies but
also to the emergence of new varieties of body cultures and identities.
Let us look at this issue more closely.

Studying Global Sport:
Issues, Questions and Dimensions

There are, as noted, several difficult conceptual issues that need to be
grasped in understanding global processes. Advocates of competing

traditions including the modernisation perspective, imperialism theories, dependency theory, world systems theory, figurational/process sociology and globalisation research have sought to compare and contrast globalising development in different societies. More recently, these traditions have found expression in the study of sport. Competing claims have been made regarding the adequacy of these traditions (Jarvie and Maguire 1994; Maguire 1999).

In reviewing these traditions, several conceptual traps are evident. The traps centre on four main areas: (1) the tendency to think in dichotomous ways; (2) the use of **monocausal** logic and explanation; (3) the propensity to view these processes as governed by either the intended or the unintended actions of groups of people; and (4) the lack of an adequate account of gender power (Wolff 1991). Several binary oppositions that structure debates about global sport development can be identified. These include universalism versus particularism, homogenisation versus differentiation, integration versus fragmentation, centralisation versus decentralisation and juxtaposition versus syncretisation. Further, the monocausal logic that is sometimes evident in research variously centres on whether global processes can be explained with prime reference to the technological, the economic, the political or the cultural. Yet we suggest that an either/or resolution of this complex structured process will not suffice. Put succinctly, a balance or blend between intended ideological practices and unplanned sets of interdependencies structures global processes.

An additional trap to avoid is the suggestion that analyses that use the term *globalisation concept* are automatically or implicitly emphasising a homogenisation thesis. Such analyses are then alleged to suggest the emergence of a global culture that will suspend or end conflict. But to associate globalisation exclusively with such a modernisation thesis, confirming a triumph of the West in some simple sense, and for advocates to assume that all parties contribute equally in this global process is itself an oversimplification of a set of complex arguments. Globalisation processes have no 'zero starting point'. It is clear that they gathered momentum between the 15th and 18th centuries (Robertson 1992) and have continued apace since the turn of the 19th century. The emergence and diffusion of sport in the 19th century is clearly interwoven with this overall process.

It would also appear that global sport processes are not solely the direct outcome of nation-state activities. Whatever its merits or failings, the International Olympic Committee (IOC) operates independently of any specific nation-state. Rather, these processes need to be accounted for in relation to how they operate independently of conventionally designated societal and sociocultural processes. In addition, while the globalisation of sport is connected to the intended ideological practices of specific groups of people from particular countries, its pattern and development cannot be reduced solely to these ideological practices. Although elite sports migrants, officials and consumers are caught up in globalisation processes, they do have the capacity to reinterpret cultural products and experiences into something distinct—the local acts back on the global. Furthermore, the receptivity of national popular cultures to nonindigenous cultural products can be active and heterogeneous—local lives make sense of global events. That is not to overlook, however, the political economy at work in the production and consumption of global sport products. Globalisation, then, is best understood as a balance and blend between diminishing contrasts and increasing varieties, a **commingling of cultures** and an attempt by more established groups to control and regulate access to global flows. Let us highlight with reference to emergence and diffusion of sport how these processes have been at work.

Globalisation and the Making of Modern Sport

In noting that early-17th-century English society was the 'cradle of modern sport', it is important to recognise that both the longer-term links of medieval European and non-Western ancient civilisations with play and games should not be overlooked (cf. Maguire 1999). Yet it is clear that modern sport did develop in England first (Guttmann 1978). Over the course of three centuries, a series of structured processes that characterise global **achievement sport** has emerged and grown in intensity. These structured processes, six of which are identified here, flow from a blend of intended and unintended social actions. While the reach and spread of these processes have varied over time and across space, they now form an interlocking fabric—that of modern achievement sport—that provides the context within which people experience global sport. Furthermore, the pattern and development of these structured processes also reflect and reinforce the prevailing balance of power within and between societies. In the emergence and diffusion of global sport, several structured processes can thus be identified:

- The long-term decline, though not disappearance, of indigenous Western and non-occidental folk body cultures
- The emergence and diffusion of a specifically gendered ideology, content, meaning, habitus and control of global sport
- The scientisation, rationalisation and valorisation of human expressiveness
- The athlete as the enhanced, efficient machine adhering to the sports ethics associated with success and the ultimate performance

- The athlete, spectator and viewer as both the consumers of scarce resources and, in certain respects, the destroyers of the environment

- The emergence of a global sport power elite and the reinforcement and enhancement of global inequalities within the West and between the West and non-Western societies

Each of these processes permeates the making of modern sport. Although there is evidence of cultic/play activities, folk games and recreations in the ancient worlds and civilisations of Europe, Asia and South America, *modern* sport, like the steam engine, emerged first in England.

The Sportisation of English Pastimes

The initial development of 'sportlike' English pastimes occurred, according to Elias and Dunning (1986), in two main phases. In the early emergence of what these sociologists have termed **sportisation,** the phase of the 17th and 18th centuries witnessed the transformation of a variety of pastimes, including cricket, fox hunting, horse racing and boxing, into recognisably modern sports. In the second phase, the early and mid-19th century, soccer, rugby, tennis and track and field began to take on modern forms. Maguire (1999) has developed this argument further and has identified a third sportisation phase during the late 19th and early 20th centuries. This 'take-off' phase overlapped with a fourth phase that lasted from the 1920s through to the 1960s. More recently, beginning in the late 1960s, a fifth phase of sportisation processes has begun to unfold. Crucially, the emergence and diffusion of these sporting forms on a global scale is closely connected to broader globalisation processes outlined earlier. In this context, we will focus on the last three phases of this **five-phase model.**

The third sportisation phase entailed the differential diffusion of English sport forms to continental Europe and to both the formal and informal British Empire. This was closely connected to two interrelated processes: the emergence of intense forms of nationalism and a spurt in globalisation processes. During this period we saw the intensification of national sentiment, the emergence of ethnic nation-states and the invention of traditions. Sport played a crucial role in this connection. The last three decades of the 19th century marked a decisive transformation in the spread of the old, the invention of the new and the institutionalisation of most sports on a national and even international stage. In this way, sport became a medium for and barometer of national identification and competitive community struggle. While the rise of sport provided new expressions of nationalism through the choice or invention of nationally specific sports, it is also important to note that such nations were doing so in the context of the dominant standard setter, the English.

Several indices of the take-off phase in globalisation processes can be identified: an increase in the number of international agencies; the growth of increasingly global forms of communication; the development of global competitions and prizes; and the development of notions of rights, **citizenship** and humanity that are increasingly standardised internationally. It is suggested that the third phase in sportisation processes is connected to this take-off phase. The last quarter of the 19th century, for example, witnessed the emergence and spread of sport, the establishment of international sports organisations, the growth of competition between national teams, the worldwide acceptance of rules governing specific—that is, Western—sport forms, and the establishment of global competitions such as the Olympic games and the men's and women's soccer World Cup. The 20th-century establishment of world championships is also indicative of the occurrence of globalisation processes in the sports world.

Several important issues are raised by these interconnections. In this phase Westerners and, in particular, the English/British—with their economic spheres of influence and their games spreading to continental Europe and the colonies—were the dominant 'players'. But they were not alone: Danish and Swedish gymnastics, the German *Turnverein* movement and the spread of *skiidraet* from Norway to North America and beyond are all examples of the Europeanisation phase in global sport development. Though the diffusion of sports personnel, forms, ideologies and images were not part of some global marketing ploy, at this stage it did reflect the prevailing balance of power in cultural interchange. Increasingly, however, North American sports personnel, forms, ideologies and images began to compete with and supersede their English equivalents. During the 1920s and 1930s, sports such as baseball, basketball, ice-hockey and volleyball diffused to those parts of the world more centrally linked to the American sphere of influence—Europe, South America and parts of the Asian Pacific rim. There has been a struggle for power and the control of culture since the 1920s, but in sport, this occurred not only between the West and the rest, but also within the West itself. The main long-term effect was a reduction in the contrasts between global sport cultures.

From the 1920s through to the late 1960s, the West regulated the field of play, sports organisations, the surplus value associated with sporting festivals and the ideological meanings associated with such events. Western and non-Western people actively embraced some aspects of the sports that originated in the Anglo/Euro-American core. Sport was and is a carrier of deep culture and structure, and in the fourth phase this culture was Western in orientation. Indeed, sport can be said to have become a **global idiom** in this phase, a form of international communication, a language readily adopted and understood across the world.

Globalising sport also entailed a specific type of Western masculine culture. Sport is thus arguably one of the most powerful transfer mechanisms for culture and structure ever known to humankind, but in suggesting this it would be unwise to overstate the extent to which Western domination of global sport cultures was and is complete. On occasion, non-Western people not only resist and reinterpret Western masculine sports personnel, forms, models and marketing, they also maintain, foster and promote, on a global scale, their indigenous recreational pursuits.

While competitive sports carry a message of Western value systems, this does not mean that people from non-occidental or indeed occidental cultures accepted them uncritically between the 1920s and the late 1960s. Studies of Trobriand cricket, baseball in Japan, the diffusion of sport to Papua New Guinea, and the early-20th-century development of Finnish baseball all highlight the dynamic interchange between the local, national and global. Indeed, indigenous cultures have proved adept at embracing a sport form, reinventing it and then recycling it back to the country of origin. Ironically, American football is a prime example of this as it evolved from an English context in the form of rugby. In turn, the core country also embraces cultural flows from the outsider culture and the reinvented sport form diffuses further around the core. It should also be observed that this phase of global sportisation witnessed the slow decline of modern sport's founding nation.

Whereas the fourth phase of sportisation clearly involved an elaborate political economy in which the control of sport was influenced by **Western hegemony,** control was never complete. Resistance took a variety of forms such as the Cold War rivalry between the West, the former Soviet Union and the Communist bloc that was also played out in the sports world. There also occurred the slow assertion of women's rights and the challenge to hegemonic masculinity. The latter stages of this fourth phase were also characterised by the rise of non-Western nations to sporting prominence and, sometimes, pre-eminence. Non-Western nations began to beat their former colonial masters, especially the English. They were doing so, however, in terms of their former masters' games, and not their own indigenous recreations, and success was confined to the sports field.

This changing balance of power intensified in the fifth phase of sportisation beginning in the late 1960s and is apparent in a range of sports including badminton, cricket, soccer, table tennis and track and field. Here, African, Asian and South American nations were and are increasingly to the fore. Anglo/Euro-American control of global sport has also waned, to a degree, off the playing field. The control of international sports organisations and the Olympic movement is beginning, although slowly and unevenly, to slip out of the exclusive hands of the West: non-Westerners now hold some of the executive positions on the IOC. Yet, it would be wise not to overstate the change that has occurred. In addition, Eastern martial arts as well as a range of folk games have diffused into and around the Western core. Yet, the media sport production complex markets 'sameness'—especially in the form of American sports—and the global political economy that regulates global flows ensures that the local people do not freely choose which cultural products are consumed.

We should, however, not overlook the point that global marketing strategies also celebrate difference. There is also reason to suggest that those national cultures and identities most affected by these processes appear to be those at the centre, not the periphery, of the global system. Just as in music and food, so too in sport: the fifth phase of global sportisation involves the 'creolisation' of sports cultures. When both national identity itself and the sport forms of the culture as a whole are undergoing a pluralisation process, it is increasingly difficult to sustain the notion that a *single* sport represents the nation. The global movement of sports labour has reinforced the problems of identity politics and multi-ethnicity. With these trends in mind, perhaps it is less surprising that Western sports personnel and administrators may be experiencing aspects of the self-doubt and uncertainty that can be detected in Western nations in general in the most recent globalisation phase. As these processes gather momentum, new power balances have emerged and new identities have been forged. In order to reinforce this preliminary outline of the making of modern sport, let us focus our attention on the part that gender relations played in this connection.

Case Study: Sport, Gender Relations and the Global Order

In tracing the emergence of modern sport, it is important to both identify and outline the state of play in the lead up to, and the key players involved in, this transition from traditional folk games. Although research has tended to focus on the activities of males involved in folk games, evidence is being accumulated that the nature and form of participation by women was more complex and widespread than previously suggested (Guttmann 1994). Some clues to the involvement of women in 'smock races', pugilism and folk pastimes more generally have emerged. Despite excellent work on aspects of the late-19th-century development of women's sports, the folk game/pastime tradition is still relatively unexplored (Hargreaves 1994).

We do know, however, far more about the key players involved in the transition to modern sport. It is clear that, initially, men from the landed aristocracy and gentry and, later, the bourgeoisie were decisive figures in the reshaping of body culture, the 'athletics craze', the 'games cult' and the implementation of 'muscular Christianity'. In both the first and second sportisation phases identified earlier, modern sport was devised on male terms, creating a 'male preserve'. That is, the content, ideology and meanings of modern achievement sport were being determined by and for elite white, Anglo-European men. Modern achievement sport was both reinforcing and developing a specific form of male body culture, what Bourdieu (1984) and Elias (1939/1978) would call habitus. During the course of the second and third sportisation phases, competing body cultures—male and female versions of European gymnastics, and indigenous folk cultures that found expression in various types of recreations—were being marginalised and, in some respects, withered away. Such a conclusion might, however, reflect our limited state of knowledge, underestimate the diversity of body cultures that diffused in the take-off phase of globalisation and, inadvertently, extinguish from history the activities of women in body forms other than modern achievement sport. That is not our intention, and studies of these possibilities are yet to be carried out.

By the third sportisation phase and the take-off globalisation phase (1870–1920), elite white men had successfully reshaped body culture in tune with what they regarded as a suitable form of sporting endeavour and physical education for 'neophyte' gentlemen. The structures of sport, its administration, organisation, control and practice, were being decided *by* men, and largely, *for* men. The role of American and non-European 'white' Commonwealth men was beginning to increase, yet the levers of power and play were still exercised by European males. By this third phase, the fabric of sport reflected and reinforced a specific Western, able-bodied, class-based male habitus. It was this body culture, in the form of modern achievement sport, that globalised across the formal and informal British Empire and to those parts of the planet that were linked through a series of other interdependency chains with Western nations. The relative ascendancy of modern achievement sport was being reinforced during the fourth sportisation phase. Arguably, however, in the fifth sportisation phase, the dynamics underpinning this Western male body culture have grown more complex and diffuse.

At one level, the political economy of global sport—finding expression in the media sport complex, migration processes and patriotic/nationalistic games of international competitions—reinforces and consolidates the grip of modern achievement sport on bodies of people and people's bodies across the planet. Yet, there are also countervailing tendencies and new varieties of body cultures emerging. These include the feminist critique and challenge to hegemonic masculinity in sport; the changing conceptions of sexuality, and counterhegemonic practices such as the Gay Games; the emergence of the Paralympics and disabled sports more generally; the diffusion of non-Western folk cultures and martial arts to the global core; the revival of traditional folk cultures within the West; and the emergence of 'extreme' sports. Each of these tendencies goes against the trend of diminishing contrasts between body cultures evident in modern achievement sport and, potentially, provides new varieties of body cultures and alternatives to the dominant Western male habitus. How do such processes relate to the flows that are part of the contemporary **global sport/gender order?**

Gender and the Contemporary Global Sport Order

The sport process is contoured by the global flow lines identified earlier. Elite labour migration, as will be highlighted in chapter 2, is a pronounced feature of global sport. In specific sports, such as golf and tennis, international circuits traverse the globe and athletes experience a range of enabling and constraining experiences. For elite women, the range of migration possibilities reflects the prevailing unequal resourcing of their sports relative to their male counterparts. Elite women also experience specific problems not faced by male athletes. In focusing on track and field, for example, the cases of the now-retired Hassiba Boulmerka from Algeria and the Syrian Ghada Shouaa highlight issues that deserve greater consideration. Both of these women, world or Olympic champions, faced issues of adjustment and dislocation as they endured the experience of foreign sojourn and the varying forms of patriarchal structures that exist in different societies. Yet, the religious and social pressures that faced them, and other athletes coming from some Arab societies, compound these challenges. Boulmerka received death threats and was seen by some Islamic fundamentalists as a threat to traditional values. So, if we are to examine the gendered nature of migration processes, several issues need attention, including domestic labour and the role of women while partners travel; exploitation, dislocation and cultural adjustment; identity politics, labour rights and differential rewards; and motivation, differential receptivity and role modelling.

Closely connected to the emergence of elite female sports migrants are questions concerning their positioning within the global media sport complex. Evidence presented in chapter 3 shows that media sport reinforces hegemonic masculinity and contributes to the symbolic annihilation, trivialisation and sexualisation of elite women. Areas of attention that need examination in global media sport include the political economy of media, particularly with reference to its white male ownership and control; the production codes characteristic of media sport; the mediated messages contained in coverage of global sport; and audience knowledgeability and receptivity.

The experience of some elite women athletes can be considered in light of the changing nature of this global media sport complex. Significant changes have occurred over the past two decades. Whatever the merits of the sports system associated with the GDR (East Germany), it is true that elite women received resources and social status that surpassed their Western counterparts. With the people's revolutions of 1989, that system was swept away. Former GDR elite women athletes were integrated into the Federal German Republic's system. In this context, these women experienced a different blend of limits and possibilities, and a different set of enabling and constraining features. In this new system, successful women athletes could expect to receive greater personal financial reward than in the past. Athletes such as Katrin Krabbe and Heiki Drechsler, the latter winning gold in the long jump in Sydney, not only maintained their performance levels, but also became glamour models for the emerging media sport advertising/endorsement complex. But not all GDR athletes could make this transition as easily to global capitalist sport. Astrid Kumbernuss, world champion shot putter in 1999 and bronze medallist in Sydney, might still make the front cover of *Athletics Weekly*, but not of *Vogue* or *Cosmopolitan*. Despite winning at the recent World Athletics Championships in Seville, Kumbernuss has had seemingly a very different experience from that of other former GDR athletes—in the media sport complex only certain female bodies count.

The contested nature of which 'bodies' count also relates to issues of identity politics, sexuality and gender relations. It is clear that the celebration of heterosexuality is an implicit part of global sport marketing, endorsements operations and media coverage (cf. chapter 3). Just occasionally, however, specific events—such as the Australian Open in January 1999, when tennis star Martina Hingis made a negative comment about opponent Amelie Mauresmo, who is a lesbian—bring to the fore questions of identity politics that subsequently ripple across the globe. As yet, we do not know how the Mauresmo/Hingis incident was transmitted, received, perceived and reacted to in different societies, but such occasions provide sociologists of gender relations, sexuality and gay theory the opportunity to explore issues in a global context and with a worldwide frame of reference. A series of classic established/outsider dynamics, prestige/charisma relations and group disgrace elements appear part of the identity politics at work on this global stage.

If the research agenda examining gender relations and global processes focused solely on the experiences of athletes and spectators/consumers, it would overlook an area worthy of equal attention. Global sport rests not only on national forms of domestic labour, but also on commodity chains, involving transnational companies in the sports goods industry that use child and women labourers to produce the equipment and clothing we consume. Companies such as Adidas, Reebok and Nike are involved in practices that exploit such groups in Third World countries. Nike is particularly worthy of attention. Given the 'sweatshop' conditions that women experience assembling Nike shoes, such practices are rather at odds with the sanitised and supposedly empowering advertising campaigns that are aimed at young Western women and designed to drive up sales in this niche of the global market (Maguire 1999). One might suggest that the Nike transnational advocacy network, so ably described by Sage (1999), could also extend its work to involve elite female athletes sponsored by Nike and other such companies. Being an empowered athlete in the West does not excuse overlooking the fate of women in Southeast Asia! Elite athletes, men and women, have to defend or gain their due rights in global sport. In so doing, however, they, along with other groups, can play a part in directing the attention of the executives of transnational corporations, national governments, consumers and students to the inequalities and exploitative practices that shape global sport. In this regard, sociologists of sport have an important part to play in focusing on this and other gendered and unequal elements of the global sport process.

Power, Citizenship and the Governance of Global Sport

We also need to consider the issues associated with how humans cope with the problems of increasing interdependence, especially as they relate to global **governance.** There are some key areas to consider. First, we must identify the structured processes that are reshaping local and national governance. It is clear that globalisation processes are placing limits on the autonomy/sovereignty of nations. However, a blurring of the boundaries of domestic politics is transforming the conditions of political decision-making. In Europe and elsewhere, globalisation processes are changing the institutional/organisational context of national politics and altering the legal framework/administrative practices of governments. What happens at the European Commission in Brussels also counts in London. Also, the lines of responsibility/accountability of nation-states are being obscured, though nation-states remain powerful players in the network of global power politics. Given these processes, we must also address another set of issues that involve rethinking notions of sovereignty, political community and citizenship—both for urban and rural dwellers. It is necessary to examine people's lives in terms of multiple identities, allegiances and loyalties. Consider the dual identities of track and field stars Cathy Freeman and Colin Jackson. Freeman of Australia and Jackson of Britain have celebrated athletic success by wrapping themselves not only in their national flags, but also the flags of, respectively, the Australian Aborigines and Wales. Increasingly, the rights / responsibilities that tied people to the local or national are now stretching to the regional and international, and also to social movements such as Greenpeace. What seems to be developing is a series of overlapping global, regional, transnational, national and local political communities that are contoured along multiple overlapping / intersecting socio-spatial **networks of power.**

These global changes have profound implications for the way we do and use the sociology of sport. We must begin the search for a global sociology that addresses the human condition by developing relatively adequate accounts based on reason, evidence and humanity. If we do not do this, then fundamentalist thinking, biological determinism or sociobiology will fill the void. Perhaps such forces are already doing so. In this light we need to map out a research agenda on global governance of sport. The focus should be on questions of sport, governance and social exclusion, and local, national and European cultural identities. Attention must be given to issues of how power and control are exercised in a top-down-and-across institutional manner (horizontal / vertical subsidiarity) and the role of national governments, the European Union (EU) and civil society. Questions concerning the regulation, control, licensing and administration of sport policy and practice also arise. The joint ownership of media corporations and sports franchises is a prime example in which such questions arise. Sport policy questions also occur in the areas of violence, drugs, pain, injury and health. Examination of sports labour migration, the production of indigenous sporting talent and the exploitation of people from non-EU societies must also be undertaken. And, given the extent to which such issues plague the planet, we must consider race / ethnicity and sport and not allow sociobehaviourism to be expressed unchallenged. Yet this challenges us as writers of this textbook—just how can we stem the tide of a return to a medieval demon-haunted world or a planet in which genetic modification, environmental pollution or global capitalism rules unchecked? We must use our social scientific knowledge as a candle in this gathering gloom—we hope this chapter provides some help for you, too.

Debating Point:
Who Is Winning the Global Game?

International sport success in the late 20th century and in the early part of this new century involves a contest between systems located within a global context. Sport success depends on several elements: the availability and identification of human resources, the methods of coaching and training, the efficiency of the sports organisation and the depth of knowledge of sports medicine and sport sciences (Heinilä 1970). These national sports system mechanisms are a necessary but not sufficient explanation of international sport success. In addition to these elements, sport development within a particular society also depends on the status of that nation in the sports international rank order. Less developed nations tend to underutilise their talent and performers or lose them to more powerful nations. Global sport processes can thus lead to under- or dependent development of a nation's talent. Kenyan athletics demonstrates this very well (Bale and Sang 1996). It is relevant to observe that while individuals inherit specific genetic qualities, ethnic groups do not. Further, in the development of an individual's sporting career, a blend of unlearned and learned elements interweave to produce performance capability. This is the 'hinge' on which sporting success is based—contoured and shaped by the national sport development system and the range of global flows outlined already.

The migration of performers, coaches, administrators and sport scientists within and between nations, continents and hemispheres is a pronounced feature of late-20th-century sport. Migration of this elite talent, as chapter 2 highlights, has become a decisive feature that structures the experience of sport in different societies. The movement of technology and the manufacture of clothing, footwear and equipment are worldwide industries that wealthier nations are able to access to a far greater degree than their poorer counterparts. The global sports industry needs to be examined in terms of the implications for sustainable sports systems. In addition to these global flows, the images of sports stars and tournaments travel round the globe via the media sport complex. The interconnected web of media and corporate interests, as chapter 3 highlights, structures but does not completely determine the sports experience for performers and consumers alike. Global sporting success not only reflects national sports systems but also reinforces national esteem. Global sport involves a form of patriot games in which images and stories are told to us, about ourselves and about others. Elite-level achievement sport also tells us something about what it is to be human. With its emphasis on rational and efficient performance, specialisation, scientisation, competition and professionalisation, achievement sport reinforces the myth of the 'super*man*'. This myth is sustained by the ideology and findings of the sport sciences that tend to be concerned with identifying the conditions necessary to produce the ultimate performance.

The global sports system accordingly involves the following mechanisms of production, experience and consumption. Achievement sport involves identification and development of talent; production on a global stage, in a single or multisport event; and consumption by direct spectators or, through the media complex, a global mass audience. Traced over time there is a tendency towards the emergence of a global achievement sport monoculture—a culture where administrators, coaches and teachers promote and foster achievement sport values and ideologies and where competitions and tournaments are structured along highly commodified and rationalised lines. Within the global sports system there is not only an international rank order of nations, but also a grouping of these nations, more or less, along political, economic and cultural lines into core, semiperipheral and peripheral blocs. At the core of most team- and individual-based sports lies the countries of Western Europe, North America—excluding Mexico—and former 'white' Commonwealth countries such as Australia. Semiperipheral countries tend to involve former socialist countries and some emerging nations such as South Korea. Peripheral countries include South Africa, most Islamic nations and the majority of African countries. Whereas the West may be challenged on the playing field by non-core countries, the control over the content, ideology and economic resources associated with sport still tends to lie within the West. Yet, through state policy, non-core countries can use major sports festivals to solidify internal national identification and enhance international recognition and prestige.

In terms of hosting events or making relevant decisions, however, it is the West that dominates in international recognition, respectability, status and prestige. The more high tech and commodified the sport, the more dependent success is on the elements of the global sport process identified earlier. As a result, the West tends to win out. Indeed the last decade has seen the recruitment by Western nations not only of sport scientists and coaches from the former Soviet bloc but also, in sports such as soccer, the drain of athletic talent from Africa and South America to the economically more powerful clubs of Europe. Non-core leagues remain in a dependent relationship with the dominant European core. In other sports, such as track and field and baseball, this drain of talent flows to the United States. The West also remains dominant in terms of the design, production and marketing of sports equipment; new innovations emerge within the West. Sports federations tend to be controlled by Western officials and global sports tournaments are usually located within the West.

In the fifth sportisation phase, there have, however, been challenges to the achievement sport ideology and to Western domination. Though no longer in existence, the Soviet bloc mounted a sustained challenge to the West for some 40 years, though it too became incorporated into the ideology of achievement sport. Despite the ideological differences between Castro's Cuba and the capitalist West, Cubans participate in, and by some measures, outperform the core capitalist countries at the Olympics. Non-Western success on the playing field, in specific sports such as badminton and middle- and long-distance athletics, is beginning to be matched in terms of involvement of non-Western personnel as coaches, officials, administrators and producers of sports goods; coverage by non-Western media outlets; and hosting of major tournaments by non-core countries. Though England was, as we noted, the cradle of modern sport, the relative decline of Great Britain on the sports field—despite the improved, if overhyped, success at the Sydney Olympic Games—is also matched by its fading influence in the corridors of power of global sport politics. This may be indicative of how things might develop in this century for Europeans and perhaps Westerners more generally. One main source of potential dispute may well be the Olympic Games. As yet, however, the West is the winner in the global sport contest—hegemonic control remains with Westerners.

Power, Cultural Struggles and Global Diversity

From what has been written so far, it is clear that the emergence and diffusion of modern sport is bound up in complex networks and interdependency chains that are marked by unequal power relations. Political, economic, cultural and social processes have affected the development of sport over the past three centuries. This global development has undoubtedly led to a degree of homogenisation—in common with broader globalisation processes. In addition, the spread of British/European/Western sports has had elements of cultural imperialism infused with it. Further, while there was no 'master plan' in the early phases of this process, transnational corporations have more recently sought to market their products to consumers across the globe. Westerners have been the global winners at their own games—both on and off the field. The male members of Western societies were acting as an established group on a world level. Their tastes and conduct, including their sports, were part of this, and these practices had effects similar to those of elite cultural activities within Western societies themselves. They are signs of distinction, prestige and power. Yet, this is not the whole story.

The rise of the West was contested and its 'triumph' was not inevitable. Furthermore, Western culture had long been permeated by non-Western cultural forms, people, technologies and knowledge. In sum, these cultural interchanges stretch back to long before the West momentarily achieved relative dominance in cultural interchange. It also needs to be recognised that both the intended and unintended aspects of global sport development need inspection. That is, while the intended acts of representatives of transnational agencies or the transnational capitalist class are potentially more significant in the *short term*, unintended and relatively autonomous transnational practices predominate over the *long term*. These practices structure the subsequent plans and actions of the personnel of transnational agencies and the transnational capitalist class.

In addition, global sport has not led to complete homogenisation: the consumption of nonindigenous cultural wares by different national groups has been both active and heterogeneous. Resistance to global sportisation processes has also been evident. Yet, there is a political economy at work in the production and consumption of global sports/leisure products that can lead to the relative ascendancy of a narrow selection of capitalist and Western sports cultures. Global sport processes can therefore be understood in terms of the attempts by more established white male groups to control and regulate access to global flows and also in terms of how indigenous peoples both resist these processes and recycle their own cultural products. We are currently witnessing the homogenisation of specific body cultures—through achievement sport, the Olympic movement and sport science programmes—and simultaneously the increase in the diversity of sports/body cultures.

It is possible, however, to overstate the extent to which the West has triumphed in terms of global sports structures, organisations, ideologies and performances. Non-Western cultures, as noted, resist and reinterpret Western sports and maintain, foster and promote, on a global scale, their own indigenous recreational pursuits (e.g., the Indian game *kabbadi*). Clearly, the speed, scale and volume of sport development are interwoven with the broader global flows of people, technology, finance, images and ideologies that are controlled by the West and by Western men. In the longer term, however, it is possible to detect signs that the disjunctures and non-isomorphic patterns that characterise global processes are also leading to the diminution of Western power in a variety of contexts. Sport may be no exception. Sport may become increasingly contested, with different civilisational blocs challenging both 19th- and 20th-century hegemonic masculine notions regarding the content, meaning, control, organisation and ideology of sport. By adopting a **multicausal,** multidirectional analysis that examines the production of both **homogeneity** and **heterogeneity,** we are better placed to probe the global cultural commingling that is taking place.

Summary

This chapter has sought to examine the concept of globalisation and how it can be applied to the emergence and diffusion of sport. Concepts such as global flows and interdependency chains help explain the structure and pattern of contemporary sport. In addition, competing approaches to globalisation all highlight how sport is embedded in wider networks of power relations. The development of sport can be connected to five main phases and a series of cultural struggles. Power is central to the ownership and control of global sport. Marked by a series of inequalities, the governance of this global sport process is highly contested. There is an urgent need to make such governance more democratic, accountable and transparent.

Key Terms and Concepts

achievement sport

citizenship

civilisational struggle

cultural commingling

established/outsider relations

five-phase model

global flows

global idiom

globalisation

global sport/gender order

governance

homogeneity/heterogeneity

interdependency chains

mono/multicausal

multidirectional

power networks

sportisation

Western hegemony

Review Questions

1. Using a 'dynamic network' of your choice, show how the concept of globalisation helps make sense of the tensions involved in sport.

2. Critically examine how the power of transnational corporations controls modern sport.

3. How might an understanding of global flows help explain the structure of a sport form of your choice?

4. Critically evaluate the strengths and weaknesses of two or more approaches to the study of globalisation. How have they been applied to sport?

5. What are the key issues at stake in competing accounts of the relationship between sport and globalisation?

6. Discuss, in detail, the connections between sportisation and globalisation.

7. In what ways are globalisation processes reshaping sport and gender relations?

8. In what ways was the emergence and diffusion of sport bound up in civilisational struggles?

9. What are the main structured processes that permeate the sportisation phases? To what extent do they help explain the character of modern achievement sport?

10. Global sport is bound up in questions of power—economic, political, cultural and social. How might the governance of global sport be made more democratic, transparent and accountable?

Projects

1. Choose a major sports industry company, such as Nike. Evaluate the extent to which the company ethos matches up to the marketing strategies and production processes that are evident.
2. Conduct a search for information on the environmental impact of a major sporting event, such as the Olympics, and critically evaluate the evidence gained.
3. Go into a local sports store and record the range of products on display. Choose one brand and a product produced by this company. Establish the ownership of this company, where the product was designed, the source of the raw materials, the manufacturing base and distribution strategy. How would you explain what you have found?
4. Using archived evidence from a sport form of your choice, trace the emergence and diffusion of this sport. How might the five-phase model and the concept of global flows explain what you have discovered?
5. Choose either a specific sport or a major sports organisation. Trace the main power brokers, the main power networks and the many winners and losers in this process.
6. Imagine you are able to replace the modern Olympics with a new global sports festival. What would it stand for and what would its content be? Who would be involved and what would they represent? Where would this festival take place and how would it be paid for? How would you evaluate the competing claims of different groups?

CHAPTER 2

SPORT, LABOUR AND MIGRATION

Objectives

After completing this chapter, you should be able to

- discuss the concept of labour migration and apply this to sport;
- evaluate the competing economic, political, cultural and social processes that contour and shape labour migration;
- connect labour migration issues to the broader process of globalisation;
- discuss issues of de-skilling, dependent development, employment rights, identity politics and cultural adjustment in explaining labour migration;
- outline the main features and trends in sports labour migration; and
- examine the sport policy implications of migration for indigenous players, employment and national team development.

Labour migration is an established feature of the sporting 'global village' (Maguire 1999). This migration centrally involves athletes but also includes coaches, officials, administrators and sport scientists. This movement of 'workers' occurs both within and between nations and continents. This phenomenon has been studied by social scientists focusing on several sports including ice-hockey (Maguire 1996), cricket (Maguire and Stead 1996), baseball (Klein 1991), basketball (Maguire 1994) and, perhaps most notably, soccer (Bromberger 1994; Lanfranchi 1994; Maguire and Stead 1997; Stead and Maguire 2000; Maguire and Pearton 2000). Consideration has been given to tracing the patterns in sports migration, how and why these patterns occur, and what meaning and significance this migration has for those involved—either as 'hosts' or 'migrants'. Although migrant labour has been a feature of the sport process for some time, it is also correct to observe that its frequency and extent have grown in complexity and intensity over recent decades. This acceleration is closely tied to the global processes referred to in chapter 1.

Initial Questions

Several issues can be used as sensitising questions in research into sports labour migration. These include the following:

1. Which sports are most involved, why have they been so affected and what structural or cultural changes have thus occurred in those sports?

2. What are the patterns of global movement and how and why have they developed in this manner?

3. What is the impact on host and donor countries?

4. Why do professional athletes become labour migrants and what do they experience along their journeys (Stead and Maguire 2000)?

The migration of athletes and others involved in the sports industry occurs at three levels: within nations, between nations located within the same continent and between nations located in different continents and hemispheres. Discernible national patterns are evident in the **recruitment** and subsequent **retention** of athletes in sports such as American football, basketball, cricket, ice-hockey, track and field and soccer (Bale and Maguire 1994). An example of intracontinental movement is the presence of athletes from the Dominican Republic on North American baseball teams (Klein 1991). The movement within Western Europe and between the EU and Eastern Europe in sports such as soccer, ice-hockey, basketball and track and field has also increased significantly over the past two decades. After the people's revolutions of 1989 and the subsequent 'opening up' of Eastern Europe, Hungarians, Czechs, Slovakians and Romanians moved west—creating a **talent pipeline.** The western move-ment of Bosnian and Croatian athletes during the civil wars in the former Yugoslavia is also part of this broader picture. The further enlargement of the EU eastwards may accelerate these processes even more.

Movement of labour also occurs in sports such as American football, baseball, basketball and soccer between North America, Europe, South America and Asia. By the mid-1990s, for example, more than 400 Americans were playing in Europe's professional men's basketball leagues, with the higher calibre of players 'residing' in Italy and Spain. A player claiming ancestral links to a specific country and the imposition of quotas on foreign players by particular national sports organisations complicate migration issues further. Anglo-Canadians and French-Canadians use their ice-hockey skills in Britain, Germany, France and Switzerland. There is also a flow of sports labour in the opposite direction. North American ice-hockey clubs recruit players from Scandinavia and the former Soviet bloc (Maguire 1996). American universities have also actively recruited European men and women in sports such as track and field, soccer, rugby, basketball and swimming (Bale and Maguire 1994). African track and field talent is also part of the American university scholarship programme. Australian, Afro-Caribbean, South Asian and South African players also figure promi-nently in English cricket, and they have done so for many decades.

In some sports, such as cricket and rugby, this migration has a seasonal pattern, with the northern and southern hemispheres offering two seasons of play. The natural rhythm of the traditional sporting calendar has thus diminished in importance. Other sports stars experience an even more transitory form of migration—their 'workplace' is constantly shifting. Take, for example, the experience of European, American and African athletes on the European track and field Grand Prix circuit or European and American skiers on the World Cup alpine skiing circuit. Other examples include cycling and motor racing, ranging from Formula One to motorcycling. In team sports, labour tends to be 'hired' by a specific club or organisation and individuals reside in the **host country** for a limited period. However, some athletes stay on and make the host country their home, either through marriage to a citizen of that country or by having stayed 'attached' to a specific country for a sufficient length of time to qualify for nationality status. Sometimes, such as in European basketball, individuals begin to play for the country in which they have become resident and for whom they subsequently claim nationality.

There are other dimensions that need consideration. Sometimes, seasonal and transitory migration patterns interweave, as with golf and tennis players (Bale and Maguire 1994). Tennis stars such as Pete Sampras and Venus Williams cross the globe in search of world ranking points and Grand Slam titles. These migratory forays tend to last no more than eight days at each tournament venue. In this respect, tennis players, along with golfers, are arguably the nomads of the sports migration process, with constantly shifting workplaces and places of residence. It also needs to be understood that men and women have separate global circuits in these sports and others such as skiing. Not only do women tend to earn less than their male counterparts, but the enabling and constraining features that characterise their experiences may be markedly different as well. Migrants in general have to do sport work in various locations and, as a group, experience degrees of exploitation, dislocation and cultural adjustment. Although women are travelling more frequently and in greater numbers, the trend of men moving more freely and in greater numbers, over time and across space, remains. This trend is based on a social structure that ensures that it is usually women who perform domestic and child-rearing labour, whether in the company of their travelling partners or waiting 'at home'. Gender relations, then, play a crucial part in contouring a migrant's life. Yet so too do national identity and ethnic affiliation—a migrant's life is patterned along the same 'fault lines' that characterise other global flows and cultural practices.

How can we make sense of these migration processes? As with global processes more broadly, it would appear that an economic analysis is a necessary but not sufficient explanation. Rather, a complex and shifting set of interdependencies contour the migrant trails of world sport. These interdependencies are multilayered and incorporate economic and political, historical, geographical, social and cultural factors. Thus, in seeking to explain global labour migration, a broad approach involving an examination of wider societal processes must be taken— not merely focusing on the economic aspects of the sports industry. Questions concerning talent pipelines, stereotyping and the ascribing of qualities to athletes from different countries and ethnic groups are also part of the decision-making process.

Case Study:
Men's World Cup Finals, France 1998

In examining the migration patterns evident at the men's World Cup held in France in 1998, five main questions can be used to guide our thinking about this case study and sport migration more generally:

1. How much of the process underpinning the patterns identified can be explained in economic terms?

2. What elements other than the economic appear to play a part in contouring and shaping these migration patterns?

3. What factors are most central in explaining relations with and between global soccer regions?

4. What are the main networks, power relationships, enabling and constraining features and labour inequalities involved in the processes described?

5. What conceptual and sport policy implications follow from the findings uncovered in this study?

Fédération Internationale de Football Association (FIFA) is the governing body of world football and administrator of the global competition known simply as the World Cup. It was formed in 1904 with 7 member nations (France, Sweden, Denmark, Switzerland, the Netherlands, Belgium and Spain) but since then has grown into a massive global organisation, with 201 full, provisional and associate member nations in 1996. World football is subdivided into 6 confederations of which UEFA (Europe) is the most powerful. Although UEFA has only about 25 percent of FIFA member states within its borders, these nations generate around 80 percent of FIFA's annual revenue (Sugden and Tomlinson 1998), making it soccer's core economy (Maguire and Stead 1997). The qualifying rounds for the World Cup finals take place within the confederations—national teams from five of the six confederations qualified for the World Cup in 1998 (Maguire and Pearton 2000).

Of the 704 players at France '98, 62 percent (436) worked in Europe. This in part reflects the fact that 15 of the 32 national teams that qualified for these final stages were from UEFA. UEFA keeps most of its own players working within its confederation. But UEFA also attracts the most players from other federations, 122 in total in 1998, and has the most movement *within* the confederation itself. Although there is movement of players between the countries that make up CONMEBOL (South America), there are no World Cup players from any of the other confederations playing there. CAF (Africa) similarly attracts no players from other confederations. AFC (Asia) and CONCACAF (North and Central America and the Caribbean) have only 9 players between them from other federations within their club systems. These figures thus emphasise the centrality of Europe in the international soccer labour market.

The most popular destinations for migrant World Cup players are the English, Italian and Spanish leagues, with the German *Bundesliga* also prominent. Clubs in these four leagues employed 270 of the players taking part in the World Cup finals. Five countries (England, Japan, Mexico, Saudi Arabia and Spain) had all 22 members of their squads playing at 'home'. In contrast, Nigeria did not have any of its players playing club football domestically, let alone any migrants. This is attributable in part to the **underdevelopment** of soccer in Nigeria but also due to the ongoing political unrest that is prevalent in that country. Several distinct patterns of labour migration were also evident at the confederation, European and national levels (Maguire and Pearton 2000).

CONMEBOL (South America) had five of its member nations at the World Cup finals (Brazil, Argentina, Paraguay, Colombia and Chile). Thus 110 players from South America were present. Of these 110 players, 41 (37.3 percent) play their club football outside South America; 30 of these 41 players (73 percent) earn their living in the Latin countries of Italy and Spain. Portugal, England and Germany are their other European destinations. In total, 83 percent of the South Americans playing outside CONMEBOL work in UEFA countries. A further 10 percent play in Mexico and, presumably, linguistic and geographical issues are significant. The remaining 7 percent work in the affluent, though not high status, Japanese and North American soccer leagues. CAF (Africa) also had five representatives at France '98 (Cameroon, Morocco, Nigeria, South Africa and Tunisia), again a total of 110 players. Clubs outside Africa employ a large proportion (67.3 percent) of these players. Overall, migration by African players is overwhelmingly to European countries, with just 4 percent of the migrants playing outside UEFA. Of the 74 African migrant players, 58 percent are located in nations with Mediterranean coastlines (France, Italy, Spain, Greece and Turkey), with France (19 percent) and Spain (18 percent) being the most popular destinations. Whilst economic factors are relevant, this is also due to the fact that these nations have historical and colonial links with North Africa.

The Eastern European talent pipeline, as already noted, has been a feature of several sports since the people's revolutions of the late 1980s. Western European soccer clubs have been some of the principal beneficiaries of this ongoing process. Of the 88 Eastern European players representing four nations (Bulgaria, Croatia, Romania and Yugoslavia) at France '98, 56 (63.6 percent) played outside Eastern Europe. Only 6 percent chose or were recruited by non-Western European clubs. Spain is their most popular destination; nearly one-third (29 percent) play for Spanish clubs. Germany, Italy and Turkey were also popular—arguably for geographical reasons, as all share borders with former Iron Curtain nations. Yet it is impossible to deduce whether the popularity of certain destinations is a function of player preference, club economics or coach selection policies. More qualitative research is required to complement this account.

Several key findings can be identified from this case study. First, UEFA (Europe) is confirmed as the core economy within world football. Europe is the principal destination for the very elite players who took part in the World Cup finals in 1998. Second, a pattern of very elite player recruitment within Europe is evident that arguably differs from migrant trails at a slightly lower level. In this study, the affluent English, Italian and Spanish clubs, which can afford the best of the elite, were found to be the major importers of soccer talent. Officials of clubs located within *Serie A*, the Premier League and the Spanish *Liga* may prefer to spend large sums of money on fewer, very elite players—those competing at the World Cup finals. In contrast, Belgian, French and German clubs may spread their cash by buying more players of a slightly lesser standard.

The rise of England as a major purchaser of elite soccer talent relates, in part, to the increased economic **power** possessed by Premier League clubs since their alliance with Rupert Murdoch's Sky TV network. This process may gather momentum with the Murdoch-owned company purchase of shares in several Premier League clubs, including Leeds United and Manchester United. This process has also been fuelled due to the re-entry of English clubs to European competitions after the ban of the late 1980s. For migrant soccer players, as shown in a study of elite cricketers, the desire to compete at the top level is also an important motivating factor. Yet, long-established talent pipelines and stereotypes held by coaches of the characteristics of players from specific nations also seem to play a part in decision-making processes. This case study confirms the well-established migrant links between Nordic countries and Britain/England (Maguire and Stead 1997). Many of the Norwegian and Danish squad members at France '98 play their club soccer in England and Scotland.

Another feature of the migration patterns identified was the number of South Americans playing in Italy and Spain. This phenomenon is a function of several factors. First, Brazilians and Argentinians make up the majority of South American immigrants to Spanish and Italian leagues. These nations have historically done very well in the World Cup and produced great players. Thus they would be an attractive proposition for the economically powerful clubs of Italy and Spain. Second, there is a linguistic and cultural link between Spain and many of the South American nations (except Brazil) because of their colonial past. This makes the assimilation of migrant players into Spanish culture much easier. This is arguably also a factor for migrants to Italy from South America. Third, perceived playing styles may have an influence on player selection. South American football is stereotypically renowned for its skill and flamboyancy. According to this stereotype, this fits in better with the playing styles of the Latin countries of Italy and Spain than in Northern Europe. Spanish clubs tend to do very little recruiting from other Western European nations (cf. Maguire and Stead 1997).

Although economics play a crucial part in contouring the patterns of soccer migration, they are by no means the only factor involved. Rather, sets of interdependencies contour and shape the global sports migration. Politics, history, geography and culture all affect the structuring of soccer migrant trails. Viewing these as interconnected processes allows a better grasp of how soccer migration patterns are bound up in global sport developments (Maguire and Pearton 2000).

Debating Point: Why Recruit and Why Move?

Several observations regarding the patterns, dimensions and issues described so far can now be made. Sports migration is bound up in a complex political economy that is itself embedded in a series of power struggles characterising the global sports system. Migration is marked by a series of political, cultural, economic and geographical issues and pressures that structure the migrant's life. These issues and pressures vary among sports played in different continents—they interweave in a fashion where no one factor dominates. Similarly, several motives are involved in the recruitment and travel choices of the migrant. In order to make sense of these choices, a typology of sports migration can be outlined. This typology provides us with a model and several ideal type-patterns to better understand the enabling and constraining features of the choices made by athletes. Neither the recruitment nor the actions of a migrant can be adequately understood without reference to a sociological model of migration.

Migrants identified as sports **pioneers** possess a passion and zeal in promoting the virtues of 'their' sport (Bromberger 1994). Their words and actions can be seen as a form of 'proselytising' by which they seek to convert local people to new sports cultures. In European soccer, migrants of this kind can be located around the turn of the 19th century. The movement of British citizens and anglophiles returning from a visit to the birthplace of soccer, and developing the game in places where clubs such as Athletic Bilbao, Zurich Grasshoppers and Djurgården (Stockholm) have subsequently developed, is a good example of pioneer activity. In sports such as ice-hockey, some Canadian migrants in Britain are perceived to be currently playing a similar role (Maguire 1996).

Some migrants can be identified as **settlers** who subsequently stayed and settled in the society where they performed their labour (Lanfranchi 1994). The Dane, Jan Molby, who migrated to play for Liverpool FC, demonstrates aspects of this migrant type—he is now resident and working as a soccer manager in the UK. Other migrants can be viewed as **mercenaries** who are motivated more by short-term gains and who use agents to secure lucrative deals with several clubs. These migrants have little or no attachment to the local, to a sense of place where they currently reside or play their sport. European soccer examples include the Bulgarian, Hristo Stoichkov; the Romanian, Gheorghe Popescu, who played for PSV Eindhoven, Tottenham Hotspur and Barcelona; and Nicholas Anelka, who moved from Paris St-Germain to Arsenal, and then, in quick succession, from Arsenal to Real Madrid before returning to Paris St-Germain.

In contrast, some migrants are **nomads** who are motivated more by a cosmopolitan engagement with migration. They use their sports career to travel and experience other cultures; they enjoy being the outsider, the stranger (Maguire and Stead 1996). Recently retired soccer players such as Eric Cantona, Jurgen Klinsmann and Ruud Gullet typified the 'cosmopolitan stranger'. Yet some cosmopolitans, along with pioneers, mercenaries and even long-term settlers, act as **returnees** in the European process. In these cases, the pull of home is strong enough that migrants eventually return to compete in their homeland. The motivation of migrants, then, is complex and multifaceted. So what is it about playing in, or for, a foreign land that is so appealing?

In probing the movement of Scandinavian soccer players to England, Stead and Maguire (2000) developed a series of questions that can also be used to consider the motivation of sports stars more generally. These questions include the following:

1. Are such moves considered a developmental stage in the personal lives of the players?

2. Do players see migration as a 'rite de passage' that will enhance their playing development?

3. Are their motives tied to financial lure or imperative?

4. Is migration part of the desire to 'be the best they can be', to perform on a global stage and to play for a nation irrespective of their own sense of national identity?

Stead and Maguire (2000) conclude that the players in their study were aware of the financially weak nature of domestic leagues in Scandinavia and the economic rewards available in England. Yet, their decision to move was influenced both by the desire to test their ability against 'the best' and a wish to experience life in different cultures. Stead and Maguire termed the Scandinavians interviewed *nomadic investors*— whose motives to move involved a complex blend of cultural, professional and economic elements. But the desire to move is one part of the migration equation—why would English soccer coaches be interested in Scandinavians and, indeed, how do coaches view potential migrants more generally?

In order to establish a fuller picture of the migration equation at the very elite level in soccer, it is also necessary to investigate the import of soccer talent. In examining the broad movement patterns identified between the EU and non-UEFA countries, several issues have to be considered in formulating an explanation (Stead and Maguire 2000; Maguire and Pearton 2000). Central among the factors that structure labour flows are the residual impact of colonial links and the reflection of these links through common language and culture, political and economic interdependencies, the residence of enclaves of nationals within the EU, and the history of both exploitation and support between countries. In addition, there is the significance of geographical proximity. This may extend further than just common borders or shorter travel routes. Consideration has to be given to the greater employment mobility arising from membership of pan-national politico-economic groupings such as the EU. Further, the cultural values of specific countries that encourage or permit people to engage in migration need examination. Equally, the cultural values of specific countries that welcome or discourage inward migration into their country have to be considered.

There are also factors specific to soccer. The relative status and reputation of the sport in different countries as defined by international playing success, quality and styles of play, characteristics of players, and economic prowess of clubs and leagues all play a part. The cosmopolitan nature of specific leagues and clubs and the clear intention by some officials to seek playing and political success by fostering inward migration must also be considered. More specifically, long-standing relationships can exist between clubs and countries based on previous player migration dealings and the exchange of coaches and officials, including missionary work undertaken in less developed soccer nations. Spectators can also demand and anticipate the inclusion of foreign players. In addition, the concept of migrant players being cash crops harvested from peripheral nations by the core soccer economies, primarily in the EU, and the development of new global talent sources by such economies are issues that require attention.

Some Eastern European countries have developed reputations as major producer nations, and powerful European clubs are constantly scouting for cheaper products they can import and exploit. Clearly, the lure of the financial gains accruing from a move to the West has provided a strong incentive and is important in explaining migration patterns. Professional opportunities in the East are usually limited. One consequence of this fact may be that the Eastern European player is regarded as a useful low-cost option for EU clubs. The increasing availability and sheer size of the resource also needs consideration. Geographical proximity, and with it, a history of shared ethnicity, culture, language and religion, also play a part in migration developments. During the Cold War era, this experience was restricted by the Iron Curtain, the dismantling of which has allowed earlier links to be rekindled. If the haemorrhaging of the East's best players continues, however, the degree to which Eastern Europe will remain a fertile source of soccer talent will be in question.

Italian and Spanish leagues are also a far more attractive employment proposition than the leagues in the Nordic countries. Glamorous, fanatically supported and with excellent facilities, clubs such as Barcelona (Spain) and AC Milan (Italy) are the power bases of European soccer. Other, more peripheral leagues are clearly less powerful and have a dependent relationship with the core clubs. Whilst some club sides such as Malmö and Göteborg (Sweden), Brondby (Denmark) and Rosenberg (Norway) have been successful in European competitions, there is not the financial infrastructure or the continuity of participation in high-level competition in Sweden, Denmark or Norway to persuade ambitious players to remain in the domestic leagues. But economics, as noted, is only part of the migration equation.

Soccer cultures foster and promote attitudes towards certain nationalities. The personal and professional characteristics attributed to Nordic players make them attractive to foreign clubs. This **ascribed status** includes high educational standards, language competencies and an aptitude for settling into new surroundings and cultures. Their indigenous playing styles are also seen as being adaptable, able to offer power and strength but with a high level of technical ability. In addition, there are the long-standing pan-European links of the Nordic nations and the game developed there through a history of exposure to coaches and players from other parts of Europe. In contrast to the attractiveness of

Nordic players, 'soccer wisdom' in the European north would suggest that the Latin temperament and style of playing would be inappropriate for the faster and more physical game to be found in northern leagues. Southern European players may also be considered by coaches, fellow players and fans as too volatile emotionally and unlikely to settle. Their level of education and competence in other languages may also be questioned. What is true of soccer may also apply to sports such as basketball and ice-hockey (Maguire 1999). The elements outlined do seem to be part of the reasons why athletes are recruited or why they migrate.

Disparities in Sports Migration

In studying sports migration beyond the question of why athletes move or the reasons why they are recruited, there are a series of issues that deserve more attention. The labour rights enjoyed by sports migrants, and indeed indigenous sports workers, vary considerably between sports and across continents. The **employment rights** achieved by players in team sports such as European soccer are minimal compared to the freedoms gained by athletes in individual sports, particularly in tennis and golf. Martina Hingis and Tiger Woods enjoy greater control over the production and exploitation of their sports talent than do EU soccer players of comparable ability such as Alessandro Del Piero or David Beckham. Not all participants in individual sports enjoy the advantages of tennis players or golfers, of course. Young female gymnasts also experience specific forms of exploitation regarding the control of their bodies, training, diet and performance (Ryan 1995).

Within team sports, employment rights also vary across sports played in different continents. Although North American athletes in sports such as American / Canadian football, ice-hockey, basketball and baseball are unionised and conduct negotiations with owners based on collective bargaining, they have not been that successful in gaining the same employment rights as other workers (Sage 1990). College athletes are still drafted or assigned to specific professional North American football and basketball teams. In comparison, the free movement of labour is now part of EU law. Individuals are free to perform and work where they wish within the EU. Employment protection legislation also applies to migrant labour. The European Court action brought by Jean-Marc Bosman against UEFA effectively secured the rights of EU sports stars to work in any country of the community without restriction (Maguire and Stead 1997; Stead and Maguire 2000). Yet, during late 2000, the European transfer system still operated, and its revision was subject to intense struggle between the players' union, the administrators of the game (UEFA and FIFA), the clubs and the European Commission. No resolution is yet in sight, but the European Commission appears deter-mined to abolish the existing system.

The rights that the Bosman case established are not applicable to all players. Individuals from countries outside the EU are subject to a selection procedure. Sports migrants have to prove international status in their respective sports. Further, as with migrants more generally, exploitative labour practices also take place. Questions concerning whether African and East European soccer players receive comparable wages and conditions to their EU counterparts need to form part of further research. Sports migration has its own highly differentiated political economy that reflects its position as part of the global sports system, and a migrant's experience is patterned along the system's fault lines.

Large-scale and prolonged migration of athletic labour can amount, in specific instances, to the **de-skilling** of **donor countries.** Latin and Central American countries, for example, regularly experience the loss of baseball stars and soccer players to the United States and Europe. Less developed countries invest in the production of athletic talent, but once these players reach maturity, more economically developed leagues, such as Major League Baseball, **recruit** the best available talent (Klein 1991). Not only is the **local** audience denied direct access to the talent nurtured and developed in their country, but, in some instances, such as with African national soccer teams, sports lose some of their quality performers when the demands of European clubs clash with interna-tional matches. Questions concerning national identity, underdevelop-ment and **dependent development** need to be addressed as part of the wider debate concerning sport migration (Bale and Sang 1996).

Reactions to and in the Host Culture

The reaction of sports labour migrants to the host culture also requires consideration. The constant moving back and forth between different cultures requires that particular types of migrants develop flexible personal controls, dispositions and means of orientation (King 1991). In developing this new kind of conduct, migrants such as tennis players and golfers face problems of intercultural communication. Major global sports festivals and tournaments involve a multilayered form of cultural communication involving interaction with other players, coaches, offi-cials, the crowd and media personnel. While some sports migrants may find the move from one culture to another relatively free of culture shock, this may not always be the case. There may be specific features of these processes that reflect broader gender inequalities that differen-tially hamper and constrain women: the gendered nature of these processes requires consideration.

Apart from leading to problems of **adjustment**, sports migration can also engender hostility in the host country. Sports labour unions, such as in European soccer, have sought to protect indigenous workers (players) by arguing for quotas and qualification thresholds to be applied to potential migrants. Despite the Bosman ruling—which, as noted, de-regulated the movement of sports labour within the EU—Gordon Taylor, general secretary of the Professional Footballers Association (PFA), continued to demand restrictions on non-EU migrants. The common themes that run through the cases of basketball, cricket, ice-hockey and soccer (Maguire 1988; Maguire and Stead 1996; Maguire 1996; Maguire and Stead 1997; Maguire and Pearton 2000; Stead and Maguire 2000) concern the perceived threat to national team perfor-mances and the underdevelopment of indigenous talent. These ques-tions are also surfacing in the contentious debate regarding the recent professionalisation of rugby union and the decision by officials of major English clubs to recruit overseas players in large numbers.

Debates of this kind also involve questions concerning national identity and **identity politics**. Issues of attachment to place, notions of self-identity and allegiance to a specific country are significant in this regard. The globalisation of capital has led to a transformation in the financial services industry (Dezalay 1990). This has led to a new category of professionals that include international lawyers, corporate tax ac-countants, financial advisers and management consultants. This group has played a pivotal role in the attempts by transnational corporations to chart and formalise the newly globalised economic arena. While the experiences of these professionals is not exactly the same as for all sports migrants, in certain respects some elite sports migrants appear to share some of the values of these financial entrepreneurs. National teams are, for some migrants, 'flags of convenience' to ensure they are able to display their talents to a worldwide audience on a global stage (Maguire and Stead 1996).

Indeed, sports migrants, such as the Americans performing in the World League of American Football or Africans recruited by American universities, may have little sense of attachment to a specific space or local community. Highly rational and technical criteria determine their status and market value and thus sports migrants embrace the ethos of hard work, differential rewards and a win-at-all-costs approach. The 'rebel' cricket and rugby tours to South Africa in the 1980s and early 1990s illustrated how sports migrants can likewise act as mercenaries for big business. Sometimes, the link between corporate business and sports migrants is only too clear. Take, for example, the Rugby Super League developed by Rupert Murdoch, where player contracts were bought to ensure a product would be displayed by the media outlet broadcasting such sports. In a deregulated transfer market, player migration may well begin to reflect the conjunction of corporate inter-ests. For example, the involvement of Nike and Sky TV with Manchester United may ensure that the sponsors and media companies can place player contracts with clubs they have a vested interest in promoting.

Debating Point: Is Importing Labour Good or Bad for Local Player Development?

Issues concerning power and control of sport arise when answering the question of whether the recruitment of foreign migrants is good or bad. What counts as good or bad depends on who decides and by what criteria—whoever defines what counts as 'success' wins the argument over player migration. Whether consideration is given to basketball, cricket, ice-hockey or soccer, similar tensions are evident (Bale and Maguire 1994; Maguire 1988; Maguire and Stead 1996; Maguire 1996; Stead and Maguire 2000; Maguire and Pearton 2000). In the develop-ment of English basketball over the past three decades, tensions have centred round three areas of conflict:

1. Between promoters of the commercial success of the clubs and promoters of the prestige associated with the national team

2. Between entrepreneurs striving for short-term viability and offi-cials concerned with long-term development

3. Between marketers of a spectacle that can be sold to the media and advocates of local identity and player development

Over the past three decades a transformation has occurred in English basketball. Elite participants have shifted from being amateur, home-based players to the majority being achievement-oriented mi-grants plus a few indigenous workers. The game itself became a com-modity, with new owners seeking to restructure the game in order to compete in the media and sponsorship marketplace. As part of this process, the cultural meaning of the game shifted in the direction of 'spectacle'. Dovetailing with this commodification of the game, an **Americanisation** process unfolded that has involved the recruitment of American sports migrants as players and coaches, the adoption of American-style marketing strategies and media coverage and a change in the ideological messages underpinning the game focusing on Ameri-can spectacle and entertainment. More recently, the National Basketball Association (NBA) has identified English basketball as a location to expand its operations (Falcous and Maguire 1999).

This transformation has been marked by conflicts between two groups. On the one hand, the desire of a new breed of club owners and their auxiliaries, the American sports migrants, is to provide an instant commercial product to 'display' to spectators. On the other, there is the aspiration of more established officials of the English Basketball Association (EBBA) to build the foundations for the long-term playing success of English basketball. As the game became subject to economic goals, its success was tied to its market value. That is, the viability of clubs became more and more dependent on income derived from spectators, sponsors and the media. The new owners of clubs actively encouraged this process and proposed structural changes to the league that led to an intensification of commodification processes. In turn, this commodification allowed the recruitment of American sports migrants to become a formal strategy of the clubs (Maguire 1988). Most groups initially supported the recruitment of American players. The hope was that the entertainment they would provide would produce several benefits, but above all more sponsorship and media coverage, increased attendance figures, greater participation rates and improved playing standards. Such arguments did not persuade those concerned with the long-term development of the local/national game.

Throughout the 1980s and 1990s, English players tended to increasingly occupy supporting positions. Exponents of migrant recruitment tended to downplay the conflict between indigenous, dual national and naturalised players competing for team positions. The strongest sides were those who combined the recruitment of top Americans with significant sponsorship from large transnational corporations. Despite some internal dissension during the 1980s, the EBBA publicly welcomed this commercialisation and praised the increased media attention and growth in sponsorship. Fear of the commercial consequences of removing American sports migrants from the league led to a relative loss of power to the increasingly commercially oriented clubs. This resulted in English players, coaches and, ironically, the EBBA becoming marginalised. Officials and coaches concerned about the development of native English players were losing ground to those who advocated the need to recruit American players to provide an entertainment package that would attract spectators, media coverage and sponsorship.

In the early stages of the National Basketball League (NBL), concern was expressed regarding the number of American imports; towards the end of the 1970s and in the early 1980s, criticism of the number of dual nationals began to rise. At issue was the fact that, while a particular team could have two foreign players on its roster, it could also add Americans who could claim British nationality. Given the rationale underpinning the commodification of basketball, it is not surprising that clubs sought to exploit this loophole. By the early 1980s, the question of dual nationals had become 'the most contentious issue in English basketball' (Maguire 1988).

Despite this, the growth in the number of migrants designated as dual nationals and 'English acquired'—players who had served a minimum residence period—continued. Not just content to frustrate attempts to reduce the recruitment of migrant Americans, the clubs sought to increase their power. This, coupled with the influx of Americans and the distribution of the wealth coming into the game, prompted several criticisms. Dave West, then coach of Stockport Thoroglaze Belgrade, writing in 1982, called on the EBBA to 'enforce regulations to safeguard the future of England's juniors'. He argued that

> We sacrifice the future of the game for the Americans.... We must have the only national team in European basketball that speaks with an American accent. The introduction of the foreign player has helped to popularise the game.... But their numbers must be controlled to create opportunities for our own players to develop. The ... Association ... must be responsible for its future development. (Maguire 1988)

Although West suggested that the English national team was the only one in Europe to speak with an American accent, the processes in question were occurring to varying degrees throughout Europe and elsewhere (McKay et al. 1993; Olin and Penttila 1994). Such comments, however, vividly highlight the contested nature of the recruitment of sports migrants and the shift of the game towards spectacle. In addition, while West argued that the future of the game lies with the Association, he overlooked the extent to which the power of the EBBA had declined. The growing power of Basketball Marketing Limited, the company set up by the EBBA and the clubs, and the growing ownership of clubs by entrepreneurs not hitherto connected with the sport were indicative of this.

The struggle over the import of American migrants continued throughout the 1980s and 1990s. The struggle between those seeking to develop the sport as media entertainment and those seeking to promote it as a participant game has continued to mark English basketball to this day. As those who sought to further commodify the game gained ground, the concomitant Americanisation of the game accelerated. In 1985, then English national coach Bill Beswick felt that this process had already gone too far. He argued that unless basketball had 'a well-thought out, properly organised structure ... [it would] fragment and alienate the various areas of development, and ... leave the NBL an over-commercialised, over-Americanised entertainment package with little or no relationship to the real game ... in this country' (Maguire 1988).

Since that time, **power** within the game has shifted even further in the direction of the owners and away from the EBBA. While the development of English basketball in the late 1990s is yet to be fully charted, the general trend towards basketball becoming a commodity to be sold and to be consumed as a spectacle provided by the labour of American migrants remains evident (Falcous and Maguire 1999). However, given the general instability of the English game, the position of the American sports migrants would appear to be marked by insecurity. The national team has enjoyed precious little success and the team remains over-reliant on dual national Americans. A similar picture holds true with regard to British ice-hockey, though the migrants in that case are Canadian (Maguire 1996). If this is true of these marginal sports, what of soccer, the so-called English 'national game'?

The debate in English and European soccer over the relative impact of migrant players has several dimensions. There are, as with basketball and ice-hockey, perceived advantages and disadvantages with regard to immigration. The advantages are perceived to lie in the better quality of performance—with foreign players improving the standards of existing players and also acting as a role model for younger players. The disadvantages are seen to stem from the lack of opportunities for indigenous players and the concomitant lack of investment in good quality talent identification and development by clubs. By employing too many foreign players the club, the league and eventually the national team enter a phase of dependent development. These disadvantages are even more pronounced in the leagues, such as the English, where indigenous player emigration is limited: elite English players are infrequently employed by other European clubs. On the other hand, with this influx of migrant players it is not uncommon for some Premier League clubs to have only one or two English players in the starting lineup. This imbalance between the import of foreign players and the export of English players exacerbates the problem. While this clearly restricts opportunities for current senior players, the impact these processes have on youth development is even greater.

With the growing commodification of European soccer, the rewards for success and the cost of failure are so great that managers cannot afford the promise of longer-term youth development. Instead, British managers go for ready-made, experienced foreign players who offer a greater chance of instant success. The response to these issues has been contradictory. Increasingly, national federations express concern that the combined effects of a rapid influx of foreign players and the absence of youth development policies equate to a decline in national playing standards (Maguire and Pearton 2000). In many instances, youth or reserve teams have been abandoned and 'nursery-club' links established in less developed soccer nations. The resistance to these processes has been matched by a concern with the development of national teams. The presence of overseas players denies indigenous players access to teams and leads, in some instances, to personal and national underdevelopment.

Cesare Maldini, then Italian under-21 national coach, highlighted this issue when he noted in 1993 that 'at youth level, our football is getting worse. We don't have the players any more. The increasing number of foreigners in our game means the opportunities for the youngsters are vanishing' (Maguire 1994). In contrast to these sentiments, major European soccer club owners seek to strengthen their position at every opportunity. In response to Maldini, Silvio Berlusconi, then owner of AC Milan, highlighted the struggles involved. He argued for no restrictions on sports migration. As part of this process, Berlusconi concluded that 'the concept of the national team will, gradually, become less and less important. It is the clubs with which the fans associate' (Maguire 1994). Given this approach, the fortunes of the national team become secondary. Corporate success is what counts. The emergence of the Champions League has reinforced these processes, and migrant labour is now an integral feature of the English Premier League. The longer-term consequences are yet to be fully appreciated.

Summary

This chapter has sought to highlight some of the broad patterns and structures that characterise global sports migration. In addition, attention has been paid to the enabling and constraining features of global sport that shape sports migration processes, and also to the experiences of migrants and the issues of power, culture and control that influence their decision to travel and their reception once they arrive. In making sense of the broad patterns and structures identified, due regard has to be paid both to the political economy of global sport and to the social and cultural flows that interweave with the political and economic. In working out the migration equation, consideration has to be given to the broader context and to those factors specific to sport.

Relevant societal processes include the ongoing impact of colonial heritages and cultural linkages and non-sport-related migrant experiences, cultural and legal encouragement or discouragement of migration, social/cultural/economic dependency and exploitation and political changes within and between societies and power blocs. Sport-related processes are multilayered and include the ascribing of status to particular sporting traditions/leagues or the playing characteristics of specific nationalities, ethnic or gender groups; the political, economic and playing ambitions of particular clubs, leagues, national associations or confederations; the role of agents, known talent pipelines and social/coaching networks; and the identification, development and exploitation of new talent sources. The speed, scale and volume of future migration will be contoured along the points outlined. Clearly these issues must be dealt with in an integrated manner—only then will the sports migration equation be more readily understood.

Key Terms and Concepts

achieved/ascribed status
Americanisation
cultural adjustment
host/donor countries
identity politics
labour migration
local/global
mercenaries
nomads
pioneers

dependent development
de-skilling
employment rights
power
recruitment/retention
returnees
settlers
talent pipelines
underdevelopment

Review Questions

1. Outline the connection between sports labour migration and globalisation processes.
2. Explain the main issues involved in sports labour migration.
3. What are the main patterns and features of sports labour migration?
4. In what ways can elite sports labour migration be described as a male preserve?
5. Account for the main reasons why elite athletes migrate, and describe what problems they encounter.
6. In seeking to explain the sports labour migration process, assess the merits of the argument that an economic analysis is a necessary but not sufficient explanation.
7. Critically examine the patterns of labour migration evident at the 1998 men's World Cup soccer tournament. How do you explain what you observe?
8. In what ways can an understanding of the typology of labour migrants help explain the patterns of migration?
9. Critically account for how the changing balance of power, ownership and control of elite sport helps explain the growth and development of migration over the past decade.
10. What are the main sport policy implications involved for those sports that are marked by a significant growth in inward and/or outward labour migration?

Projects

1. Choose a major sport and document, using player rosters, the nature and extent of player migration. Compare this data with similar evidence from an earlier period. What are the similarities and differences?

2. Select a sport where both men and women migrate. Using a variety of sources, compare and contrast the experience of the athletes involved. What do your findings tell you about gender and global sport processes?

3. Contact your local professional club. Arrange to conduct interviews with a sample of elite players. Draw up a set of questions that will explore their reasons for migrating and their experience of living in another country.

4. Examine a sport where the issue of migration is controversial. Identify the main individuals involved in the decision-making process concerning the recruitment and retention of migrants. Highlight how these people and their decisions are contested by less powerful groups.

5. Choose one elite labour migrant from a developing country. Using a variety of sources, explain the career of this athlete. What factors will you have to take into account and what concepts will you use?

6. Interview a sample of sports fans and ask them their views on the costs and benefits associated with migrants representing their local club or national team. Explore the extent to which local and national identities are strengthened or weakened by such migrants.

SPORT, MEDIA AND SOCIETY

Objectives

After completing this chapter, you should be able to

- discuss the historical development of media sport relations;
- evaluate the extent to which sport is interdependent with the media industry;
- describe and explain the dimensions of the media sport complex;
- critically analyse competing claims that mediated sport can reinforce or challenge established social relations;
- analyse the power networks that characterise media sport relations; and
- discuss the impact of sponsorship, advertising and marketing on the organisation, structure and content of sport.

The **mass media** is part of our everyday lives. We experience its various forms on a daily basis whether we are reading a newspaper or magazine, watching television, listening to the radio or accessing the Internet. And it seems impossible to reject the immense influence that the media has had on sport. This is not to say that sport has not left its mark on the media. Rather, sport and the media are interdependent social institutions. Some sports are attractive to the media, particularly television, as a source of **advertising** revenue and a boost to viewership. And, of course, the media creates financial benefits and publicity for many sports (Coakley 1998; Lobmeyer and Weidinger 1992; Nixon 1984; Nixon and Frey 1996). Mediated sport constitutes an important part of our existence. It informs us about sport and sportspeople, which in turn influences the way that we think about our world. And the great spectacle of mediated sport provides us with entertainment.

Growth and Development of Mediated Sport

The mass media takes many forms including newspapers, magazines, books, film, television (terrestrial, satellite, cable and digital), radio, video and the Internet. Throughout the 20th century, both the media and sport have become increasingly diverse and pervasive. That is to say, there has been an increase in the range of media and sport forms and a growing influence of each in our daily lives. These are cultural institutions with long and complex histories. There are many excellent reviews of the historical processes that have been influential in shaping modern media sport relations (Barnett 1990; Boyle and Haynes 2000; Goldlust

1987; Rowe 1999; Horne et al. 1999). Whilst each institution has distinct and different organisations, practices, ideologies and personnel, there has always been some connection between the two. Understanding these interactions, in their historical context, can help unravel the complexities of mediated sport in contemporary society.

With the rise of industrialisation, technological innovation and commercial practices and values in Western societies, the mass media has developed into a profit-oriented institution that has immense cultural importance as a means of communication (Rowe 1999). Whilst images of 18th-century sport were depicted in paintings, sketches and poetic literature, mass communication of sporting information developed during the late 19th century with the emergence of the print media: newspapers, sporting magazines and books. In Great Britain, what we have come to know as the popular press began in 1896 when *The Daily Mail* came into circulation (Horne et al. 1999). The growth of spectator sports and the associated emphasis on gambling in the late 18th century helped to increase the popularity of the press. Newspapers provided news, results and a betting market in horse racing, prize fighting and animal blood sports (Boyle and Haynes 2000).

Only some sports enjoyed greater visibility through media attention. In the main, those sports that were patronised by the aristocracy (such as hunting, coursing and fishing) and those that attracted a working-class betting dimension (such as horse racing and prize fighting), benefited from press promotion. **Commercial processes** were evident in the development of mediated sport from around the 1870s. The sporting press, which included such literature as *The Field Magazine* and *The Shooting Times* (Boyle and Haynes 2000), *Sporting Life* and *The Sporting Chronicle* (Horne et al. 1999), featured numerous commercial advertisements. In addition, the increasing influence of newspapers began to popularise the economic values of sport. Whannel (1992) notes that radio broadcasting slowly established itself as a competitor to the print press for sport news and commentary from 1925. The first radio broadcasts of outside sports included major events such as the Grand National, the Boat Race and Wimbledon and sports such as rugby union and amateur golf. At the beginning of the 20th century, technological innovations in the film industry had a significant effect in providing **audiences** with information and entertainment of a sporting nature. Moving sports images such as action from Derby Day or Football Cup finals were captured on film, particularly on newsreel, for the first time.

The relationships between sport and television became especially intense throughout the 20th century, although they developed relatively slowly. Technical difficulties with the quality and range of transmitted images were not successfully overcome until the 1950s, even though television was launched in the late 1930s, and the FA Cup final was first broadcast by the British Broadcasting Corporation in 1939 (Wagg 1984). Improvements in camera technology and transmission coupled with the introduction of commercial television in 1955 provided more entertaining sports programmes (Whannel 1992). The development of the electronic media continued more rapidly from the 1960s, as is evident in the development of video and satellite, and later, cable, digital networks and the Internet. Significant changes in the British press were also happening from the 1960s onwards. In particular, the tabloid revolution increased the popularity and coverage of sport. That is to say, sensation and scandal began to characterise sports journalism in an attempt to gain greater reader numbers in an increasingly competitive media market (Horne et al. 1999).

The development towards what we can now define as a global media sport network has been marked by further technological expansion, especially in electronic media, and such innovations as pay-per-view events and sports channels such as Sky Sports. As Maguire highlights, modern mediated sports are global media spectacles. World Cup soccer tournaments and the Olympic Games, for example, are broadcast to more than 200 countries across the globe (Maguire 1999). ESPN International (Entertainment Sports Network, a subsidiary of ABC, the American Broadcasting Companies) goes 'on air' to more than 127 million houses in 150 countries around the world (Bellamy 1998), and 17 of the top 20 television programmes in history are sports events (Coakley 1998).

The global nature of media sport is connected with its development into big business. Mediated sport is a rapidly expanding commercial industry. Television companies pay in excess of $800 million for the right to screen the Summer Olympics. The television industry directly finances sports such as soccer and rugby in the United Kingdom and the 'big four' (baseball, American football, ice-hockey and basketball) in the United States via TV-rights fees that reach multimillion-pound (and multimillion-dollar) sums. In addition, advertising and merchandising associated with sport provide growing revenue for global commercial sports and media institutions.

Towards an Understanding of Media Sport: The Media Sport Complex

One way to make sense of the relationships between sport, the media and society is to adopt a theoretical framework called the **media sport complex** (Jhally 1989; Maguire 1999; Wenner 1989). This is represented in generalised diagrammatic form in figure 3.1.

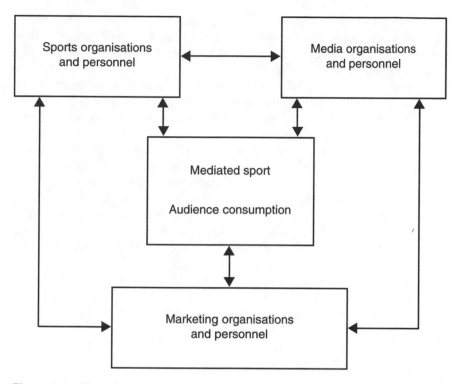

Figure 3.1   The media sport complex.
Adapted from Wenner (1989).

In figure 3.1, the three groups that form the basis of media sport **production** and **consumption** are media organisations and personnel, sports organisations and personnel and marketing organisations and personnel. Sociologists of sport study these groups to get a more accurate understanding of the complexities of media sport **marketing** relations. Two key elements of mediated sport are often considered. First, there is a great deal of interest in media sport production—that is, the way in which mediated sport is packaged, represented and transmitted for television, radio, newspapers, journals, magazines and the Internet. More specific lines of inquiry into media sport production focus on the technical dimensions and narrative techniques associated with sports **representation.** Analyses of technical dimensions centre on what is selected and highlighted for audience viewing, the numbers and angles of cameras and the use of zoom lenses, split screens and replays (Gruneau 1989; Horne et al. 1999; Rowe 1999). The study of narrative techniques in mediated sport concerns what is said during sports commentaries, who is saying it and who is being spoken about. These studies argue that rather than relaying a simple reflection of the world, mediated sport constructs particular images and presents specific messages about the world in which we live (Creedon 1994; Kinkema and Harris 1992).

Second, there is a rising interest in the perceptions and reactions of those who watch, read or listen to mediated sport. Audience figures for the Olympics, World Cup events and Wimbledon exceed 10 million. But why do people watch, read or listen? Of interest here are the ways in which mediated sport forms are consumed by their audiences. Questions concern the composition of particular audiences in terms of class, gender and age; the motivations of audiences—the reasons why they watch or read or listen; and the ways in which media sport shapes people's perceptions of reality. Wider issues of **ownership** power and **control,** including the extent to which some key groups have more or less power in deciding which sports are mediated and how they are reproduced, are also important. Other fundamental issues include whose interests are being served in these decision-making processes; the impact of mediated sport on the people who watch, read and hear about it; and the degree of freedom and choice that audiences have as they consume mediated sport. It is important to keep in mind that sport and the media are social institutions that have come into being through human interaction. People shape sports and media organisations and practices and they give meaning to them. Hence, all of the groups represented in the media sport complex should be viewed as interdependent and located within a larger cultural, political and economic sphere.

Debating Point:
Does Sport Depend on the Media?

The study of media sport concerns questions about the nature of power relationships among sports, the mass media, commercial interests and audiences. Much of the literature on media sport relations concerns the effects of the media on sport and the ways in which sport relies on the media for its survival. However, the degree to which sport is dependent on the media and the extent to which the media controls sport varies between sports, over time and according to particular cultural contexts. Some professional sports, for example, are relatively dependent on the media as a secure source of income. These sports include soccer, rugby and cricket in Britain and basketball, American football, ice-hockey and baseball in the United States. But these sports are also reliant on other commercial agencies such as sponsors and advertisers as a source of revenue. For sports whose survival is grounded in profit maximisation,

then, media finance is important but not sin_
ing organisations also have an impact on t_

Two key arguments, primarily focuse_
identified in this area of study. First, te_
agencies have changed and will continu_
own financial interests. Second, these cl_
sion sport product that persuades audiences _
tural values. That is, audiences are so captivated by _
spectacle of television sport that they are manipulated by _
systems integral to both the sports programmes and associated adver_
tising.

Sport has, over time, changed to meet the demands of television production. For example, the summer Olympic Games have been extended by 2 days to 17 days so that sports can be programmed over two extra weekends, making maximum use of (U.S.) prime-time television. This can boost audience figures and increase revenue sales from the associated increase in advertising commitment. Television companies also influence the location of the Olympic Games. Locations in the United States have tended to dominate the choice of Olympic venue since 1968 (Coakley 1998). It is U.S. television companies such as the National Broadcasting Company (NBC) that are guaranteeing the greatest amount of money for the rights to screen the Olympic Games. Securing these exclusive screening rights will raise profits through **sponsorship** and advertising and increase the global status of NBC, which has paid approximately $3.6 billion for the television rights for the Olympic Games until 2008 (Coakley 1998). Given this, it can be claimed that scheduling of Olympic events is, in the main, determined by U.S. prime-time viewing. The timing of events can, in some instances, be changed so that live broadcasts can be presented at prime times, thus increasing the chance of advertising revenue.

Seeking to attract a casual audience, and hence sponsors and advertisers, intensifies the need to package media sport in an exciting, entertaining manner. Audiences tend to change their viewing in response to scheduling and timing of programmes, type of competition, possibility of national success and the presence of personalities. The media selects, interprets and explains sports action in order to engage and hold the audience. Visual, verbal and auditory techniques are utilised in the creation of dramatic sports **spectacles** that have viewers sitting on the edge of their seats in the comfort of their own homes. Rather like a theatrical production, drama is created in several ways. Often sports events take place at spectacular venues. Focusing on the *live* event is a key feature of the packaging of sport for entertainment. So too is the immediate presentation of performances and analyses. Setting the scene is made easier when events occur in cities and countries that have

ng and recognisable landmarks. The Opera House in Sydney
ed a captivating backdrop for mediated productions of the 2000
pics. Showing highlights from past action, in particular those that
ture emotional crisis or triumph, is a method of constructing tension
nd excitement. Long-lasting images of Paul Gascoigne's emotions at
the 1990 World Cup or the joyful tears of Garry Herbert (cox to the Searle
brothers, Olympic champions in coxed pairs rowing, Barcelona 1992)
were created by media replays, close-ups and slow-motion representations (Whannel 1992). Maximising the connection between sports performers and the audience is another technique aimed at attracting
audiences. Heroes such as English soccer player Gary Lineker and
villains such as Vinnie Jones are good examples of the creation of sports
stars. This technique can be based on a single dramatic performance or
on a series of episodes, rather like the telling of a story. Camera technique, lighting, sound and commentary make an important contribution to the production of dramatic sports action.

Sports have undergone many changes in the interests of the media,
advertisers and sponsors. These changes have created opportunities for
high scoring, such as the three-point shot in basketball, and rapid action
scoring, such as rally (American) scoring in squash and the tie-break in
tennis. The intensification of tensions between players and teams, such
as that produced by medal play rather than stroke play in golf, whereby
the former produces an exciting climax at every hole, is also indicative
of these changes. There are other ways in which television has changed
aspects of sport in order to retain audience interest. Two examples are
the introduction of players' names on shirts and the use of visible
numbers identifiable by commentators in athletic events.

Power, Control and Ownership in Media Sport

So, it is clear that sport has changed in the interests of television. Sport
is represented on the screen in ways that are attractive to the viewers.
Some more commercially oriented sports have become increasingly
dependent on television, sponsorship and advertising revenue. The
balance of power in these cases tends to rest with those holding the purse
strings. In Britain, processes of professionalisation in rugby union have
been influenced by the global demands of television. The Rugby Football Union (RFU) and British Sky Broadcasting (BSkyB) had a contract
worth £87.5 million for exclusive screening of England's International
Games and the five national championships from 1996–2001 (Boyle and
Haynes 2000). This secured revenue for players and administrators of
the game. Yet, as Maguire and Tuck (1998) note, it also congested the
scheduling of games, extended the traditional league season and, thus,
increased the demands and pressures on the players. Professionalisation

of rugby union and the associated demands of media, sponsorship and advertising agencies have served to shift the ideals of the game away from its traditional amateur roots and towards values of the commercial world of modern sport. This apparent dependence of sport on the media and business organisations is never total. Rather, media sport relations are characterised by interdependent **commercial** relationships.

Athelaide and Snow (1979) claim that the nature and character of sport has changed in response to the commercial interests of the media. In this sense, the mediated sport product is less about the action, skill and performances on the field of play and more about the creation of a theatrical display for the purpose of attracting an audience that can be 'exchanged' for large sums of money from advertising revenue. For Chandler (1988), however, it is arguable that television has turned sports into nothing more than another dimension of the entertainment industry devoid of value and unworthy of our attention. Sports viewers can, of course, choose what they watch. Sports governing bodies and governments can also make decisions about changes to the organisation and structure of sports. In Britain, the traditional association of rugby union with the BBC was removed with the aforementioned BSkyB deal. Several politicians and advocates of sporting tradition vehemently resisted the exclusion of rugby union from a terrestrial television channel widely accessible to the British nation. Games involving Scotland, Wales, Ireland, France and Italy continue to be screened on the BBC (Boyle and Haynes 2000).

Wider political decisions and legislation can also influence the extent to which the media has control over sport. For example, laws governing monopolistic business practices, whereby one organisation is deemed to be autonomous in its control over a particular commercial sector, have restricted the impact of some media institutions in the world of sport. In 1998, the £623.4 million ($1.05 billion) offer from BSkyB for Manchester United was referred by the then UK Trade Secretary, Peter Mandelson, to the Monopolies and Mergers Commission (MMC). Stephen Byers, UK Secretary of State for Trade and Industry blocked the proposal on the basis that this media sport merger would enable BSkyB to secure Premier League football rights in the future, restrict entry of other media interests into the pay-per-view market, cause prices of BSkyB sports to rise, and restrict viewing choice and innovation. In addition, it was claimed that such a merger would raise ticket prices, intensify fixtures, further increase the inequality in wealth between clubs and give BSkyB influence over the organisation of football that may not be in the interests of the game (Finbow 1999).

It can be argued that the media is of benefit to sport for reasons other than profit. Television sports for example are enjoyable, stimulating and interesting for many people. As the influence of the media has intensified, sport has become more accessible to an increasing number of people. Media sport informs people about the teams they support and, perhaps, might fuel their interest in sporting activity. For Chandler (1988), media sport has made public the reality of professional, commercially oriented sport and exposed it for open criticism. This, she concludes, helps to destroy the myth that sport is always an inspirational, harmonious activity. Thus, media sport may be more, rather than less, of a real representation.

The interdependent relationships between sports organisations, media companies and marketing agencies are fundamental to the survival of commercial spectator sports. Yet, the mass media does not have an impact on all sports: sports that do not depend on media, sponsorship or advertising are played all over the world. These sports and games, including amateur and voluntary sports and leisure / recreational activities, may reflect particular personal and community ideals and identities. It is also the case that some sports can provide an immense benefit to the mass media. Sports programmes make a significant contribution to increased television ratings. People watch, read about and listen to mediated sports in large, sometimes vast, numbers. Major events such as World Cup competitions and the Olympic Games attract millions of viewers (Wenner 1989).

People 'tune in' to sports for many reasons. Many people watch television because they have nothing better to do or they want to relax. In this sense, watching sports programmes may be defined as a 'default' activity. That is, people often watch sports just because they are on the television at a time when they happen to be watching. Committed fans, however, want to see particular teams or individual performers succeed. From the comfort of their own armchairs, often in the company of other fans, they can follow the action, offer vocal support, share in the excitement, tension and drama, comment on specific aspects of performance and learn more about particular players and sports (Wenner and Gantz 1989). Whatever the motivations for watching, reading about or listening to sports, audience share is increased. As a result, sports have a high recognition factor (Lash and Urry 1994).

Sports news and stories can provide increased circulation of print media forms such as newspapers and sports magazines and there can be long-term scheduling benefits to television stations (Coakley 1998). With a large, captive audience, television companies have the opportunity to advertise future programmes and schedules to attract greater audience numbers over longer periods of time. In addition, sports audiences can be 'sold' in lucrative deals to advertisers and sponsors. Companies such as McDonald's, Budweiser, Coca-Cola and large tobacco and brewery corporations invest heavily in sports advertising in order to sell their products. There seems to be an interdependent relationship between the media and sport. And in countries where sports have become forms of commercial entertainment and where the importance of power and money prevail, the interrelationships between the media and sport have become intensified.

These relations represent situations of conflict and co-operation over the ways in which sport is represented. Tensions and harmonies prevail and reveal a complex network of power relations characterised by accommodation, resistance and negotiation. This reflects the distinct historical roots of the mass media and sport and their different agendas (Boyle and Haynes 2000). Indeed, media sport relations differ between sports and according to the means of mediation. The interaction between the two institutions has been described as one of 'mutual interest' (Coakley 1998; Rowe 1999). That is, the relationships between sport and the media are characterised by enabling and constraining features for both institutions.

Debating Point: Does Media Sport Reflect and Reinforce Dominant Social Values?

There are many different techniques, styles and forms for representing sport in the media. **Visual techniques** include zoom lenses, split screens, slow-motion replay and the use of graphics. **Narrative techniques** are utilised in commentaries and feature different uses and styles of language and sound. Visual and narrative techniques serve to inform the audience about the process and outcome of the game or event and to create a drama and spectacle for audience entertainment. It is true to say that mediated sports are not simple presentations of reality but are representations of selected, highlighted and edited sports constructed to inform and entertain the viewers (Whannel 1992).

Mediated productions of sport reflect certain people's ideas and values about particular sports and the societies in which they are located. The style and content of these programmes focuses on entertaining the audience, who often become so involved with what they read, hear and see that they accept it as reality. This point is summarised by Boyle and Haynes (2000) who explain that mediated sport is saturated with images and ideals which at times reflect, construct and legitimise but also challenge and (re)constitute attitudes which permeate wider society. Work of this kind addresses the more general debate as to whether audiences are **skilled consumers** or **cultural dupes**. At the heart of this debate are questions of power and **knowledgeability**. Research suggests that the selected forms of sport that we have access to through the media articulate beliefs about many social issues including age, class, gender, race, ethnicity, nationalism, (dis)ability and other diverse aspects of personal and social identities (Coakley 1998; Chandler 1988; Hargreaves 1986; Kinkema and Harris 1992; Whannel 1992). These underlying messages can influence people's ideas about their social world even though audiences tend not to think consciously about it in this way.

Race and Ethnic Relations in Media Sport

It is often argued that media coverage of sport represents established ideas about race and ethnic relations. In particular, the media tends to discuss the participation of black racial groups in terms of their 'apparent' and 'natural' physical superiority. Cashmore (1996) states that stereotypes of the natural black athlete have commonly been used by media personnel as explanations for the dominance (overrepresentation) of black people in some sports. This ideology represents what Coakley (1998) refers to as *race logic*. He notes that this way of thinking began to develop during the 17th century when white Europeans were attempting to explain why some people in the world looked and behaved very differently from them. The common belief at this time was that black people were savage, primitive and uncivilised with underdeveloped intellectual capabilities. White people considered themselves to be intellectually superior and this justified their oppression of black people. Throughout history this race logic has permeated ideology about colour of skin, character and intellectual and physical capability. It has formed the basis of white dominance and prejudice against black people in many spheres of society including sport, and there is evidence that it exists, albeit in covert ways, in today's society. These ideas are perpetuated in current media sport stereotypes. Davis and Harris (1998) argue that race and ethnicity are not central points of discussion in media coverage of sport. Rather, there is a tendency to focus on the commercial success and star status of black athletes. The successes of British boxers, such as Frank Bruno, Chris Eubank and Lennox Lewis, and soccer players, such as Paul Ince, Ian Wright and Andy Cole, certainly represent positive images of black sportspeople. These stand in stark contrast with the cultural myths and links made between being black and inner-city deprivation and criminal activity.

Media coverage of black sportspeople also serves to reflect common-sense racial stereotypes concerning their innate physical capabilities. In addition, there have been several editorial comments and leading articles concerning the dominance of black athletes (Anthony 2000; Richardson 1995; Walker 1995). In 1995, Sir Roger Bannister, Britain's first four-minute miler and, for some, a respected sport scientist, presented the theory that black athletes have natural anatomical and physiological advantages over white athletes, which explains the success of black athletes on the track. Yet this line of thinking is based on unsubstantiated racial generalisations. In response to this theory, British athlete Mark Richardson (400m) highlights that more convincing explanations of black athletic success are connected to sociological arguments. As Richardson (1995) suggests, the appeal of athletics to many black people is that it is accessible and offers a context in which recognition is based on objective measures of success. In addition, the emergence of black athletic talent and the media publicity that surrounds these achievements has served to raise the profile of black athletes and create more visible role models for black communities. As Walker (1995) notes, the rise in prominence of successful black athletes may also help to construct a self-perpetuating belief that black people *can* and *will* achieve results in particular social spheres such as sports.

A self-fulfilling belief may also be reinforced amongst white people that the odds are stacked against them in particular events and they would be better off in sports that were not dominated by black athletes. In addition to this type of direct, public discussion, television commentary and print media stories about sports and sportspeople often reinforce stereotypical ideas about the 'natural' physical skill, 'animal-like' aggression and intellectual naivety of black performers (Whannel 1992). As Boyle and Haynes (2000) note, the brutal fighting style of Nigel Benn and his publicised violence outside the boxing ring constructed a media image around him that reflected the stereotypical notions of black men as overtly violent. A character of savage aggression and primitive violence was signified by his media title as the 'Dark Destroyer'.

That popular sports programmes are, in the main, presented by white commentators suggests that the controlling force behind the content and style of media coverage remains with white people. There seems to be an increase of black and Asian presenters in other areas of the media, such as business, news, children's productions and current affairs, but not in sport. What makes this point more striking is that the success of black British sportswomen and -men has been particularly visible in the buildup to, participation in and achievements at the 2000 Olympic Games. Whilst opportunities to participate and excel in sport may be characterised by a more level racial/ethnic playing field, career opportunities in media sport seem to be out of bounds for some racial groups. This is also the case in the context of careers in coaching or sports administration. Coakley (1998) offers two reasons that might explain this situation. First, he notes that coaches and managers have often played sports in central 'thinking' positions. Since the stereotype of black people includes the idea that they are intellectually inferior, they tend not to play in 'thinking' positions in sports. This creates a disadvantage when it comes to careers in coaching or sports management. Careers in the media also require thought and written or verbal analysis. Given this, it would not be unreasonable to suggest that Coakley's first point is useful in explaining why black people are underrepresented in media sport careers such as journalism and television presentation. Second, Coakley (1998) highlights that selection for coaching and management is often based on the subjective ideals of those doing the hiring. When racial prejudice and stereotyping prevail, members of minority ethnic groups are often overlooked for jobs in coaching, management and arguably the media because they are not considered to have the intellectual capability required.

Gender Relations in Media Sport

Media sport can also reflect **dominant ideologies** and cultural ideas about gender and gender relations. Indeed, mediated sport seems to reflect the balance of power between the sexes in sport and society more broadly. That is, media sport reflects a cultural trend whereby many women are afforded relatively inferior status to men. Women's sports receive less coverage than men's in both the print media and on television (Hargreaves 1994; Creedon 1994). Whilst increasing numbers of women are playing a variety of sports, achieving notable success and watching sports, they remain underrepresented in terms of media attention. The amount of space in national daily newspapers dedicated to women's sports is extremely low. Most hours dedicated to sports viewing on British television are filled with male-dominated sports such as soccer, rugby, cricket, horse racing and motor racing. When stories and news items about women's sports are included they tend to focus on aspects of appearance rather than performance. More specifically, media coverage of sport tends to reinforce ideals of masculinity and femininity.

Established images of manliness tend to frame representations of sport in the media. Masculine ideals such as strength, toughness and aggression are celebrated and reinforced in media sport. Violence and aggression on the playing field are often the focus of media photographs and narrative. There tends to be an emphasis on male power, strength and aggression as markers of masculinity. Slow-motion replays and close-up camera shots of aggressive physical contact in soccer, rugby and boxing and the occurrence of injuries are commonly featured in television presentations. This type of 'ritualised' aggression has strong links with the values and behaviours of maleness and masculinity. The media often characterises the bodies of sportsmen as powerful weapons of destruction and domination symbolising both the mental and physical toughness that defines established images of masculinity.

Traditional ideals of femininity are reflected in media coverage of sportswomen that are often dominated by references to grace, beauty and finesse. Writing in *The Times* newspaper of London during the 2000 Sydney Olympic Games, Oliver Holt profiles Denise Lewis (Great Britain, 2000 Olympic gold medallist in heptathlon) using established ideals of femininity. He states that 'Lewis has beauty and she has grace and now the world knows she has guts too'. Reflecting on the complex interaction of gender and racial dimensions, Holt continues: 'She was brought up in adversity in Wolverhampton by an equally determined single mother and last night she drew on all her survival instincts to salvage the dream they have dreamt of for so long'. Not only does this media article reinforce traditional ideas about femininity but it also reflects established ideals that sport is a sphere in which some minority racial groups can gain success out of limited life chances by channelling their natural energies and physicality into sport.

Tennis is a good example of a sport in which media attention for sportswomen centres on feminine beauty. Players such as Anna Kournikova gain more attention for their (hetero)sexual attractiveness than players whose physiques are muscular and powerful, such as Martina Navratilova and Amelie Mauresmo. Writing in *The Observer* newspaper of London on 29 June 1997, Emma Lindsey highlights that the most lucrative financial sponsorships and the greatest amount of positive media coverage go to successful and sexy players. She writes the following:

> Anna Kournikova slinks slim hipped about the baseline. Twirling tendrils of her fringe, flicking her long blond pony tail and sashaying in a sexy little number constructed as a tennis dress, she's got what it takes to get male fans going.... without the usual chunky legs ... Kournikova breaks away from the hairy-lipped eastern European archetype. She is one of the new breed of sports babes.

The sex appeal of these 'sports babes' reinforces the established values of heterosexual female beauty. It is this, rather than performance, that tends to be central to media representation about them. It is often the case that photographs of sportswomen feature sexualised images rather than action photos. These images of the female body beautiful are also accompanied by commentary and narrative that tend to highlight other traditional values of femininity such as being married or having a (male) partner and issues of child rearing (Hargreaves 1994).

When successful female athletes are perceived to be a challenge to established gender ideology, such as being lesbian or being heavily muscled, they can receive negative media commentary. For example, in an article titled 'Marion Beats the Clock with Big Ben's Legs' (*London Evening Standard*, 23 July 1998), Herd makes derogatory remarks about the muscled physique of American Marion Jones (world and Olympic 100m champion). Arguably, Jones is the greatest female athlete in the world, yet Herd comments that

> There was a photograph of her in a newspaper this week. I put my hand over her head and I'm damned if I could tell whether it was a male or female.... No breasts, no feminine contours. Just power. Hugely muscled thighs.... All things considered, though, give me Joyce Grenfell any time.

Reflecting the idea that women's bodies should be feminine, in the traditional sense of the word, this example demonstrates the way that performances of successful sportswomen are marginalised. As such they reinforce established views about what women should and should not do with their bodies and what they should and should not look like. The predominance of men's sports and the marginalisation and trivialisation of women's sports in the media most often serve to reinforce traditional gender relations. That is, media sport representations reflect the message that women's sports are less important than men's sports and that they are only worthy of attention if the sportswomen in question are both successful and sexy.

This debating point demonstrates some of the ways in which race/ethnic and gender relations are represented in media sport productions. In many cases, the literature analyses a particular issue such as race/ethnicity, gender, social class, age or (dis)ability as distinct and seemingly separate from the others. At any time, one of these particular issues may come to the fore and submerge the existence of the others. Yet it should be emphasised that these dimensions interconnect in a complex network of processes that can serve to both reinforce and at times resist traditional social values.

Case Study: Formula One Racing and Media Marketing Relations

Formula One motor racing is a good example of the interdependent relationship between a sports organisation and media and marketing agencies. This case study addresses issues of ownership, power and control in the context of a highly commercialised sport. It focuses on the ways in which Formula One has been shaped by a network of media and marketing interests. The key groups and personnel in this relationship are defined in figure 3.2.

Bernie Ecclestone has been the most influential in the development of Formula One into a global commercial enterprise that continues to expand its profits and influence on the worldwide sporting stage.

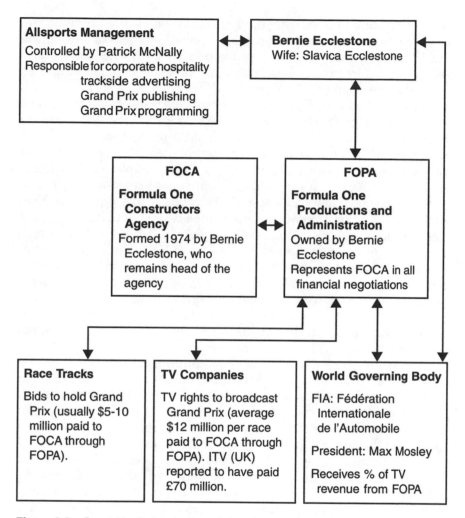

Figure 3.2   Sport-Media-Marketing relationships: The case of Formula One racing.
Data from Williams (1998) and Maguire (1999).

Keeping his affairs 'in the family' has been one tactic for securing control over the organisation and practices of motor racing over the past two decades. His wife, Slavica, holds offshore trusts in which profits from Formula One are held; his ally, Patrick McNally, controls Allsports Management; and another friend, Max Mosley, is President of FIA (Fédération Internationale de l'Automobile), the world motorsports governing body.

Bernie Ecclestone began to expand his web of power 20 years ago when, as boss of Formula One team Brabham, he became chief executive of the Formula One Constructors Agency (FOCA). Unhappy that race organisers were financially exploiting teams, he directed united team pressure on the organisers, effectively persuading them to buy a package of motor racing designed and produced by the teams. He also entered into more profitable negotiations over television rights to screen Formula One racing.

In the 1980s it was FIA that sold Formula One to television. Ecclestone successfully negotiated an alternative arrangement whereby the teams secured TV-rights deals and FIA was paid a percentage of profits. A relatively high degree of power and control was shifting to the teams and to Bernie Ecclestone. Over time, his influence over media organisations grew. He was able to push TV companies to pay more each time a contract was renewed. If the TV companies did not agree, then Ecclestone would approach a rival company. His network of control over motorsports strengthened in 1987 when he became FIA vice president in charge of promotional affairs (Saward 1997). Ecclestone's entrepreneurial abilities and his risk-taking style were coupled with the other teams' increasing fear of taking financial risks. Motorsports teams were happy for him to take control of negotiations with media and marketing organisations. So, at the same time as Ecclestone was working on expanding his power base, other teams were effectively putting him in the 'driving seat' (Williams 1998).

It was the inception of the agency Formula One Productions and Administration (FOPA) that enabled the profits from Formula One to soar from the late 1980s. Bernie Ecclestone owned 100 percent of this company, effectively controlling motor racing. The increasing popularity of Formula One at this time contributed to Ecclestone's ability to raise TV-rights fees and demand more from race circuit owners wanting to hold a Formula One event. At a fee of approximately $10 million/year for each race, the annual income secured by FOPA is $160 million (Saward 1997). To hold a race, circuit owners are persuaded to allow Allsports Management to organise all trackside advertising and hospitality.

Influential in these business interests is Patrick McNally, a former motorsports journalist and sponsorship negotiator (Saward 1997). He has developed corporate entertainment through the creation of a facility known as the Paddock Club, where business groups and people can entertain and be entertained within the exciting and spectacular atmosphere that is Formula One racing. As Saward (1997) notes, the activities of FOPA created an extremely profitable Formula One company with an annual turnover of approximately $30 million and an 80% profit ratio at the beginning of the 1990s. Ecclestone was in control and in 1993 paid himself a vast salary of $45 million (Saward 1997). Yet, he continues to invest money in the motorsports industry to the benefit of Formula One. In 1994 he allocated $40 million in research and development. Ecclestone seems particularly keen to expand the influence of media technology in the sport. Indeed, he has been influential in the development of a multichannel digital TV system for pay-per-view races. So, the interrelationships between the media, marketing and motorsports have been and continue to be shaped by Ecclestone's big business ideologies and technological advances. He has already experimented with 'virtual advertising', whereby a multitude of electronic images can be superimposed onto trackside hoarding. There are 30 hoardings at each race venue that are sold for advertising income. At around $100,000 a billboard in 75 countries, that's an estimated annual advertising income of $225 million (Saward 1997).

We can see in this case study that Formula One motor racing is an exemplar of the complex network of power relations that characterise media sport relations. The interconnections among Bernie Ecclestone; the world motorsports governing body, FIA; marketing companies, FOCA, FOPA and Allsports Management; the racetrack owners; TV companies; sponsors; advertisers; and the teams developed via long-term intended and unintended processes. Formula One is global big business. It relies on business interests to remain a viable commercial sport. In addition, media and marketing organisations have secured a great deal of financial wealth by being connected with Formula One. In summary, approximately $160 million in fees are earned from racetrack owners and $36 million from advertising and merchandising activities of the Paddock Club. The annual income of Formula One reaches half a billion dollars. In the near future, pay-per-view and digital TV technology will help to generate further income.

The vast revenue of Formula One racing is not shared in equal proportions amongst the teams. Several teams are dissatisfied with a balance of power that has shifted in favour of Bernie Ecclestone. The Concorde Agreement between Formula One teams and FOCA sets out particular terms of financial payment to the teams from FOCA. For example, signatory teams receive 47 percent of TV income paid to FOCA (Saward 1997). In the renegotiation of the 1997–2001 Concorde Agreement, Williams, McClaren and Tyrell did not sign the terms by way of a protest at the organisation and structure of Formula One business activities. Yet they excluded themselves from sharing in TV income. The seven remaining teams earn $22 million just to be at the races. The agreement does not include prize money, which is paid separately. Some in Formula One argue that too much money is going out of motorsports and into the Ecclestone 'household' (Williams 1997; 1998). There is much evidence of this. For example, in a recent restructuring, Formula One Holdings (FOH) was transferred to SLEC Holdings owned by Valper Holdings, a company controlled by the offshore trusts of Ecclestone's wife. The battles for wealth, status and control between key people within Formula One, media and marketing organisations are on-going. In recent moves to float Formula One on the stock exchange, the interdependence between FOH and FIA has been questioned by some banks that claim them to be acting as a cartel and preventing other business interests from entering negotiations. Flotation may lead to more long-term stability, but the nature of **power networks** in sporting spheres is dynamic. Ecclestone would still be chief executive of a 'floated' Formula One. Yet another of his allies, Helmut Werner, has been identified as the likely person to be appointed to expand the sporting business via even more wide-reaching processes of global development.

Summary

The media is an immense cultural institution. In its diversity of print and electronic forms, the media pervades many aspects of our everyday life including our experiences of sport. Furthering an understanding of sport and social life requires investigation of media sport relations. Sociologists of sport have investigated media sport relations as a way of furthering an understanding of sport and social life. Several scholars have done this by critically analysing the interdependent aspects of the media sport complex. The key groups that have an impact on the processes and outcomes of media sport relations are media organisations, sports organisations and marketing organisations. The relationships between these groups have developed over time and across cultures. They also vary in degree and characteristics according to particular sport contexts.

Media sport relations have intensified during the 20th century to the extent that some more commercially oriented sports may not exist, at least in the same way, without the financial support of the media and television in particular. It is the case that both sport and the media benefit from their associations. Sports are guaranteed substantial, often long-term fees and increased global visibility from their involvement with the media. The media can gain increased and extensive viewing numbers and also increased revenue from associated advertising and sponsorship. This chapter has emphasised that media sport relations are characterised by interdependence. Yet, the balance of power can often be seen to shift in favour of media and marketing organisations, the groups that hold the greatest financial purses. Media and marketing organisations offer extremely large sums of money to be involved in sport. On this basis they can make several demands that have led to changes in the organisation, structure and character (content) of sport. These changes reflect the shift in sport to the profit-maximisation ideology of big business. Media sport is packaged to effectively captivate large audiences: sports are selected, highlighted and edited to create an entertaining media product. In addition, the sports we watch, read about and listen to contain images that tend to reflect dominant cultural ideals. Whilst watching sports on the television, or reading about them in the newspapers, or listening to them on the radio, is no measure of the attention paid to the messages portrayed in the presentation, they do have a significant influence on the way that we think about our social world.

Key Terms and Concepts

advertising   media sport complex
audience   ownership/control
commercial processes   power networks
cultural dupes   production/consumption
dominant ideologies   representation
knowledgeability   skilled consumers
marketing   sponsorship
mass media   visual/narrative techniques
media spectacle

Review Questions

1. Summarise the historical development of the mass media and mediated sport in modern societies.
2. Define and explain the key features of the mass media.
3. Describe and explain the key dimensions and issues that characterise the media sport complex.
4. How might an understanding of the media sport complex help explain the impact of media and marketing agencies in a sport of your choice?
5. With reference to at least two sports, critically analyse the extent to which sport is interdependent with media and marketing organisations.
6. Examine the competing claims that mediated sport reinforces and/or resists dominant cultural beliefs about either gender or race/ethnicity.
7. Explain how visual, verbal and auditory techniques are used in the creation of mediated sport spectacles.
8. Discuss the reasons why sport is 'packaged' for television.
9. Discuss the impact of sponsorship and advertising on a sport of your choice.
10. Critically evaluate how the structure, organisation and content of sport have changed to meet the demands of television production.

Projects

1. Using newspaper reports of the Wimbledon tennis championships, compare and contrast the ways in which women players were portrayed in a selected year from each of the following: 1930s, 1960s and 1990s.

2. Videotape the opening or closing ceremony of a winter or summer Olympic Games or other major sporting event such as the World Cup. Using content analysis, describe and explain the ways in which a media spectacle has been created out of the selected event.

3. Videotape a televised sports programme. Using qualitative content analysis, examine how racial/ethnic stereotypes are framed and represented.

4. Establish the ways in which the print and electronic media represent and package a major sports event in your country. Do this by choosing a sample of and interviewing key media personnel involved in the process of planning and production.

5. In a sport form of your choice, and using the Internet as a source of information, produce a diagram that traces the network of media, marketing, advertising and sponsorship interests and relationships that characterise the sport. What does the network you have represented in the diagram reveal about issues of ownership and control in your sport?

6. Form a focus group of students who will be watching a major sports programme in your country. Identify specific themes and questions for discussion that focus on such aspects as gender, race/ethnicity, social class, (dis)ability, age or national identity. What did the discussion reveal about the ways in which the media constructs and represents the selected themes?

CHAPTER
4

SPORT, POLITICS AND DEMOCRACY

Objectives

After completing this chapter, you should be able to

- understand the relationship between politics and sport;
- explain some of the differences between a classical and a modern political economy of sport;
- discuss the politics of sport in different comparative contexts;
- explain the relationship between sport, privilege and class;
- evaluate the extent to which sport is democratic; and
- discuss the extent to which the politics of sport has changed over the last 50 years or more.

This chapter briefly discusses the changing relationship between sport and **politics** and critically evaluates one of the central concepts associated with the politics of sport. It draws on comparative examples of sports from Sweden and Denmark as a basis for reflecting on the democratic nature and organisation of sport. The chapter suggests that the very notion of **democracy** has to be examined more closely, and that sport no longer needs to be defined as reflecting a particular political system. In fact, there is no longer a need to think in terms of systems, whether this is with due reference to **capitalism** or a planned economy. Present-day politics of sport concern whether sport should be viewed as a set of values, as a social movement or as political practice. Sport, for example, might not be defined as a social democratic system, but the promise of sport might be that it can be an inspiration, a way of being, a manner of acting that is based on both democratic and **social values.**

Debating Point:
Should Sport Be Used for Political Purposes?

Yes. Sport is an exceptional mechanism for testing **diplomatic relations** between regions or nations. Sport and specifically sportspeople can serve as national representatives not just for sport but also for ideology and identity. They become symbols of a particular way of life and serve as a potential vehicle for dialogue and integration when other forms of negotiation have failed. Sport may at times be a vehicle for promoting dialogue and therefore provides a means to political ends. Because of its popular appeal, sport has potential benefits at both micro- and macro-political levels. Sport both contributes to and is constitutive of various political economies and values. The notion of sport being autonomous from politics is mythical.

No. Sport is not important enough in terms of making a significant difference to international relations or resolving national tensions and conflict. Sport is of limited diplomatic value because when nations choose to exercise their full economic and political power, sport is relatively insignificant. The use of sport for political purposes detracts from the classical essence of sport. Many sports organisations choose to operate at arm's length from government, thus illustrating sport's essential **autonomy.** The politics of sport itself is a different issue from whether sport should be used for social purposes by local or central governments. Sport is essentially social as opposed to political.

The Changing Politics of Sport

The dominant postwar commentaries on the relationship between sport, politics and the state have also reflected the changing ways in which academic disciplines have approached debates about sport. In the early 1980s, the notable growth of interest in the study of sport and politics was thought to have been derived from the fact that the then socialist countries with fully supported sports programmes had experienced remarkable successes in international sport since at least the 1950s; sports activities had become increasingly incorporated into the domestic welfare **policies** of the then capitalist liberal democracies; and sport had been increasingly used as an element of foreign policy by various nation-states throughout the world (Cantelon and Gruneau 1982; Petrie 1975). From this point of view, politics was what occurred when the political elite were also the leading figures and defining managers in the significance of sport within the activities of various governments.

To say that an area of activity, such as sport, is not part of politics or has nothing to do with politics is to make a particular kind of political point. By at least 1986, the myth of autonomy so often associated with the **politics of sport** had been marginalised as utopian ideology. In other words, as Lincoln Allison (1993) described in *The Changing Politics of Sport,* the myth of autonomy 'was the persistent assertion that sport was somehow separate from society' and that it transcended or had nothing to do with politics or social conflict. The influence of pluralist and Marxist perspectives on the state throughout the 1980s and 1990s further consolidated the notion that it was not enough to recognise that sport did not take place in a social vacuum, but that it related to economy and society. Like politics, sport could not be understood as a distinct field of activity, but in fact it needed to be grasped as part of a broader field of social relations. As a consequence, it has become increasingly impossible to think of sport being defined as a *system*. More importantly, it is necessary to consider the values and ideas associated with sport in particular settings and at particular times or periods of contemporary history. For example, it is becoming impossible in the 21st century to talk of a socialist sports system, but nonetheless **socialism** can be viewed as a set of values that informs **sport policy** and practice within and between certain state formations.

Politics has been variously described as centrally concerned with civil government, the state and public affairs; **human conflict** and its resolution; or the sources and exercise of **power.** There are two fundamental test questions, argues Allison (1996), that can be applied to the concept of politics. First, do creatures other than human beings have politics and, second, can there be societies without politics? The implication of the latter might be viewed as utopian in the sense that while such a society might be conceivable it is not practically possible. A modern mainstream view in the late 1990s might have been that politics only applies to human beings or at least to those beings that can communicate symbolically and thus make statements, invoke principles, argue and disagree. Politics therefore occurs in practice when people disagree about the distribution of resources and have at least some procedures for the resolution of such disagreements. It is thus not just present in and between states.

The issue of **political economy** deserves particular attention, not necessarily in the strict Marxist sense of the term, and not just because of the particular relationship between politics and economics or the politics of economics, but also because of the influence of political economy on the politics of sport. The border between politics and economics is peculiarly open because, for obvious reasons, states dispose of substantial material resources while production and exchange across the globe can hardly take place without some framework of security. Correspondingly, argues Jones (1996), definitions of economics have generally focused on systems of production and exchange, rational behaviour directed towards the maximisation of utility through an optimal allocation of scarce resources, or the accumulation and distribution of wealth. Much of the conventional liberal thinking into the economics of sport has been underpinned by certain forms of utilitarian thinking that are present within both politics and economics (Gratton and Taylor 2000).

By contrast, the political economy of sport has been dominated by the social sciences. By this we do not mean classical Marxist political economy; as Horne, Tomlinson, and Whannel (1999) suggest, we are all pluralists now. As such, modern political economy might be better served by focusing on the making of the state as a process rather than revering the state as some monolithic structure. Drawing on the work of MacLennan (1995), they suggest a synthesis between elements of Marxism and critical **pluralism** as a means of explaining the politics of sport and sport policy. A modern political economy of sport might therefore acknowledge some or all of the following concerns: the fundamental political issues that arise from the accumulation and distribution of wealth derived from sports production and consumption; the continuing influence of capitalism on sport; the relationship between sport and global poverty; the state's sport policy agenda in relation to the interests of the business sector and the perception that states and governments are important interest groups not just in the determination of sports policy but also the essential regulation of capitalism. The traditions of classical and Marxian political economy and notions of the political economy of sport continue to survive precisely because neoclassical economics is often reluctant to consider the political basis and social implications of capitalist production and distribution in the 21st century.

Finally, in one of the most comprehensive and recent overviews of politics and sport, Houlihan (2000) outlines some of the major themes that have influenced the literature on the relationship between politics and sport. These are divided into two broad schools of thought: (1) politics in sport that direct our attention to how governments use sport and the process by which public policy is made and implemented and (2) politics in sport that leads to a consideration of the way in which sports organisations use power to pursue their own sectional interests at the expense of other social groups. Contained within the former group would be themes essentially relating to the role of the state, including issues of sport and national identity, sport and economic development, sport and foreign policy and the promotion of individual state interests. By contrast, the latter would include an examination of the power of sports organisations in determining the nature of sporting opportunity, and an examination of sport not just as a source of profit but also as a vehicle for the transmission of capitalist values and issues of equality. Whatever definition of politics is used, it is likely to be highly contested because there is considerable disagreement as to which aspects of social life are to be considered political. Consequently, the content and approach to the politics of sport is never static but ever-changing, and any true comprehension of the processes involved requires a historical imagination.

The issue of democracy has been readily debated within the politics of sport. There are various national sports organisations that claim to be more democratic because they operate at arm's length from government, and yet the notion and future of democracy is rarely in itself questioned. Furthermore, the connotations of the word in modern times are so favourable that organisations and forms of state control that have no claim to being democratic still use the term. As a descriptive term, democracy is closely associated with majority rule, although there is no real consensus as to what majority rule really means. For example, do issues relating to majority rule or the democratic nature of sport include the following: Who counts as the people and what is a 'majority' of them? Why, if at all, should majorities rule minorities? Should a direct or representative system of democracy be preferred? What are the dangers of majority rule for minority rights? The organisation of sport in Sweden has often been heralded as being based on a model of **social welfare** and being more democratic in terms of its organisation.

Case Study:
Swedish Athletes Test the Swedish Tax System

Some small countries have been successful in achieving complete independence from central government without the need for an intermediate agency. The Nordic countries have a long history of democratic popular sports movements. Sensibly, their independence has been protected in legislation. The Swedish Sports Confederation (SSC), formed in 1903, has metamorphosed as an umbrella organisation representing 40,000 clubs. It is claimed that half of Sweden's 7 million inhabitants are members of sports clubs (Thomson 1992). Some 2 million of these are active sportspeople, of whom about 650,000 engage in competitive sports at various levels and 7,000 are at the elite, national championship level and above.

Every tier of the SSC is based on a system of democratic elections leading to the national executive group of 11 that represents the sport community at home and abroad (see figure 4.1). The SSC and the Swedish Olympic Committee work jointly in provision for elite sport. They run an elite training centre at Bosön near Stockholm. Sweden's model of an independent, democratic, popular sports movement has no exact equivalent outside Nordic countries (Thomson 1992).

Yet even in Sweden the system of democracy is under attack from within the Swedish sports world. For many, politics is defined in terms of the actions of governments that have the authoritative use of power to make rules and law. For almost five decades, Sweden has been known for its social welfare model that has often been viewed as an ambitious 'third way' for what has been a hypothetical compromise between communism and capitalism. In practice, it has meant far-reaching government involvement in the private sphere, fuelled by a strong conviction that social engineering can achieve the kind of justice that the ruling political party holds to be the ultimate truth. One of the main characteristics is the assumed right of politicians not only to alleviate

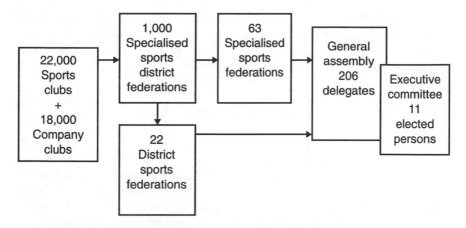

Figure 4.1   The Swedish Sports Confederation's democratic structure.
Data from *Sport in Sweden,* Thomson, 1992: 15.

poverty but to redistribute wealth across society. These values remain high on the agenda of New Labour in Britain, but in Sweden this social welfare model is changing, or at least is being challenged.

One element of the social welfare model that has stubbornly refused to disappear has been the tax rates that are the highest amongst the industrial nations. As such, it is not difficult to imagine the personal income tax burdens for Sweden's top sports personalities (King 2000). It is equally easy to anticipate the proportionate commitment of the Swedish tax authorities to collect its share of the escalating revenues within sport. They have been particularly vigilant with regard to sports clubs and personalities. Recently, the Swedish tax authorities received a boost when the Stockholm District Administrative Court upheld the tax inspector's decision in a case involving Pernilla Wiberg, one of Sweden's top downhill skiers. The skier had been assessed on tax from undeclared income between 1993 and 1996 and decided to appeal the decision to the highest administrative court, the Regeringsratten. The action could delay for up to two years what many believe will be a landmark decision.

This case is of significant consequence in Sweden for the evolution of its dominant political values as well as the tax issues involved. For many, the courts, in giving effect to the tax legislation created by years of social democratic leadership, have essentially created a tax system in which politicians are able to confiscate private property and where the tendency is to stop people from using fully legal ways of tax planning. If the Wiberg case rules in favour of the skier, it is widely believed that legislature would immediately step in to prevent what might amount to a mass exodus of capital from sport into offshore trusts. If Wiberg loses the case, then she and other sports stars will also be losers. This will then highlight the need to regulate agents and managers, particularly for younger athletes. But as this practice is not yet in place, many will follow what Wiberg and others have done in response to the personal income tax burden in Sweden, namely, move to Monaco or other lower-tax jurisdictions.

The Changing Nature of Democracy

Contemporary ideas relating to the democratic nature of sport are mixed. Nearly all sports organisations at an ideological level like to think of themselves as being democratic despite operating sports policies that exclude certain groups. In this sense democracy remains one of the key ideologies for sport and society in the early 21st century, and it remains crucial to realise that the content and nature of democracy is ever-changing. It could be suggested that contemporary liberal democracy as practised throughout Western sport is lacking in a number of fundamental ways, notably in its inability to control the ways in which global sports companies such as Nike exploit world labour markets and the way in which certain sports fail to recognise individual differences of, for example, age, ethnicity, gender and even **class.** Furthermore, sport in the West tends to be undemocratic in that large sections of the population remain disenfranchised when it comes to voting for positions of power and influence within sporting clubs and organisations. For example, the football authorities and even governments view sceptically the setting up of supporter-owned football trusts or an increased community stake in the sports Public Limited Company. There is no opportunity in Britain or the United States to develop the sort of ownership pattern practised within Barcelona Football Club or to develop a system of free associations that characterise the very essence of democratic sport in certain Scandinavian countries such as Sweden or Denmark.

Case Study: Danish Sport As the 'Third Way'

In at least two ways, sport in Denmark might be viewed as constituting a 'third way'. In terms of policy, sport deliberately rejects the notion of any unified sports culture (Boje and Eichberg 1996). Sport is defined within a much broader notion encompassing sport and body culture within an overall framework of cultural policy. Sport as body culture is not restricted only to competitive sports, with its problematic dualism between elite and mass sport; or fitness- and health-promoting initiatives; or popular games, forms of play and ritualistic festivals. Rather, sport as body culture is seen to exist in a progressive tri-athletic way involving an interplay among three independent forms of movement culture: performance- and result-orientated sport, lifestyle-promoting movement for exercise and fitness, and popular activities of body culture at the level of informal, playful bodily experiences. Thus, sport cannot be served by a cultural policy that predominantly attends to the interests of only athletic associations and elite sports clubs. Cultural policy in Denmark, it is argued, must acknowledge the tri-athletic development of body culture in order to serve the interests of the entire population.

Finally, Danish sport might also be said to be more democratic in terms of its organisational structures when compared to, say, British sporting structures. To a large extent, the public sector in Denmark provides the framework by creating and managing sports activities at local, regional and national levels. The sports sector is also highly decentralised and operates at arm's length from government. The government recognises three organisations for the development of sport and provides funding through the Ministry of Culture from the Danish Pools Organisation. The Danish Sport Federation (DIF) and Danish Gymnastics and Sports Associations (DGI) both claim membership of about 1.5 million. They and the Danish government are joint owners of the Pools Organisation, which provides about £55 million for sport annually. DIF represents 57 governing bodies of sport and its share of the annual allocation is about £25 million. It distributes 70 percent to its members and uses a further 20 percent for services such as training courses and materials, publications, consulting and assistance with legal, accounting, insurance and regulatory issues. The remaining 10 percent goes to the DIF's administration and the operation of the House of Sport at Bronby, which accommodates the governing bodies of sport and the DIF offices. The democratic nature of the distribution of wealth is illustrated by the allocation of funds: the smaller governing bodies, which have difficulty in attracting sponsors and TV money, receive proportionately more of the resources (Jarvie and Thomson 1999).

More important, however, than the nature and content of any forms of democracy is recognition that the concept of democracy is itself ever-changing. Not only should we continually question the application of the same criteria for what constitutes democracy and appropriate demo-cratic values, but we should also recognise that such values change from one decade to the next. In the first place, modern technology and modern wealth have thrown up a plethora of problems that classical thinkers never dreamt of. Just as Athenian democracy was not designed to resolve the issue of rights in America or Canada, so the sustaining values of the Cold War may not now, or ever, have much long-term applicability on the West Bank.

The West desperately seeks to identify a democratic aspiration in Russia, and institutions exist to give substance to the idea. Yet whatever system the Russian Federation practises, it is likely to have little relation to liberal democracy as the West understands it. In the same sense, what we understand as democracy has in reality always been on the move. In Britain, mid-20th-century democracy was substantially different from early-19th-century democracy, when the term was seldom used. Britain today is probably more democratic than it has ever been, given the devolved local arrangements of administration in Ireland, Scotland and Wales. And yet, it would be stretching the imagination to claim that the citizens feel any sort of ownership of the institutions, including the sporting institutions, that make up 21st-century Britain.

Sport, Privilege and Democracy

Sport has long been viewed as a graphic symbol of **meritocracy** despite the fact that sociologists and others have been questioning the substantive basis for such a claim for more than quarter of a century. Writing in 1976, Canadian sociologist and cultural critic Richard Gruneau questioned the extent to which taken-for-granted claims about sport's meritocratic basis could be substantiated. Thus the popular image of sport as an unquestioned democracy of ability and practice is somewhat overexaggerated, if not mythical. Generally speaking, the term *democratisation* tends to imply a widening degree of opportunity or a diminishing degree of separatism in varying forms of sports involvement. The term has also been used to describe the process whereby employees or clients have more control over sporting decisions and sporting bodies. The expansion of opportunities in sport over the last quarter of the 20th century might be used at one level to argue that sport, at least in the West, has become more open. But, as Moffat (1999) suggests, the reality in Britain is that the extremes of **privilege** and poverty remain sharply drawn. An emphasis on social class cannot explain all aspects of the development of British sport—it tends, for example, to occlude the place of women in sport—but there is good reason for believing that sport and class have been mutually reinforcing categories in British society for a long time. Indeed, the claim that the secular decline of British sport in the international arena during the 20th century is partly the result of the exclusionary nature of sport in Britain cannot lightly be dismissed (Hill 2000).

The following examples show the extent to which some sports in Britain and North America might be viewed as reflecting privilege, class and **status** within the sporting body politic. Nowhere is this better illustrated than in the case of access to private golf clubs in Britain. The secretary of the Honourable Company of Edinburgh Golfers resides at Muirfield, host to the 2000 Open Golf Championship and one of the most difficult clubs of which to gain membership. Despite the current popular image that Scotland is somehow a more egalitarian society than class-cleavage England, in golfing terms the assertion could be challenged. Hiding behind the façade of the Honourable Company is an important segment of Scottish society, mainly the privileged, who have particular attitudes towards open participation and club membership. The secretary of the club, remarking on the exclusivity of the membership, tells the story 'of a distinguished group of visitors who approached the secretary to ask if they might be permitted to play a round as guests ... the official looked over the near deserted 18 holes to see three foursomes playing and replied that the course was busy' (Jarvie and Burnett 2000). The Muirfield Golf Club and, more particularly, the Honourable Company of Golfers continue to practise a closed-door policy in terms of membership. The secretive and mysterious nature of the inner workings of the Scottish establishment are hard to track and yet it is evidenced on the public face of a place such as Muirfield, which shows little respect for the simple goals of equality of regard and sporting opportunity, values allegedly held dear by the Scottish electorate.

The title 'What's in a Game? Class and History' recently captioned an article explaining the extent to which the game of lacrosse had strived to become a more meritocratic sport in North America (Stephen 2000). The earliest documented reference to lacrosse dates from the mid-1600s but, given its folk origins in the cultural practices of the Huron, Chippewa and Iroquois, such a date might be deemed conservative. At one point, lacrosse was made illegal in order to prevent Native Americans using it for warlike purposes. Geographically, Montreal is considered to be the cradle of modern lacrosse, although the French, according to Jackson (1996), are likely to have engaged in informal competition long before the Montreal Lacrosse Club was formed in 1856. By the 19th century, lacrosse had grown into one of the most exclusive sports in the United States, fashionable among the elite schools and colleges and a mainstay of the White Anglo-Saxon Protestant Ivy League Universities. In 2000, lacrosse is a chic status sport in the United States and remains a mainstream sport of the northeastern private schools and colleges while slowly filtering into state schools. It is still practised by marginalised sectors of North American culture that conveniently overlook the origins of the game.

While such cases, one from Britain and one from the United States, allow for the assertion that sport has been transformed by the changing social conditions of modern life, it would seem premature to state that sport in all its different forms is democratic. A significant amount of substantive evidence exists that challenges the notion of meritocratic sporting practices permeating both U.S. and British sporting cultures. The contemporary scene has changed dramatically when one compares 21st-century sport with 19th-century sport. The case can be made that extreme class- and status-linked barriers to sports participation have been greatly challenged by the changing nature of democracy in Britain, the United States and other places. Such an argument can be made without necessarily accepting that sport is widely available to all.

Whether it be golf, lacrosse or another sport, at least two points are important to note. The first is that while class, democracy and privilege are always on the move, the gap between privilege and poverty remains, whether referring to Britain or the United States. Unlike the British, Americans do not tend to conceive of their society hierarchically. By comparison with British society, Americans are not interested in the language of class or in the models of society. The result, as Lord Beaverbrook once remarked, is that in the New World, unlike the old, the only difference between rich and poor is that the rich have more money. This remains a shrewd insight. Britain, or at least parts of Britain, remains besotted with issues of class, privilege and how the rest of the world perceives Britain to be. A nation that debated whether the late Princess of Wales, after her divorce, should be allowed to retain the prefix Her Royal Highness is clearly concerned with its class image. A nation that was gripped by a courtroom battle between two cricketers, Imran Khan and Ian Botham, a large part of which was devoted to considering their social origins, is as equally obsessed with class in the late 20th century as it was with gentlemen versus players in the 19th century. Neither of these examples illustrates an overwhelming desire to be rid of divisive social distinctions such as class, poverty and privilege.

The second point is that while there have been inequalities in wealth and power in most societies throughout history, it seems unreasonable to define a classless society as one in which inequalities have been abolished. Instead it might be useful to adopt an approach that Bourdieu (1998) has described as a 'reasoned Utopia'. As these examples serve to remind us, we need to think more carefully about how we consider ourselves as social individuals or as social groups, how previous social groups thought about themselves and what future patterns of involvement in sport will say about particular societies. Only then will we better understand the complexities of sport privilege and democracy that have operated within sporting worlds and what remains to be done to achieve more meritocratic sports cultures.

Summary

This chapter has explored the ever-changing relationship between sport, politics and democracy. The social values associated with 21st-century sport need to be examined before accepting broad generalisations about the meritocratic or democratic nature of today's sporting world.

There remains a good deal of uncertainty about terms such as *democracy* but the relationship between sport and politics has been the subject of much debate in sociology for more than quarter of a century. *Politics*, like *democracy*, used to be a word that was rarely used in the context of sport. This is no longer the case. More importantly, however, it is not so much the extent to which sport has become more or less political or democratic but that the concept of democracy itself has changed over time. Not only should we wonder at the viability of applying the same criteria to different sports or countries between one decade or the next, it is not necessarily desirable that we should.

As indicated earlier, sport is probably more democratic, in terms of representation, than it has ever been, but it would stretch the language of democracy beyond reason to suggest that the ownership of sport or patterns of recruitment into powerful positions have changed dramatically. The new republicanism that is reflected in much of British or U.S. politics has hardly penetrated the world of sport in terms of a federal system of administration, such as those operated within the Nordic countries. On the other hand, the issue of whether sport is or is not political tends in the 21st century to be a moribund question that, in practice, has been replaced by whichever politics of sport tends to be dominant within changing sporting worlds.

Key Terms and Concepts

autonomy

capitalism

class

democracy

diplomatic relations

human conflict

meritocracy

pluralism

policies

political economy

politics

politics of sport

power

privilege

socialism

social values

social welfare

sport policy

status

third way

Review Questions

1. Review the arguments for and against sport being used for political purposes.
2. What were some of the themes that dominated the early sport and politics debate?
3. What themes reflect the politics of sport today?

4. Evaluate the differences between classical and modern political economies of sport.
5. Describe and critique Houlihan's (2000) description of politics and sports literature.
6. Discuss the two ways in which the Danish sports system might be viewed as a third, more democratic way for sport.
7. To what extent does sport in either Britain or the United States reflect privilege, class and status?
8. To what extent is the argument that sport is meritocratic overexaggerated?
9. Compare and contrast the sports system in Scandinavia with that of Britain, the United States or one other country of your choice.
10. What social values should be associated with sport in the 21st century?

Projects

1. Examine the committee structure of your local sports club and the process by which individuals become elected. Comment on the extent to which your local sports club committee is both representative and democratic.
2. Form a discussion group of four people from your club or your area and highlight the core issues that constitute the politics of sport in your club or area.
3. Identify between 8 and 10 points that would form the basis of any antiracist sports policy in your local sports organisation, school or university.
4. Find out how much money is spent on sport in your country and the rationale for spending that money on certain sports or activities.
5. In your country of residence, describe the sports policies of both the main opposition political party and the party or coalition forming the government. Comment on the ways that these policies reflect the core political values of the respective parties.
6. Examine the content of the sports coverage reported in two major newspapers of your choice for a month and report on the major national political sports issues reported in these two newspapers.

CHAPTER
5

SPORT, THE ENVIRONMENT AND 'GREEN' ISSUES

© Joe Robbins

Objectives

After completing this chapter, you should be able to

- discuss aspects of environmentalism and 'green' issues in relation to sport;
- explain the concept of sustainable development and its application to sport;
- understand the ways in which sportspeople, cultures and practices can be managed within the principles of sustainable development;
- discuss the interconnections between local and global environmental concerns as they relate to sport;
- critically evaluate the extent to which sport is a threat to the environment; and
- assess the degree to which sport is underpinned by 'green' ideologies and practices.

Concerns about the environment have become prominent in recent years. The social, economic and political profile of **'green' issues** such as the destruction of the ozone layer, recycling, **pollution** from motor vehicles and depletion of energy resources have become familiar topics of local and worldwide debate. Over the past decade, the growing awareness of environmental threats has focused on the damage caused by human beings that affects human, plant and animal life, natural ecological habitats and the earth's resources. The earth has finite resources that are being exploited, depleted and often exhausted by human activity. Industry, housing, transport and leisure, recreation and sporting activities all utilise the physical environment. The unmanaged use of the environment could be a threat to human social life, plant and animal populations and possibly to planetary existence.

When people speak of possible solutions to these threats, they focus their attention on the idea of **sustainable development.** Selman (1996) defines this concept by three fundamental principles: (1) **intergenerational equity** highlights a need to pass on the earth to future generations in a condition equal to that which was inherited; (2) **intragenerational equity** implies that methods of sustainable development should take into account the needs of all people around the globe regardless of social status; and (3) **transfrontier responsibility** requires individuals to live within the limits of their local resources rather than exploiting those of others. Put simply, sustainable living and development is primarily concerned with managing and living with the environment in such a way as to maintain its capacity now and in the future.

The growth of **environmentalism** over the last two decades and the increasing importance of sustainability seem to have been influential in the development of 'green' policies, practices and images. Many of these are associated with the activities of large-scale commercial organisations and government parties. For example, in Britain, and indeed in many countries of the world, the problem of air pollution from motor vehicle emissions has concerned government and industries for some time. Policies such as the sale of unleaded petrol, reduction in supply of leaded petrol, associated vehicle design changes, and emissions-monitoring schemes have been implemented to combat poor air quality.

Sports organisations have also begun to address wider environmental concerns. For example, the Olympic Co-ordination Authority for the 2000 Sydney games included 'green' commitments in the form of **environmental guidelines** as part of the bid to host the Games. Yearley (1992) highlights that environmental pressure groups, environmental organisations and **'green' politics** have raised the profile of several environmental concerns, helped to define many of the problems and attempted to offer solutions to them. For example, in Australia, a nongovernmental environmental watchdog for the 2000 Sydney Olympic Games emerged. Named Green Games Watch 2000 (GGW2000), it represented a coalition of the Australian Conservation Foundation, Nature Conservation Council of New South Wales, the National Parks Association, the National Toxics Network and the Total Environmental Centre (Symington and Angel 2000a). Sports organisations such as GGW2000 work in conjunction with groups concerned with both **local** and **global environmentalism** to achieve the ecologically sustainable development of sport. Nevertheless, environmental threats posed by sportspeople and the practices they engage in have not, as yet, received a great deal of recognition. Whilst the literature concerning sport, the environment and 'green' issues is scarce, environmental concerns are interconnected with sportspeople, sports cultures and sports practices.

Debating Point:
Is Sport a Threat to the Environment?

It seems that our lives are increasingly influenced by concerns about the environment and the development of 'green' ideals, beliefs and values. There is a tendency to think that past societies were more in touch with natural ecosystems and, hence, lived more harmoniously with them. Environmentalists commonly claim that present society is engaged in the wanton destruction of the earth. It is argued that modern ways of living, such as increased urbanisation and industrialisation, intensive agricultural methods and sport, leisure and recreation practices, use the environment in unsustainable and ineffectively managed ways.

Past societies are often noted for their sustainable living practices. It is suggested that, historically, ways of living were less likely to result in elimination of species, long-term pollution or irreversible depletion of the earth's resources. Yet, Yearley (1992) highlights that the decline of some civilisations was, in part, due to extensive and irreparable damage to the land. The Romans, for example, engaged in extensive deforestation and exploitative agricultural practices that destroyed land fertility and rendered the soil incapable of food crop production. Historical records rarely touch on **ecological degradation** and environmental threat but there is evidence that, throughout history, human beings have had a destructive impact on the earth (Yearley, 1996).

Present society, then, is not alone in battling ecological problems. Selman (1996) notes that the recognition of the finite nature and vulnerability of the earth's ecosystems and the desire to sustain and conserve the landscape for production, aesthetics and recreational use was certainly a feature of life in the 18th century. But policies aimed at managing and conserving the earth and the introduction of ideas about sustainable living and development have rapidly become more prominent and formalised in many areas of life during the 20th century, including leisure, recreation and sport. This is connected with increasing exploration and knowledge of the environment, mainly in relation to rapid industrialisation of social life.

The environmental revolution of the 1960s and 1970s focused on **conservation,** especially in relation to tourism and recreational activities such as walking, cycling, horse riding, fishing, hunting and bird watching. Yet, there were earlier attempts to protect the environment from recreational use. For example, concerns about the impact of human activity in the natural environment are evident in the establishment of the Sierra Club in 1892 in the United States. This led to the development of the Yosemite National Park and the expansion of other national park conservation areas. In the United Kingdom, the National Parks and Access to the Countryside Act and the National Parks Commission of 1949 established government legislation concerning **environmental protection** from leisure activities (Plimmer et al. 1996).

Sport and Sustainable Development

Many leisure activities use the open countryside and the seaside. Recreational use places great pressure on land, water and air resources. Vast numbers of people walking, cycling, driving, water skiing, jet skiing and diving, for example, can destroy land and water vegetation, cause extensive erosion and disrupt the existence of wildlife. This has been a common problem in the English Lake District and Yosemite Park in the United States. Some leisure activities are associated with the development of artificial environments such as zoos, wildlife parks and aquatic complexes.

Whilst the construction of some of these has occurred over large areas of land, some have also been developed in response to demands for environmental conservation. National parks and nature reserves, for example, represent attempts to preserve plant and animal species, habitats and ecological systems whilst protecting the legal rights of landowners and tenants and accommodating extremely large numbers of people who want to experience the natural environment at their leisure. The National Parks Commission establishes, develops and protects specific areas of the natural environment in sustainable ways in accordance with countryside codes of conduct and other government legislation (Plimmer et al. 1996). Yet these intended measures of environmental protection can have unintended destructive consequences, including overuse of footpaths and coastal walkways; accidental damage to hedgerows, fences and crops; pollution of land, water and air from litter; disruption of animal life; and destruction by vandalism.

Many popular sporting activities have necessitated extensive construction of indoor and outdoor leisure facilities on large areas of already scarce land. This type of development can destroy natural habitats and thus threaten existing plant and animal species. Sport practices themselves can be an environmental hazard. Recent research has found that even if shooting practices do not kill or cripple ducks, geese and wading birds directly, many of them are poisoned by ingesting highly toxic lead shot. Smith (1991) highlights that 'shot is one of the remaining sources of lead in the environment'. Wider concern about the polluting and health-damaging potential of lead has resulted in its removal from pencils, paint and motor vehicle fuel in recent years. The British Association for Shooting and Conservation has made some attempts to provide safe, nontoxic alternatives to lead by conducting research into the possibility of steel or tungsten/plastic shot (Smith 1991). Yet still, lead poisoning has been identified in wild fowl and birds of prey, some of which are already experiencing a decline in species numbers.

Sports and leisure activities, then, pose environmental threats that need to be addressed if they are to continue in an ecologically sustainable manner. Issues of power characterise environmental decision-making, policy and practice. Conflict between two or more competing groups whose environmental agendas differ is common. Indeed, whilst this chapter highlights the environmental benefits of sustainable development of sport, even this is a paradox. Sustainability (the conservation of the earth and its resources) and development (the commercially effective growth of industrial nations) are conflicting in relation to the activities and practices required to achieve each one. In the past two decades, the central concerns of environmentalists have been the escalating

economic endeavours of human beings and their subsequent exploitation, depletion and pollution of the natural environment. Until this time
it was assumed that economic growth and development should take
priority over **environmental management** and protection. For many
people, it is taken for granted that the natural environment is a place of
recreation where they can 'escape' from the stresses of everyday urban
and industrial life.

Whilst there is a need to protect the environment by advocating
sustainable sport practices, such practices, sportspeople and sports
culture are interdependent with the ideologies of global commercialisation, whereby economic development and profit often take precedence over environmental preservation. There is a tendency for develo-
pers, state departments and transnational corporations to have greater
influence than individual citizens and voluntary environmental pressure groups when struggles over the environment prevail.

Policy and decision-making governing the development of leisure
facilities, such as sports centres and artificial outdoor courts and pitches,
is characterised by issues of power. These facilities consume large areas
of land (Edwards 2000) and their location is crucial to economic success.
They need to be both accessible and attractive to the people who use
them if they are to be financially viable. Land available for sport and
recreational development tends to be on the 'urban fringe'. However,
much of this land is located in greenbelt areas, which are marked for
protection against inappropriate urban development. Policies concerning environmental protection are often in conflict with policies that seek
to involve more people in sport at recreational and elite levels. As sport
becomes increasingly more important in our social lives, strategies for
the sustainable development of sports facilities and practices need to
balance demands for accessible and attractive venues with policies for
environmental protection (Edwards 2000).

There is evidence of an increase in responses to environmental
problems at local, national and international levels. Global action of
governments and large commercial organisations tends to create more
marked success in combating particular environmental threats and
problems than the activities of local groups. Recently, there has been a
greater commitment at both local and global levels in the belief that
people should lead sports and leisure lifestyles that are harmonious
with the sustainable development of natural ecosystems.

Debating Point: How 'Green' Is Sport?

There is an increasing acceptance that many aspects of sport development are unsustainable because they destroy natural ecosystems and
resources. Habitat loss, threats to the continuation of animal and plant

species and land, air and water pollution all support this argument (Plimmer et al. 1996; Richardson 2000; Smith 1991; Symington and Angel 2000b). Along with increased awareness of and response to environmental threats in a broader social context, sportspeople and the organisations that they form have begun to pay more serious attention to the impact of sport on the environment.

There has been a growth of 'green' consciousness, policy and practice in the context of sport. For example, the environmental dimension was one crucial element of Sydney's winning bid to host the 2000 Olympics. Sydney won by a small margin of votes, and its commitment to environmental issues, defined in its Environmental Guidelines for the Summer Olympics seemed to be influential in swaying some voters (Symington and Angel 2000c). These guidelines focused on environmental protection and sustainable development of Olympic sites. They included commitments to the preservation of natural ecosystems; the protection of existing landscapes, habitats and animal and plant species; rehabilitation of wetlands; replanting of indigenous flora and fauna; and control of pests and weeds using nontoxic substances (Symington and Angel 2000d). Sydney now claims to be a 'world-first Green Games' (Richardson 2000). Indeed, the 2000 Olympics successfully implemented more environmental protection schemes than any other Games. At Homebush Bay, for example, the development of the Olympic Park occurred in conjunction with the preservation of unique features of wetland, woodland and grassland. This venue won the Gold Banksia Environment Award for the habitat replacement scheme designed to protect the Green and Golden Bell Frog protected under the New South Wales Threatened Species Act of 1995 (Symington and Angel 2000e). The issue captured public attention and brought to the fore the plight of an endangered species, resulting in the adoption of 'Izzy' the Golden Bell Frog as an icon for public transport during the Games.

In addition to **resource management** and species conservation, several other aspects of sustainable development were achieved during the 2000 Olympic preparations. The Olympic village extensively utilised solar power as a primary energy source, and construction work widely used recycled and plantation timber and adopted ecologically sustainable design and building methods (Symington and Angel 2000f). Major tree-planting projects have been planned throughout Australia so that the financial benefits of the Games can be experienced by the nation. Improvements in public transport systems have arguably reduced the need to use motor cars, and the minimisation and extensive recycling of waste was achieved by using cardboard food containers and cornstarch utensils (Richardson 2000). These examples highlight a successful attempt at the sustainable development of sport and leisure. Concerns about inter-generational equity (Selman 1996) are addressed in schemes such as the Olympic Landcare Program, which implemented the afore-mentioned tree-planting project.

In addition, Sydney's new international sporting facilities will provide benefits for the elite sportspeople of the future. A wider community of sportspeople may also feel the legacy of the 2000 Olympics. Arguably, 'ordinary' Australians will be encouraged to participate in more active lifestyles via an increased focus of attention on and perhaps increased funding for community sports and leisure (Symington and Angel 2000g). This is an example of intra-generational equity (Selman 1996) in the sustainable development of sport. It must be emphasised that equality of access and funding for sports and leisure for the Australian people still needs further attention. Symington and Angel (2000g) note that in the context of the 2000 Sydney Olympic Games, 'The economic and social costs of preparations have fallen disproportionately on lower income groups, particularly in inner western Sydney'. Money invested in sport tends to come from private sponsors interested in elite professional performers. Community and youth sport programmes remain largely underfunded. There is also evidence of wider social inequities such as increases in rents, evictions and the 'removal' of the homeless due to tourist demands and a need to improve Sydney's 'image' before and during the Games. These issues have also been highlighted in analyses of the negative social impacts created by preparations for previous Olympic Games (Jennings 2000).

Examples of environmental degradation and a series of broken policy promises have tainted the environmental successes of the Sydney Olympic Games. Since there were no clear means of measuring the success and failure of the environmental guidelines, it was difficult to ensure that policies were adhered to. Environmental groups claim that after the success of the Sydney bid, the guidelines were weakened so that they were 'easier to work with' (Symington and Angel 2000h). There were several incidences of environmental threat and damage associated with hosting the 2000 Games. For example, part of a rare type of forest consisting of 220 plant species, the Cooks River Clay Plain Scrub Forest, was cleared so that the Criterium Olympic cycling track could be constructed at Bankstown, Sydney (Symington and Angel 2000i). This destruction represented a threat to the **biodiversity** (biological diversity) of the region. That is, the species and ecosystems of the region were reduced and in some instances eradicated (Clubbe 1996). In this case, sport practices and sportspeople have threatened the earth's biological diversity and contributed to a biologically impoverished environment for future generations.

On another topic, there were no 'green' cars at the 2000 Olympics, even though the 1996 Atlanta Olympics succeeded in ensuring that 20 percent of its courtesy cars used liquid petroleum gas as an alternative to conventional fuels. Symington and Angel (2000j) suggest that if the International Olympic Committee (IOC) and the Sydney Organising Committee were serious about their environmental guidelines and the 'greening' of sport, they would have ensured that they used environmentally friendly modes of transport. Furthermore, while there was a reduction in the use of toxic Poly Vinyl Chloride (PVC) plastic in many of the Olympic constructions, it was still used in large amounts even though environmentally friendly alternatives such as polypropylene and polyethylene have been found to be durable and cost-effective in the long term (Symington and Angel 2000k). PVC is known to produce toxins such as dioxin and phthalates when burnt, which can disrupt hormone balances in humans. In the buildup to the Games, Greenpeace activists found the water of Homebush Bay to contain dangerously high levels of toxic pollutants and heavy metals. Richardson (2000) notes that Homebush Bay is one of the world's most contaminated waterways. PVC was also present in Olympic merchandise such as children's soft toys and some souvenirs despite recommendations and policies aimed at a worldwide ban on its use in these types of products (Symington and Angel 2000l). Given this, it is worth restating that commercial imperatives dominating the culture of sport can often override practices that may protect the environment and human health. This argument is also supported by evidence of the limited environmental effort and co-operation of Olympic sponsors (Symington and Angel 2000m). The Olympic Sponsors Forum excluded environmental groups from its meetings. Not wishing to upset global corporate sponsors that contribute vast sums of money to the Olympic cause, the Sydney Organising Committee for the Olympic Games (SOCOG) was reluctant to intervene. Given this, Olympic sponsors tended to have little knowledge of, and little time for, the environmental guidelines for the Games.

The idea that Sydney 2000 represented the first 'Green Games' was not a feature of the extensive advertising associated with Olympic sponsorship. Corporate sponsors such as Fuji have made some advances in the area of recycling, but this type of environmentally friendly practice is the exception amongst commercial organisations associated with the Olympics. Environmental groups have noted the disappointing efforts of the Coca-Cola Company to fulfil its commitment to avoid the use of ozone-depleting refrigeration equipment. The 2000 Olympics was an ideal opportunity for large corporations, such as Coca-Cola, to demonstrate their environmental integrity and advance sustainable development as a global commercial issue as well as placing it more centrally within the ideology and structure of sport. Nevertheless, Coca-Cola has stated that continued research and development and a partnership with the New Zealand refrigeration company, Skope, will mean the eradication of ozone-damaging cooling systems at the 2004 Olympics in Athens (Richardson 2000).

This section has demonstrated that there has been some progress towards the 'greening' of sport. Yet, policy and practice associated with sustainable development vary according to which environmental issues are prioritised, by whom, for what reason and the depth of commitment. It can be argued that the environmental management of sport and leisure varies in shade from dark to light green. Broadly speaking, the culture of sport is coloured a shade of light green. Making sport sustainable must involve planning and management, but aspects of its development may even need to stop in order to conserve the environment. Global sports events such as the Olympics provide a unique opportunity to do something to protect landscapes, animal and plant species, habitats and resources. Incorporating 'greener' ideas, beliefs, policies and processes into the wider culture of sport may help to preserve and enhance the environment now and in the future. Symington and Angel (2000n) support this idea by stating that 'it is not acceptable to simply claim to be "green", "environmentally friendly" or "energy efficient"—it is necessary and expected to quantify performance to prove these assertions'.

Case Study: Environmental Issues and the Global Anti-Golf Movement

Golf provides millions of people around the world with the opportunity to exercise outdoors as well as experience the beauty of the natural environment. Globally, 350 golf courses are built each year, about 1 new golf course each day (Chamberlain 1999). Figures from the **Global Anti-Golf Movement** demonstrate the rapid increase in the popularity of the game amongst a diversity of people. For example, in Japan before World War II there were 23 golf courses; in 1956 there was a total of 72. Today, there are 1,700 completed courses with another 330 under construction and 1,000 more being planned. Golf is a multibillion-dollar industry involving several transnational corporations associated with the game itself, construction, agriculture, entertainment, hospitality, marketing and advertising. It is rapidly developing as a professional sport and as a leisure and tourism activity that uses large areas of land, including environmentally sensitive areas around lakes and seashores and on mountains.

At first sight it might seem that golf courses represent a positive recreational use and management of the environment. Trees, shrubs and hedgerows that line the fairways create habitats for wildlife. Turf can protect soil from water and wind erosion, absorb water that can maintain the earth's supply, reduce weed growth and discourage pests such as mosquitoes But golf provides a good example of the ways in which sport can damage and even destroy natural ecosystems, pollute the environment and present a threat to human health (Chamberlain 1999).

Several environmental groups strongly oppose the construction of golf courses worldwide. These organisations are especially proactive in Southeast Asia, where golf course construction has been prolific in the past decade. The Asian Tourism Network (ANTENNA; Thailand) and the Asia-Pacific People's Environmental Network (APPEN; Malaysia) have been influential in raising awareness about and challenging the environmental threats of building and maintaining golf courses (Chamberlain 1999; Chatterjee 1993). Particularly well documented is the opposition of the Japan-based organisation, the Global Anti-Golf Movement (GAG'M), which incorporates three sponsoring organisations, ANTENNA, APPEN and the Global Network for Anti-Golf Course Action (GNAGA). Launched on World No-Golf Day (29 April 1993) the Movement is committed to investigating, exposing and challenging the environmental dangers associated with golf course and golf tourism development. These environmental problems include destruction of natural ecosystems, intensive use of water resources, pollution of land, water and air, human health problems, threats to biodiversity and 'social pollution' associated with the promotion of what is claimed to be an elitist and exclusive leisure activity (Chatterjee 1993).

Building a golf course involves the clearing of natural vegetation and destroys natural landscapes and habitats. Trees, shrubs, hedgerows and plants are destroyed, hilltops are bulldozed and valleys are filled in to create an artificial golf landscape. In Pebble Beach, California, the proposed construction of the Forest Golf Course caused intense political and legal debate over the destruction of 25 percent of the native Monterey Pine trees, considered to be an endangered species by the California Native Plant Society (Achenbach 1996). In addition, golf course construction represents a threat to biodiversity. That is, the destruction of natural ecosystems can irreversibly damage plant and animal life. This situation is further exaggerated by the pollution of waterways and poisoning of aquatic life associated with the use of toxic chemicals required in the maintenance of golf courses. An 18-hole golf course requires three to four tons of chemicals, including various fertilisers and pesticides, to ensure that the fairways and greens are in suitable condition (Chamberlain 1999; Chatterjee 1993).

Chamberlain (1999) notes that, per treated acre of land, golf courses use seven times the amount of chemicals used in large-scale agriculture. Intensive chemical usage is reported to have poisoned many fish species through exposure to nitrogen, phosphorus and other chemical compounds. For example, copper-based compounds were used to protect the golf course from winter snow in Sapporo Kokusai Country Club in Hiroshima, Japan. However, rainwater runoff polluted with the chemical killed more than 90,000 fish in a nearby aquatic project (Chatterjee 2000). Many of the chemicals in pesticides are carcinogenic (cancer-causing) and the GAG'M claims that some are known to cause nerve damage, birth defects and heart disturbances.

Several reports from golf caddies and greenkeepers note the incidence of irritated eyes and blurred vision, chronic nasal congestion and asthma, skin rashes and headaches associated with exposure to chemical substances. Chamberlain (1999) notes that a study by the Golf Superintendents Association of America recorded an 'alarmingly high rate of cancer deaths among former users.' Reports of increased cases of breast cancer among women professional golfers has led the Ladies Professional Golf Association to offer free cancer screening to its members. One death has also been attributed directly to the use of pesticides on golf courses. American George Prior became ill after playing a round of golf and died one month later. The postmortem stated the cause of death as exposure to the pesticide chlorothalonil, which is widely used on golf courses (Chatterjee 2000). Despite the promotion of environmentally friendly methods of golf course maintenance, chemical pesticides are still used extensively.

In addition, golf course construction and management inherently requires high levels of water consumption. Typically, one 18-hole course needs 3,000 cubic metres of water per day to keep fairways and greens healthy. This demand for water can intensify water shortages and threaten the existence of people who live rural subsistence lifestyles. It can be argued that golf courses are environmentally unsound because they destroy natural ecosystems and use vast amounts of natural land and water resources. The development of golf courses replaces the natural landscape with exotic soil and grass, which creates further environmental damage through the use of toxic chemical pesticides and fertilisers.

Golf course development may also be defined as a 'social pollutant'. That is, the growth of golf as a global commercial sports, leisure and tourism activity benefits only a minority of people at the expense of many and with little regard for the environment. Chamberlain (1999) explains how golf endangers Hawaiian culture as well as the natural ecology. An extensive resort complex including three nine-hole golf courses has been built in the South Kona district on Hawaii's west coast. Apart from destroying indigenous plant species still used for medicinal purposes and intensifying water shortages by consuming 500,000 to 800,000 gallons of water per day, this construction contributes to the subordination of local residents. They may be forced to take menial jobs as environmental damage destroys their rural, agricultural and subsistence fishing lifestyle.

The construction of golf courses in sensitive areas is often associated with dubious land and property transactions that are detrimental to local communities and indigenous people (Chatterjee 2000). Powerful corporations are often able to gain political assistance from local governments in buying land from local communities. Exclusive golf club memberships are often offered as incentives for this political help. Local people tend to be excluded from decision-making processes involved in golf course development. In addition, most of the profits earned from golf courses and golf tourism do not remain in the local economy. A few already wealthy business people most often gain financial benefits.

This case study has demonstrated that golf courses and golf tourism are becoming a major environmental and social issue. These problems seem to outweigh the benefits of golf provision, which are arguably experienced by a minority of people. Those who have the time and financial resources to play golf and those who use golf and its associated hospitality facilities to improve their business success represent this minority. On this basis, GAG'M claims that 'The golf industry aggressively promotes an elitist and exclusive resort lifestyle and notion of leisure' (Chatterjee 2000). Golf is increasingly becoming a resource-intensive and environmentally harmful activity and, hence, may be defined as an *unsustainable* sport, leisure and tourism activity. There is much evidence that golf is a threat to natural ecosystems, biodiversity and human health. Yet, as with other sports and leisure pursuits, golf can be developed in sustainable ways. What is required is an increased awareness of the environmental threats posed by the ideas and practices of people involved in the development of golf at local and global levels. There needs to be an increased commitment to methods of golf course construction and maintenance that can contribute to the sustainable development of the game.

Summary

The environmental agenda for sport, leisure and recreation is wide and varied. It includes such issues as population growth, air and water quality, land use and degradation, resource depletion, habitat loss and species extinction. As this chapter has highlighted, sportspeople and sporting activities create environmental threats in each of these categories. Yet, increasingly, there are policies and practices that attempt to address these sporting environmental problems. Such sport-related schemes aim to conserve the earth's resources so that the ecological processes on which life depends are maintained now and in the future. These represent part of a growing awareness of the environmental threat of sports, leisure and recreation activities and of the potential ecological damage posed by sport's economic growth and development. Put simply, there is increasing evidence of a commitment to the sustainable development of sport. The environmental procedures of governments, sports organisations and the **sports industry** have been relatively successful in achieving their aims.

As previously noted, the paradox of sustainable development often means that environmental issues are sidelined in favour of economic development when the latter is more convenient, more commercially attractive and supported by more powerful interest groups. The degree of success in combating particular environmental threats and problems is to a large extent dependent on government policy and global action. But there is also a strengthening of local beliefs in the need to lead sporting lifestyles that are harmonious with the sustainable development of natural ecosystems. There is still criticism that environmental efforts in the context of sport are superficial and that more needs to be done to recognise, understand and do something about the threats that sport and recreation pose to the land, air and water.

Key Terms and Concepts

biodiversity

conservation

ecological degradation

environmental guidelines

environmentalism

environmental management

environmental protection

Global Anti-Golf Movement

global/local environmentalism

'green' issues

'green' politics

inter-generational equity

intra-generational equity

pollution

resource management

sports industry

sustainable development

transfrontier responsibility

Review Questions

1. Using specific examples from sport, describe and explain how the concept of environmentalism can further an understanding of global sport development.

2. Identify and explain selected 'green' issues as they relate to two sports of your choice.

3. Evaluate the extent to which sportspeople, cultures and practices are a threat to local and global environments.

4. How might the concept of sustainable development be applied to the ideology and practice of sport?

5. Identify the ways in which sport development on your campus can be understood within the theoretical framework of sustainability.

6. Discuss the evidence to support the contention that modern sport forms have become increasingly environmentally 'unfriendly'.

7. Critically evaluate the claim that the Sydney 2000 Olympic Games were the first 'Green Games'.

8. Discuss the extent to which economic concerns outweigh environmental considerations in the planning and development of sport.

9. Identify the principles of the Global Anti-Golf Movement and relate them to wider 'green' issues.

10. Discuss the extent to which local environmental concerns are subordinated to the commercial and political interests of more powerful global groups.

Projects

1. Critically examine the environmental impact of a sport of your choice. Identify the principles, policies and practices necessary to reduce the destructive effects on the environment. Produce a report detailing your approach.

2. There is a planned sports stadium development in your local area at a site that has been traditionally used as a public footpath and bridleway. Identify the relevant environmental issues. Draft a letter to a local newspaper detailing why the development is a threat to the environment. Suggest other ways in which local people can voice their objection to this development.

3. Assess the extent of environmental pollution created by a local sports event. Your analysis should address the consumption of resources and the disposal of waste.

4. Write to selected sports organisations and ask them to outline their environmental guidelines. Collect evidence that will help you assess the degree to which these policies are implemented.

5. You are appointed Minister of Sport. You have to prioritise access, provision of facilities and use of a national park for a range of competing groups. These groups include hikers, bikers, horse riders and bird watchers. What criteria would you use in prioritising the claims of competing groups?

6. Go into your local sports store and select a named sports shoe. Identify the process required to produce and sell the shoe. Examine the extent to which these processes conform to the environmental principle of sustainable development.

CHAPTER 6

SPORT, COMMUNITARIANISM AND SOCIAL CAPITAL

© Human Kinetics

Objectives

After completing this chapter, you should be able to

- understand the ways in which sport contributes to the notion of community;

- evaluate the meaning of mutuality in relation to sport;

- explain the relationship between sport and social capital;

- understand different theoretical approaches to sport in the community;

- think critically about the communitarian value of sport; and

- provide several case studies of the ways in which communities have held a stake in the ownership of sports clubs.

This chapter provides a critical comment on the notions of **community** and **social capital,** both of which have been freely used in discussions about the sporting world. The theme of community has always had a central and prominent place in social theory. Social and political theorists have at various times tackled the following classical sociological questions: Should collective or individual interests have priority? Can the ideal of community be realised within contemporary social and political conditions? The relationship between the community and the individual might be seen to be anachronistic, but on both sides of the Atlantic, pressure groups and politicians have pushed **communitarianism** to the forefront of the early-21st-century political agenda. The press has championed policies promoting the notion of strong communities or active citizenship, while politicians such as Bill Clinton, Tony Blair, Gordon Brown, Jessie Jackson and even traditional socialists have all explicitly stated their commitment to community.

At the same time, the resurgence of interest in the role that sport has to play in the regeneration of community has also become a popular theme for many sports organisations that seek to capitalise on sources of government funding for local and regional communities. The implicit notion that participation in sport can make a contribution to the development of active citizenship and community regeneration is central to many wider policy agendas involving urban welfare and **social inclusion.** Such strategies often implicitly involve an ideological investment in social capital without a prior testing of the actual outcomes of such an investment. At the heart of this chapter are some straightforward questions: Does sport contribute to social capital and, if so, how? Does sport contribute to notions of community? The terms *community* and *social* *capital* have been used synonymously in relation to **civil society,** but other terms that are often linked to this topic are **civic engagement** and *civic involvement. Communitarianism,* which draws together developments in social theory, practical politics and in this instance the sporting world, has emerged as the collective term—but what does it mean?

Communitarianism As Social Theory and Political Practice

Communitarianism is a very good example of a phenomenon that reveals common ground in the relationship between academic, political and social theory and practical politics. The idea of community is central to numerous strands of communitarian thought and action. Numerous traditions of social and political thought, such as socialism, Marxism, conservatism and even one-nation Toryism, have all emphasised the ideal of community. Communitarians tend to view community not simply as an object of analysis but as the true source of **normative values,** particularly of self-reliance and self-help. Recurring themes include social justice, **mutuality,** rejection of individualism, social networks, devolved power to local communities and emphasis on family, neighbourhood and kin (Etzioni 1995). Furthermore, it is suggested that community rather than the individual or the state should be the main focus of analysis.

This community approach might be best thought of as divided into three categories, the social, the political and the vernacular, all of which overlap (Frazer 2000). Social communitarianism consists of a core group of texts or abstract cannons that have developed a sustained attack on the philosophy of **liberal individualism.** The central arguments focus on a number of abstract notions that question our knowledge of social processes and values (epistemology); the nature of the individual and the social world (ontology and metaphysics); and the nature or issue of what we *do* value and what we *should* value (ethics). Political communitarianism, on the other hand, relates to a core set of policy ideals or arguments adopted by politicians who have attempted to propel the notion of communitarianism on the 21st-century political agenda. The alleged strength of such a policy is that it lies beyond left and right politics (Giddens 1994). Its aim works towards what a communitarian public policy would mean, for example, for education and welfare, taxation and the ownership and regulation of professional sport. Vernacular communitarianism is more concerned with the ideas, ideals and values of a range of social actors and movements that think their central raison d'être is being community activists and that community building is the most important political project.

Liberal individualism is the natural target for any form of communitarianism that seeks to establish solidarity and mutuality. The critique of liberal individualism also arises out of its assumed dominant position, not simply within academic thought but also key political institutions such as the free market and the rule of law. The individual, according to liberal thought in general, must be protected from the state. Communitarian engagement with liberal individualism tends to include some or all of the following: that liberal theories of rights are overtly individualistic and fail to recognise not only that bonds of obligation are not necessarily freely chosen but that mutuality, reciprocity and co-operation are preconditions of human life; that while individual-rights culture is historically admirable, it has nonetheless gone too far to the extent that it produces a society that has encouraged people to think of themselves as separate and disconnected from others, possibly leading to a distortion or misunderstanding of the real meaning of rights per se; and that liberal individualism has produced a wholly undesirable and unintended upshot of a society that emphasises too many rights and too little duty or mutuality. Communitarianism as social theory and political practice has therefore become popular within the gap between the state or governmental provision and free market ideals, and the perception of their twin failure.

Communitarian ideals have been widely debated and are not without criticism. The emphasis on community rather than the individual or the state has raised questions about the lack of definition of community. Are we talking about community as a place or community as a set of interests? Some feminists, while supporting the notion of communitarianism, have implied that terms such as community are authoritarian and hierarchical and that communitarian arguments are reactionary and non-egalitarian. The claims of individual liberty and rights versus the claims of community raise difficult issues of the common good, public interest, and justice and exclusion (Pahl and Spencer 1998). Is social inclusion most likely to be formed through friendship or friendship-like relations arising through work and associational ties? If so, then one might expect notions of community to be closely tied to issues of social capital and civil society. Furthermore, borrowing Anderson's concept of **imagined communities** (1991), writers such as Alexander (1996) suggest that the very ideal of local imagined communities remains highly emotive and a potent political and social symbol to those it includes and those it excludes. Others such as Krieger (2000) tend to simply refer to two categories of community, actual and imagined. Yet both are at the heart of New Labour's normative ideal of British communities. In response to many of these criticisms, communitarians stress the importance of community, social capital and a strong civil society, and the practical goal of an inclusive community with layered loyalties. Whatever the perspective, communitarianism and community are likely to remain active principles within contemporary social thought and political practice.

The place of sport in the making of communities has also been the subject of some debate and reflection (Coalter 2000; Gruneau and Whitson 1993; Metcalfe 1996). The word *community* has often been associated with British sports policy. It has been suggested that sport contributes to community in at least two ways. First, there is the notion of a distinct sports community in its own right and, second, the notion that sport itself contributes to the regeneration of, for example, urban communities. Sport is viewed as contributing to civic as opposed to ethnic pride. Cup-winning teams are often provided with the freedom of the home city. Both the community and local politicians, who use sport to reinforce notions of civic pride and loyalty to the town or area, share sporting success.

The relationship between West Ham Football Club and the community is borne out in the work of Korr (1990), who describes the meaning of the club to one of the poorest inner-city areas of London in the early 1920s. Graham Walker's (1994) account of swimming in Motherwell in the 1940s shows how the swimming club tapped into notions of local civic pride and the need to swim well for the community, whether it is Motherwell, Scotland or Great Britain. Jeff Hill's research highlights the town of Nelson in the northwest of England and the place of sport in the process of building civic identity between 1870 and 1950 (Hill 1999).

The history of British sport shows that an often-idealised notion of community has overlooked the fact that there has nearly always been tension between sport for its own sake and sport as a means to an end. Historically, the provision of sports facilities in Britain has often been rationalised on the grounds that sport will promote healthy communities or reduce crime rates or help with **urban regeneration** or promote community integration or social inclusion. For example, the New Labour agenda for sport states that 'Sport can make a unique contribution to tackling social exclusion in our society'. Rarely is sport viewed in terms of sport for sport's sake but rather as a means to an end because it is seen to deliver something else other than just sport.

In general, the issue of sport's contribution to communitarian thinking has tended to rely on some or all of the following arguments: that local sports clubs provide communities with a sense of place and identity; that the associational nature of sport helps in the production and reproduction of social capital; that sport contributes to a sense of civic pride and civic boosterism; that sport has a vital role to play in the regeneration of deprived urban communities; that sports facilities can provide an important contribution to the physical infrastructure of communities and provide a social focus for community, consequently influencing people's perceptions of neighbourhood; that the power of sport has been diminished along with the decline of civil society and social capital; that a strong sense of collective identification with specific teams has been divisive; that sport alone cannot sustain vibrant living communities; that global sporting markets and patterns of consumption have marginalised and replaced local sporting identity and taste; and, finally, that mutual ownership of sports clubs can contribute to social capital within the community.

Debating Point:
Is Sport Good for the Community?

As Gruneau and Whitson (1993) point out, the word *community* tends to express an ideal in Western social thought that often evokes a nostalgic and honoured way of life. Few people if any have generally had anything bad to say about the notion of community. The social and economic benefits that sport allegedly brings to the ideal of community often revolve around notions of civic pride, identity and the role that sport plays in the regeneration of deprived, often urban, communities. Community regeneration is often framed as being about improving the social, economic and environmental aspects of a neighbourhood or area. Sport is rarely the solution in many circumstances, but in many cases sport is perceived as being part of the solution. For instance, it is often suggested that there is a relationship between sports involvement and the reduction of crime, that sport is a valuable medium for promoting education and citizenship or that involvement with local sports clubs often helps to sustain a sense of community identity for both men and women.

Thus to answer the question whether sport is good for the community, we might suggest that sport can play a positive role in a number of wide-ranging community initiatives that can help to sustain a sense of community; sport on its own is not the solution to community social and economic problems but it can be part of the solution; sociologists need to empirically test a number of statements concerning the role of sport and its associated outcomes in specific settings before concluding on the issue of sport's relationship to communities; and communities themselves change over time and, whether one is talking about a community of Internet sport enthusiasts or the place and space associated with sport in the geography of communities, recognition must be given to the fact that the relationship between sport and the community is never static but always changing. Finally, there also remains the case of sport for sport's sake without necessarily tying sport to any specific social or economic outcome.

Mutual Sport in Demutualised Communities

The issue of ownership of community-based sports clubs needs more careful consideration. The importance of a sports club to a city or community has been widely recognised, and yet in the increasingly commercial global sport marketplace there remains the danger of certain sports clubs becoming distanced from the local or grassroots fan base. Increasingly demutualised societies and communities have failed in most cases to give sports fans any form of stakeholding in the community sports club. The conventional wisdom in relationship to the ownership of sports clubs remains that of the profit-maximizing, investor-owned Public Limited Company, with the public sector remaining the natural and unchallengeable giants of the modern economy (Morrow 2000). Yet in the 21st-century global economy, a number of third-sector, non–profit-making organisations continue to flourish.

When it comes to building sustainable forms of social capital, generated by a sense of local self-responsibility, neither the private sector nor the public sector seems to offer the ideal solution. The private sector has a history of crowding out the third sector from capital markets, and the public sector of bludgeoning mutual or **co-operative** ventures out of existence. There will continue to be many areas of economic activity where investor-owned, profit-maximising companies will remain dominant, but there are many other instances where there remains a need for stronger state/civil regulation or a different form of ownership, or possibly a combination of both. When consumers or employees become owners, their sense of self-esteem, responsibility and participation can be transformed.

The issue of **community ownership** or the community as a significant stakeholder in the ownership and running of sports clubs has only recently been investigated. The ultimate form of fan or community involvement would be to have a mutual structure where the fans or community own the club itself rather than the private Public Limited Company model. In the United States, the example of the Green Bay Packers may be cited as an example of a club that maintained local fan and community involvement whilst becoming one of the most successful teams in American football. The three-time winners of the Super Bowl (and runner-up in 1998) represent a small Wisconsin city of about 100,000 people in open competition with the country's population giants in Washington, New York and elsewhere. First established in 1919, the not-for-profit organisation evolved into a formidable force in American football.

In 1935 a fan fell from the stands, sued and won a $5,000 verdict, and the insurance company went out of business. The Packers went into receivership and were just about to declare bankruptcy when the Green

Bay business community came to the rescue, raised $15,000 in new capital and reorganised the club. In 1949, a further $125,000 was raised in a giant stock sale all over the state. The team's 4,634 shares are fixed in value at $25 and are subject to strict transfer rules. They can be left to relatives but cannot be sold to outsiders without first offering them to the team. Any one person can hold a maximum of 200 shares. If the team is sold, the proceeds must go towards a local war memorial. In the 21st century, where teams routinely relocate based on profit-maximising motives, the Green Bay Packers serve as an example of the need to anchor community-owned assets locally.

The Catalan football club in Barcelona is another example of a mutual community club, owned and run, in part, by its members. According to its statutes, the club exists for the pursuit of sporting excellence (Michie 1999). It can be dissolved on approval of the general assembly of its members, in which case its unmovable assets are transferred to the local councils in whose premises the club resides and the movable assets, after payment of the club debts, are donated to the Catalan government. An elected body runs the club for a term of five years. However, the annual reports of this elected body have to be reviewed and approved by the general assembly of members' representatives and this latter body also fixes the entrance and subscription fees and has to approve various other matters including TV rights, media agreements and proposals in respect of mergers or takeovers. However, with well over 100,000 members, the method of election of these representatives to form a general assembly with a manageable number of delegates is key. There is disquiet amongst some supporters that the current management would like to move the club away from its democratic foundations towards increased commercialism and that they have attempted to influence the composition of the general assembly to make it conducive to such attempts. Thus a group of supporters have established a pressure group named the 'blue elephant' organisation to uphold the democratic traditions of the club in the face of increasing attempts to commercialise.

The community **stakeholder model** provides but one model of possible conduct for sports clubs who, first, aim to demonstrate that they are a vital part of the community and, second, aim to promote and sustain social and economic capital through facilitating the community role in the decision-making structures of the sports club (Morrow 2000). The organisational thinking behind increasing community ownership of sports clubs, such as **co-operatives,** owes much to the principles of mutuality. The above cases question the inaccurate assumption that the profit-maximising investor Public Limited Company is the natural form of organisation for the professional sports club. Co-operative, mutual philosophies work best when there is a clear opportunity and incentive for people to work closely together for practical, mutual interest in increasingly demutualised societies. In truth, few democratic governments have grasped the important issue of community ownership of sports clubs and organisations. Government's natural pragmatism whispers that what works is right, but there is a danger that in rejecting the sterility of the polarized argument about state versus private ownership, the case for diversity in forms of ownership goes unexamined. Ownership matters. The socially excluded need a sense of ownership. One of the most intransigent aspects of 21st-century welfare reforms in Britain is that the poorest 15 percent cannot afford to put cash aside to save for retirement because they lack capital, either in terms of savings or real estate (Hargreaves 1999). In all the meanings of the word ownership, how it is applied to specific communities lies at the very heart of a larger debate concerning sport's contribution to civil society.

Sport and Civil Society

Interest in civil society and its relationship to the state is not new. The view that it was good to have sources of power in society that were independent of the state was both popular and controversial in the 18th century (Keane 1988). Hegel (1975) used the term *civil society* to denote the sphere of contact or of free association amongst individuals. For Antonio Gramsci (1971), civil society was the bastion of class hegemony and ultimately viewed as being supportive of the state. Danish and British sporting policies have often been premised on the principle of an 'arm's length approach' from government. For definitional purposes, civil society is an arena between the spheres of the state on the one hand and domestic or interpersonal relations on the other.

Case Study:
Sport, Civil Society and Community in Denmark

Sport in Denmark is financed partly through sport itself—clubs, federations and organisations—partly by local authorities and partly by funds derived from public betting, football pools and lotteries. The profits from these gambling activities are allocated by law to various cultural activities, among which the three national sports organisations dispose freely of the money according to their autonomy (Moller and Anderson 1998). Sport in Denmark belongs to the nongovernmental sector and is largely based on voluntarism. The voluntary contribution is regarded as a valued aspect of democracy within Danish civil society. Sports associations, like all cultural associations in Denmark, are approached from an ideal perspective characterised by notions of solidarity, reciprocity and personal initiative. Solidarity in a sports association can be manifested as responsibility for the whole, which each individual is part of. The whole that the association is part of will often be a local community, and association and solidarity through sport necessitates a broader sense of awareness of the needs of the broader local community. Sport occupies a central position in the consciousness of young Danish people and, therefore, it is deemed as having the opportunity to inspire the form of solidarity and responsibility inherent within Danish democracy.

But is sport an arena of civil society through which individuals interact with one another in ways that have an impact on them collectively or on society at large? By the 21st century, civil society had come to be defined in not just social but political and economic terms. Thus civil societies today have been described as a constellation of forces that provide a series of checks and balances on the power of the nation-state or the local state. However, at a micro-level, civil society is also the terrain of **civic associations** that are potential forces of civic engagement and mutuality. These forces might include the market in all its forms, professional associations, mutual societies, voluntary public bodies or sports associations, to name but a few of the bodies that actively hold the middle ground between the state and the individual. Sport has often been viewed as a focal point of civic engagement.

The idea that sport and other forms of cultural activity may be viewed as sites of civic engagement has often led to the suggestion that such activities might be viewed as important arenas of social inclusion or community revitalization. Community fun-runs and sponsored marathons are often used as a means of subsidising sporting provision in areas where state provision for sport is inadequate. Such perspectives reflect a change of emphasis from viewing urban regeneration or community development in purely economic terms to placing a greater emphasis on people and the development of social capital. Yet the role of professionals in the development of civil society or the development of social capital may be paradoxical. As Harris (1998) suggests, the horizontal, equitable nature of civil society makes professional efforts to strengthen it somewhat problematic because professionals usually have more power than the people they often serve, and the conventional top-down approach to the development of community and civil society is not likely to bring about the desired outcomes.

Sporting activity has historically been associated with political protests that have championed **human rights,** progressive socialism and social inequality. Kidd and Donnelly (2000) have recently explored the contribution that sport has made to the struggle for human rights. They provide examples citing sports contributions to campaigns against apartheid and racism, for gender equity and athletes' rights and finally for the rights of children and workers. They argue that the aspirations for democracy and liberation evoked under the banner of human rights cannot be achieved without human rights in sport. Kidd and Donnelly conclude by drawing attention to the Sports Act in Finland, which came into force in 1998. The purpose of the act is to promote equality and tolerance; support cultural diversity and sustainable development of the environment through sport; promote recreational, competitive and top-level sports and associated civic activity; promote the population's welfare and health; and support the growth and development of children and young people through sport (Kidd and Donnelly 2000).

Sport and physical activity, as Harris (1998) has recently asserted, have played their part in 'fostering self-esteem, human agency and social equity... an important step toward strengthening and expanding civil society'. Daniel Tarschys, then Secretary General to the Council of Europe, suggested in 1995 'that the hidden face of sport is also the tens of thousands of enthusiasts who find, in their football, rowing, athletics and rock climbing clubs, a place for meeting and exchange, but above all, the training ground for community life'. Harris goes on to assert that within this microcosm, people learn to take responsibility, to follow rules, to accept one another, to look for consensus and to take on democracy—seen in this light, 'sport is par excellence, the ideal school for democracy' (Sport England 1998). It is precisely these notions that have been central to the ideal of sport as social capital.

Sport and Social Capital

James Coleman's (1988) concept of social capital has become popular within contemporary policy-orientated discourses about sport and leisure (Coalter 2000; Harris 1998). Coleman introduced his now well-known concept in a discussion of a society's capacity for educational achievement, but implicit within his notion of social capital was a potential meaning that extends well beyond education in that social capital can be found in any sphere that involves **trust.** Developing social capital has, since the late 1980s, been viewed as a way of renewing democracy (Hirst 1994; Hutton 1995; Marquand 1988; Putnam 1995; Schuller 1997). More specifically, social capital refers to the network of social groups and relationships that fosters co-operative working and community well-being. It involves communities and other social groups exercising a certain degree of trust through taking on mutual obligations. In both British and U.S. contexts, one liberal argument has been that economic regeneration flourishes best in communities where there is seen to be a high degree of social capital.

There are at least two reasons why social capital has attracted so much attention. On the one hand, civil society and communities depend on it. Social groups and individuals learn more when they can draw on the cultural resources of people around them. They learn from each other directly, but they also learn to trust that social arrangements are in place to ensure that learning, through a multitude of mediums including sport, will benefit them for cultural and employment purposes. They also trust that their own family or friends will live in a community that is intellectually stimulating. Social capital can have these effects most readily where it is embodied in the social structure—most notably, formal educational institutions and cultural organisations that have a commitment to learning.

On the other hand, democracy depends on social capital. This is true in one very obvious sense, that democracy depends on everyone trusting that everyone else will operate the system constructively. When that trust breaks down—for example, as a reaction to certain screening practices aimed at the control of drugs in athletes or the failure to deliver sustainable sporting and economic benefits for deprived inner-city urban ghettos—the result is cynicism about democracy in general. But the potential role of social capital is more profound than this because **citizenship** requires knowledge and co-operation towards common goals. Consider the following example: The Aneurin Bevin Lodge Children's Home was established in 1997 to return to the local community young children who had been placed in care. A project to promote involvement in activities within the community provided a wide range of sporting activities for these children. The evaluation report of the project concluded that 'it is clear that those involved in the project have had positive outcomes in that sport has helped to develop confidence, awareness, self-esteem, trust, ability to value negotiation between people and reliance on self and others' (Sport England 1998). In this sense it might be suggested that the project is an attempt to produce and sustain a notion of social capital involving sport.

The importance of sustaining successful sports clubs in the community has often been an argument that has been implicated in this liberal-minded thinking that uncritically supports the notion of sport as being good. A more critical concern is the extent to which participatory involvement and social capital can result in ties between people who are neither benign nor civic-minded and whose self-interest or alienation might in itself reflect a decline in social capital. Sport, perhaps ideally, may be seen to contribute to a wide range of ideals such as civil society, voluntarism, citizenship, community well-being and social capital. Yet clarity is needed about the kinds of networks and associations required to foster community well-being or social capital. To what extent does sport or can sport help to sustain a sense of mutuality or obligation amongst people in an increasingly individualised global culture? This has been a challenge to the 'third way' of thinking closely associated with both the Blair and Clinton administrations in Britain and the United States in the early part of the 21st century.

Case Study: The Decline of Social Capital in the United States

Political scientist David Putnam (1995) recently documented the decline of social capital in the United States, which he defined as those features of social life—networks, norms and trusts—that enable participants to work together more effectively to pursue shared objectives. Putnam used this notion to analyse the phenomenon of what he calls civic disengagement: the decline in participation not just in formal political activity but also in social activities, including sport and physical activity. The decline of social capital allegedly includes decreased membership in voluntary organisations, decreased participation in organised activities and decreased time spent in informal socialising and visiting. Fitness participation declined about 10 percent between 1985 and 1990. Close to 10 percent of free time was devoted to sports and exercise, while an increasingly substantial amount of time was devoted to more sedentary forms of sport such as fishing or bowling, but even this, argued Putnam, was less than in other countries. Americans were viewed as becoming less trusting of one another with a close correlation existing between social trust and membership of civic associations. Television emerged as the prime suspect in the decline of social capital, with a 50 percent increase in viewing time in comparison to the 1950s. Television privatised time for sport and other activities and, in doing so, destroyed the networks and values that supported social capital and the pursuit of shared objectives.

Debating Point: Does Sport Promote Social Inclusion and Social Capital?

Much of the research to date has implied that sport has a place in strengthening the internal structures and relationships within and between communities. In this sense, sport can be said to both promote social inclusion and contribute to the development of social capital, but not in an unqualified sense. If social inclusion is taken to mean participation in wider society, then sport at an ideological level, and in some cases at a normative level, has a part to play. The 27th Olympiad from Australia was heralded as a great success, not least of which was the part played by the thousands of volunteers, but also by the symbolic significance of Cathy Freeman lighting the torch at the opening ceremony and then winning gold in the women's 400m. Perhaps more importantly, this athlete stamped an indelible impression on a country that, despite lack of direction from then-Prime Minister John Howard, was moving towards accepting the proposition of social inclusion as involving a mandatory acceptance of the contribution made by Aborigines to a modern, socially inclusive Australia.

Maria Isabel Urrutia was another medal winner at the Sydney Olympic Games, having lifted 75 kg in the clean and jerk weightlifting category. The Olympic gold medallist represents a country where young athletes have had to pass through guerrilla and paramilitary roadblocks while travelling between cities to national competitions. Colombia holds the unfortunate distinction of being the world's leading country in terms of kidnapping, with some 3,000 reported cases per year. Commenting on her gold medal victory in the Glasgow-based *Herald* newspaper (1 October 2000, 24), Urrutia said 'that she hoped that her victory would reach others like her—poor, black and female'. She went on:

> [A]s a poor person, I hope others see that you can make a living, see the world and get an education through sports or even music and other arts. As a woman I hope that girls who are now 13, like I was when I started, now realise that they don't have to become teenage mothers and as a black person I hope the country sees that there's another Urrutia besides the white man who signs our pesos.

Both of these cases illustrate the normative potential of sport at a particular time in particular communities. However Forrest and Kearns (1999) raise a more complex issue. For them, social and spatial links to the world beyond one's immediate neighbourhood are vital if communities are to be socially inclusive. At another level, if sport is deemed as being important in sustaining a long-term sense of social capital and civic engagement, then the traditional inward-looking view of the neighbourhood community needs to be questioned. The neighbourhood represents only a small part of an increasingly diverse web of relationships involving kin, friends, colleagues and contacts, and these need to be developed out with the immediate neighbourhood if the benefits of sport are to be sustained. Sport cannot sustain social capital on its own, but it can make a contribution.

Summary

This chapter evaluated the relationship between sport, communitarianism and social capital; questioned some of the taken-for-granted assumptions about the positive influence that sport has on various communities; discussed the contribution that sport can make to the regeneration and reproduction of social capital; outlined the community stakeholder model of sports clubs as a potential model of good practice and recognised some of the dangers associated with such an approach; and provided a theoretical and conceptual summary of the key approaches to sport and the community.

The themes of community and the place of sport in the community have been commented on for more than half a century. From at least the 1950s, the sociological analysis of community has existed in the work of writers such as Tonnies, who distinguished between relations of *gemeinschaft* and *gesellschaft*, through to the 1990s, where writers such as Etzioni sought to push a modern communitarian agenda that drew on concepts such as cohesion and mutuality. There remains a substantive moral and political disagreement between those who value community in itself and those who value it instrumentally. The notions of social capital and citizenship have been associated contemporaneously with the above agenda. Sport's role in the regeneration of 21st-century communities also remains well documented but problematic. We have argued in this chapter that it is unrealistic to expect sport to be responsible for sustaining a sense of community or citizenship or even to reinforce notions of social capital. However, sports projects and the place of sport within both imagined and active senses of community can make a valuable contribution. Yet perhaps more important is the potential contribution that sport makes to civil society, the space between the state and the individual that provides sport with the opportunity to promote a communitarian philosophy based on mutuality and obligations rather than individualism and rights.

Key Terms and Concepts

citizenship	imagined communities
civic associations	liberal individualism
civic engagement	mutuality
civil society	normative values
communitarianism	social capital
community	social inclusion
community ownership	stakeholder model
co-operative	trust
human rights	urban regeneration

Review Questions

1. Does sport help to sustain or reproduce social capital and, if so, how?
2. What arguments would a communitarian philosophy use in a critique of a liberal individual approach to sport?

3. Argue for and against the notion that sport is good for the community.
4. Critically discuss two examples of the ways in which sport produces social capital.
5. Why has the relationship between sport and social capital become important?
6. To what extent can sport help to sustain a sense of mutuality?
7. What contribution has sport made to our thinking about communitarianism?
8. Provide at least one criticism of current communitarian ideals.
9. What do you understand by the term *active citizenship*?
10. What contribution has sport made to the struggle for human rights?

Projects

1. Interview no fewer than 10 people about the role of sport in your neighbourhood. Compile a list of up to 10 different points that reflects the information you are given.
2. Identify a sports club of your choice, read the club constitution and develop a case study explaining what the club does for the local community.
3. Carry out a content analysis of the sports coverage in your local newspaper for a period of two weeks. Use the data that you have collected to discuss how the newspaper privileges certain parts of the community in its sports coverage.
4. Examine the original constitution of a professional sports club. Identify what the club pledges to do and critically discuss how the original constitution outlines ways that the club will work or contribute to some or all of the community.
5. Interview 10 different sport development officers or coaches, asking them about the ways in which participation in sport helps with the issue of leadership in the community. Use the material from your interviews to discuss how sport contributes to social capital.
6. Identify one socially excluded group in your area. Develop a sport policy document that protects their rights to sport and empowers this group to participate in sport.

INSIDE THE
WORLDS
OF SPORT

Local and National Communities

Chapter 7   Sport, Place and Space

Chapter 8   Sport, Civic and Ethnic Passions

Chapter 9   Sport in the Making of Nations

Personal Troubles and Everyday Experiences

Chapter 10   Sporting Subcultures

Chapter 11   Sport, Emotions and Societies

Chapter 12   Sport, Gender and Social Relations

SPORT, PLACE AND SPACE

© Jim Whitmer

Objectives

After completing this chapter, you should be able to

- identify the changing functions of sport;
- critically evaluate whether sport reflects the society in which it is located;
- discuss the significance of sport in Cuba and one other nation;
- discuss how sport contributes to the American dream;
- discuss the relationship between sport and consumerism; and
- evaluate how sport space is contested terrain.

When we think of space, many of us focus on the stars, planets and cosmos. However, **space** is a concept integral to ideas of who, what and where we are. No matter where you are reading this you are inhabiting 'space'. It may be in a lecture theatre, in a library or sitting on a park bench. All of these constitute a particular space, **place** and **time.** Our relevant environment can be identified by the ideas that exist in our conceptual languages regarding locality. Indeed, the ideas of space and place are essential to our existence and our capacity to communicate.

Time and space are human constructs; they are rarely as natural or as inevitable as we often think. In fact, like other constructs, time and space are essentially means of orientation to aid our understanding and control of the social and physical worlds. They help us make sense of the past, present and future; they provide sites for negotiation between individuals and groups and as such are forever open to change: they are unfixed and indefinite features of society that are constantly shifting. This is important in relation to sport.

It is difficult to imagine a place or time when humans had no concept of 'space to oneself', or 'living' or 'resting space'. There is plenty of evidence during the 19th and 20th centuries of efforts to divide aspects of life: as Eileen and Stephen Yeo describe it, 'performing from spectating, street space from play space, education and welfare from recreation, politics from the rest of life, values and choices from production, work from creativity' (Rojek 1989). These kinds of spatial divisions and tensions have always been present and are ongoing. For example, in a perceived materialistic, capitalist, self-centred and career-oriented society, there is a constant battle for hegemonic **lifestyles** to be divided up among family life, leisure time and work time (if we consider religion as less important in secular societies, then, for the time being, it has gained a relegated place in this equation). The first two might be considered 'people' time, while the last frequently concerns a vision of the self that has become a hegemonic characteristic of late-20th- and early-21st-century Western lifestyles. Indeed, some critics might argue that the self has become dominant as the centre of both time and space.

Western **lifestyles** have become increasingly ordered, and the cynic might argue that such ordering and systematisation has been to accommodate those who organise society to suit their positions of influence, power and financial resources. For example, the police have a wide range of powers to enforce authoritative perceptions of who goes where and when, an ongoing conflict in many societies. Such examples do not occur in a social, economic or political vacuum and for most people they can become what Rojek calls **natural** and **inevitable.** In other words, 'history is turned into nature' (1989): we grow through socialisation to expect certain relevant aspects of our **culture** and we internalise them in relation to our own lives. They become part of our 'natural' world. This chapter is concerned with those aspects of space and time that have come to help define sport as an essential part of the world we are constantly constructing.

Case Study: The Development of Soccer in Britain

Professional **soccer,** more commonly called **football** outside North America, is the most popular competitive sport in Britain and Europe. This is not natural in the sense that it is inevitable, having evolved because of a particular process of social construction. A sociocultural context and the concepts of time and space are essential to understanding this development.

Soccer evolved into the sport we recognise today because of a series of conditions and events that contributed to its constitution. In its earliest forms, it was a rough, rowdy and popular pastime that involved uncontrolled numbers of people, a mixture of rules, and areas that would make little sense to our modern understanding of a soccer match. The game was often attacked as morally degrading and perilous by a variety of authorities who in turn attempted to proscribe it, sometimes outlawing the game in spaces within borough boundaries.

For figurational sociologists such as Elias, one of the prime exponents of theories of the civilising processes involved in human history (Dunning 1999), the uninhibited nature of football of the past became subject to restraint, regulation and transformation. This gained impetus because of the evolution of 'mutually oriented and dependent people' (Horne et al. 1999), whose new-found social and political interests could be best protected and developed in a more controlled and regulated society. Street soccer gradually became an unacceptable form of public spectacle. As one space disappeared in response to cultural changes, another was to be created as the game itself changed.

The transformation wrought by industrialist capitalist society helped create the conditions for the development of the game we now recognise as soccer. Nineteenth-century British society gradually came under the influence and control of those such as the new middle classes, who sought to curtail the time and space of the working-class masses and their forms of popular recreation. In turn, this hegemonic influence would ensure their security and capacity to make social and economic gain. Although there are varying interpretations of this process, how it was planned, instigated and policed, who was in control and who subjected themselves to events, there is broad agreement about the conflict involving time and space. For example, Hargreaves (1986) informs us of the development of 19th-century soccer in the English town of Derby and the clashes between the authorities and the populace over the right to assemble and participate in desired leisure activities. Throughout this period, street soccer was viewed as a site for conflict between those who wanted to play the game and those who sought to suppress it. Walvin's history of soccer describes how

> new policing systems, policemen on the beat and local Watch Committees armed with punitive local by-laws all served to drive traditional games from the streets of urban Britain.... Even in the countryside, the game [football] was under pressure from the changing rural economy. Football [noted someone in 1838] seems to have almost gone out of use with the enclosure wastes and commons, requiring a wide space for its exercise. (Walvin 1994)

Soccer had to change as a game if it was to survive. It could not be played under such conditions and in terms of the environment that it was used to. The new physical, social and economic circumstances being shaped by the Industrial Revolution, urbanisation and the changing goals of the growing middle classes meant that time and space in terms of sporting pastimes would also undergo reformation. The creation of a half-day off work on Saturday, established by the Factory Act of 1850, was a significant development. For Walvin (1994), in this overall process 'the pre-industrial game was gradually transmuted into a team game which demanded rigid discipline, selflessness, teamwork and physical prowess, and in which the strengths and skills of the individual were subsumed by the greater needs of the team'. From this, a set of rules developed that gave rise to standardised soccer pitches and, eventually, stadiums that could hold one hundred thousand or more spectators. A century and a half later, the place of soccer at a world level renders it the most popular and global sport of the early 21st century.

The Place of Sport in Nations, States and Society

Written histories inform us about the place of sport in ancient Greek and Roman societies. Although perceptions of sport in these societies were different from those of the early 21st century, gladiatorial contests and the first Olympics still convey an idea that sport, for thousands of years, has held a significant place in human history. Nonetheless, as societies have evolved and changed, the meanings of sport and games have likewise altered.

Historians have traced the trajectories of sporting pursuits from such times up until the Industrial Revolution and to the present day. Apart from its artistic, competitive and physical attributes, sport has had a profound influence on modern lifestyles, both in terms of active participation and spectating. For Coakley (1998),

> sports have never been so pervasive and influential in the lives of people as they are in many societies today, and never before have physical activities and games been so closely linked to profit making, character building, patriotism, and personal health. Organised sports in the United States have become a combination of business, entertainment, education, moral training, masculinity rituals, technology transfer, declarations of identity, and endorsements of allegiance to countries and corporate sponsors.

Another aspect not mentioned specifically by Coakley might be considered the ideological dimensions of **modern sport,** which has a primary place in the history of the 20th century.

The place of boxing in Cuba serves as a good example of how sport can gain significance in contemporary society. Since the Revolution of 1959, Cuba has grown to be a world leader in amateur boxing. This has been achieved under continued U.S. economic, military and political involvement in the condition and affairs of the state of Cuba: historically a situation bitterly resented by many Cubans. In the period after the revolution, Fidel Castro began to influence Cuban sport, aiming to produce champions and bring sport to the masses. For a number of decades, Cuba has invested heavily in its athletes. Although professional boxing was outlawed, at an amateur level the sport became one of the prime targets of the new regime. It was viewed as having the capacity to increase Cuban achievement and produce Olympic champions (Sugden 1996) and amateur victors who would participate purely for the love of country and people. In itself, this was an ideological foresight. Nationalism and **socialism** have been carried on the back of Cuban boxing successes, and the place of boxing in Cuban society has been invoked as a metaphor for the new and successful socialist identity. Isolated, and under a perceived constant economic attack by the United

States, continued boxing successes serve to raise the esteem of Cubans while showing the rest of the world that socialism can win in the face of hegemonic **capitalism.** Although such ideological nuances can be drawn and constructed from many sports in other countries over hundreds of years, the ideological clash through sport between East and West during the years of the Cold War serves as an apposite example of how intense and significant these struggles can become. Cuban socialism's conflict with U.S. capitalism has many theatres, and the place of sport, particularly boxing, in this struggle has become crucial for many in Cuban society.

Historical Changes to Sport

It is possible that prehistoric societies engaged in organised sport. By the time **ancient sport** was organised in Rome and Greece, a few aspects began to resemble sport as we know it today, particularly the involvement of money. By the Middle Ages, sport changed substantially to become something that was organised by the nobility or the peasant masses. Many of the games that dominate world sport today have a peasant background, including soccer, rugby, baseball and cricket.

The meaning of sport changed throughout these periods. Although there is some debate over links to sport in centuries and millenniums gone by, it is an undoubted fact that physical expression and competition have long characterised human societies. The brutal nature of Roman 'sport' became the unorganised but still often violent sport of the peasantry of the Middle Ages. The motivation behind organisation, who participated and why, as well as the spaces designated for sporting occasions, all changed until the impact of the Industrial Revolution. Eventually, sport became more organised, systematic and widespread to become the large-scale spectator phenomenon we currently know.

Debating Point: Has Sport Always Provided the Same Functions?

Sport has provided different **functions** to societies over the course of the centuries. Although there has probably always been physically expressive, artistic and competitive roles inherent in sport, these have changed in relation to meaning and functions served. As society changes, power shifts and people become more organised and regulated in their lives. Sport's links to society as an integral part of relationships have simultaneously altered. Spiritual and supernatural beliefs appear to have been the main functions of early Greek sport. Wealth was also an important prerequisite to sporting participation in ancient Greece, and this stratification was added to by the dominance of male athletes. Eventually, sport in Greece gradually became more visible, popular, political and even commercial.

In ancient Rome, the function of sport was mainly one of mass entertainment. However, this had underlying motivations that may have meaning for people today. The spectacles of early Rome were designed to entertain and preoccupy the unemployed and idle masses. They also functioned as symbols of **power** for political leaders. Roman sport became an avenue for the disposal of troublesome sections of the population, such as Christians, criminals or rebellious parties, and also functioned as occasions for the training of the military might of the Empire (sometimes for discovering 'new talent').

During the Middle Ages (A.D. 500 to 1300), sporting tournaments were held by the ruling military classes primarily as entertainment but also as a means of military training. These same classes viewed the more popular activities pursued by the peasant masses, often violent and brutal, as safety valves for peasant discontent. For Coakley (1998), the warlike nature of many of these activities was gradually 'softened by colourful ceremonies and pageantry, and entertainment and chivalry took priority'. Although it was more recent times before these features became the dominant aspects of sport, there is a clear trajectory in their development in sporting history.

The functions of sport over time often bear a semblance of similarity despite their variations in context and meaning. From the times of the ancient Greeks and Romans, from the Middle Ages through the Industrial Revolution and on to the globalised and capitalist world of today, sport has provided exercise, artistry, competition and entertainment. Some of sport's other important functions, namely, displaying national and ideological dominance or superiority, occupying, diverting and asserting a form of control on the masses, and bringing together an otherwise diverse group of people to display 'sameness', have been constant themes throughout the history of sport. Although circumstances, conditions and environments have all changed, as have the time and space inhabited by sport in societies, the history of human sport reflects a remarkable set of constants.

Televised Sport in Time and Space

The media (newspapers, magazines, radio, television, the Internet and video games), particularly television, has come to play a crucial role in our society. Many of us own several television sets, a technology that has potential to shape some of our cultural and personal characteristics as well as determine how we view various aspects of life, including space. Without television, our lives would be very different. The space we give to TV in Western cultures and the time it consumes in our lifestyles means that the links between television and sports broadcasting are important to our assessments of the place of sport in the contemporary world.

Televised sport is central to the contemporary media environment. With the proliferation of television channels, and heightened competition for an increasingly fragmenting audience, quality programme content is at a premium (Boyle and Haynes 2000). As television is engaged in an increasingly competitive environment, sport has the potential to provide a ready-made supply of attractive programming. So powerful is TV in relation to sport that it is often this medium that helps us decide what is sport and what is not. For many years in Britain, darts was viewed as a pastime participated in almost solely by people in bars and public houses. However, in the 1980s it became a favourite sport watched by millions on television. In the early 1990s, in many parts of Britain it became easier for Gaelic football activists, promoting a minority sport to a multi-generational Irish community, to introduce the game to schoolchildren. One of the reasons was the broadcasting and popularising of Gaelic Games on Channel Four television. Likewise, TV owners and controllers decide what we should watch by way of selection, so even our perceptions of choice are affected in ways we rarely take time to consider. This of course has a controlling, or dominating, influence on the choices made by consumers and participants in sport.

This power to influence and dominate is a significant one. Some analysts believe that what is being constructed through sporting events is the equivalent of a TV movie, a soap opera that becomes a topic of interest and conversation to the exclusion and detriment of other significant life matters and, ultimately, human relationships. In addition, the way sport is presented on TV can often be different from that viewed by the immediate sporting audience. These presentations involve economic, social and political ideas that in turn invoke dominant notions concerning race, gender and class. What the TV viewer sees and what the immediate audience witnesses can often be two quite different spectacles.

Television has been a great boon to the spread and popularising of various sports. In turn, sport clearly provides a significant source of entertainment and pleasure as well as personal and community stimulation and gathering. The money released into sport on the part of TV companies has helped improve facilities and also helped sports teams and clubs retain some of their biggest star players. However, this also means that the nature and development of sport in the future is more open to question. Although sport itself doesn't depend on television, it has transformed our sense of time and space, as well as sport.

The commercialisation of a number of sports means that the influence that TV exerts on major events and personalities has the capacity to make sport exist only for the very best, for the most successful and as an avenue primarily for fame and fortune. It might even be judged to contribute to the creation of a greater level of elitism in sport and society. Many aspects of people's time increasingly revolve around sporting events on TV. The timing of these events and even where they take place is often determined by TV schedules. One of the most significant complaints on the part of many soccer fans in Britain in recent years has been the moving of soccer from traditional Saturday afternoons and Wednesday evenings to any time of the week, even Friday nights and Sunday mornings. Many sporting events have become privatised affairs as people watch the action in the space of their own homes, though in less affluent societies a crowd gathered round a TV set in a local bar may be more recognisable. Among other factors, the commercialisation of soccer was one of the main reasons why the World Cup of 1994 was played in the United States, a country with no significant soccer history.

Sport As Consumption

Consumerism is one of the dominant features of Western capitalist society: a **culture** centered on the promotion, sale and acquisition of consumer goods. The onset of 20th-century mass consumption has included the production of goods and services for national and international trade, mass marketing, advertising and the establishment of trademarks and brand names. All of these have relevance for the place and space of sport in today's world. Consumers are consciously and unconsciously fashioned by people who produce goods, entertainment, and services. Consumer products have material and cultural meanings that are translated or interpreted in terms of class, age, gender and a number of other stratifications and social messages. Fashion is probably one of the most outstanding of modern consumerist products that invokes such messages and meanings.

Elite sports have become an integral part of the commercialism involved in consumer societies. The media coverage given to these sports has become essential to their revenue generation and related popularity. Spectator tickets, team and player merchandise and corporate business involvement have all experienced an increasing **dependency** on TV and the rest of the media selling and updating the sporting 'story'. For example, the significance of the relationship between TV and soccer was evident by the 1998 World Cup final being broadcast to 190 countries and watched by nearly 1.3 billion viewers (Coakley 1998). The money generated by this is virtually incalculable. On its own, this constituted a TV product that was 'bought' by huge numbers of people.

Likewise, in the United States the National Football League brings in nearly 60 percent of its revenues from television.

The connection between advertising and the generation of income and wealth from mass sporting events means that the contemporary communications revolution has as much to do with modern perceptions of sport as the skills demonstrated by sportspersons or sports teams. This raises an issue of what some commentators consider to be a number of dangers involved in the monumental relationship between TV and sport. Over the past few decades, the amount of money being earned by a few elite athletes in American football, basketball, boxing, golf, and soccer has rapidly made them millionaires. This money has been gained primarily from TV, though some people might question the morality involved in such high earnings from what might be considered entertaining, uplifting and admirable instances of skill and fortitude. Nonetheless, besides these qualities on display, has sport lost its soul and sold out to individuals and companies whose motives are solely governed by profits?

Debating Point: Has the Media Corrupted Sport?

The kind of dependence that has evolved between sport and TV raises concerns for many people. Clearly, this relationship is more significant for commercial sports than for noncommercial ones. Social, political and economic interests have acquired an influence in sport via the media, particularly television. Coakley (1998) believes that 'the sports selected for national and global coverage have been and continue to be dependent on the media for their commercial success, and the salaries and endorsements of athletes in those sports also will depend on the media'.

The cry from some people is 'it's not sport anymore, it's business'. To some extent this ignores that business has long held some influence in sport, clearly demonstrated by the move from amateurism to professionalism on the part of many sports during the course of the 20th century. Nonetheless, the degree of influence that business has on sport has undoubtedly changed in recent decades. When top American football, basketball and world soccer stars can make more money in a week than the average teacher, medical doctor or family does in a year, and so many people seem prepared to pay more and more to watch their sporting heroes, these are signals that sport has changed dramatically. It seems true that elite sports have fallen prey to commercial interests. Two areas of sport help demonstrate this change.

The influence of business, promoters and agents in modern sport has become a significant factor, an unlikely development without the power of television. Although people making money from the commercialisation of sport have long been around (for example, boxing promoters were making huge sums of money in the United States in the 19th century), the modern omnipotent role of agents in the buying and selling of sports stars raises many issues. These include player loyalty, greed, representativeness and manipulation of the stars as well as their audiences. Television plays a role in the building of star reputations. Likewise, in terms of business, it has become a trend in North America and Britain for corporations to own, jointly possess or have an important say in the nature and direction of sports clubs. In North America, the Toronto Blue Jays have become important as a vehicle for the promotion of Labatt beer, while in Britain, NTL and Sky TV are buying into soccer clubs, partly to influence contractual arrangements between the TV companies and the soccer clubs' respective leagues. Such a level of advertising and the selling and branding of sports and sports stars depends largely on the power of television to relay appropriate images.

This takes us to another area of sport that has been affected by the influx of finance via television: the creation of sporting heroes. For several decades, sporting stars have been associated with a variety of products. However, the examples of sportspeople such as basketball player Michael Jordan in the United States and David Beckham in British soccer show that selling is often the name of the game. Little consideration is given to the morality behind many of these changes. Is it right that human beings should make so much from a relatively small contribution to human progress? Have sporting achievements gained a recognition totally undeserved and misplaced? Promoted by financial considerations, what damage can such devotion to sport do in terms of human relationships? How damaged do sportspeople become if they see themselves as something special or unique? What damage to their families? These and other questions are invariably related to the amount of money now flowing into elite sports across the globe. Whether such questions point to a further corruption of sport on the part of the growing influence of the media, particularly TV, is a matter of on-going debate. Undoubtedly, the place and space in our everyday lives occupied by modern sport and its elite participants have assumed new heights and purposes. This is primarily due to the effects of the media and commercialisation.

The Context of Culture in Time and Space

When discussing heroes and sports stars, Horne, Tomlinson and Whannel (1999) state that the process of image construction is considerably complex. As well as helping create culture, the media, especially television, taps into the 'moods, aspirations or fantasies of an audience'. The media and sporting stars exist within particular socio-historic junctures of time and space. It would be easy to condemn the lifestyle, including illicit drug-taking, of someone such as the 1980s and 1990s Argentinean soccer star Diego Maradona. However, it is much harder to understand the personal, economic and social contexts from which Maradona has emerged and lived. What is without doubt is that in one sense, the stage of world soccer, and its parallel fame, became a site where the complexities involved in Maradona's sporting lifestyle were expressed. The cultural place and space occupied by the superstar are important to our understanding of Maradona as a social product of his time.

Sport is a site for cultural expression because audiences can relate to the atmosphere that surrounds a particular sport. This is one of the reasons some sports are popular in the United States but not in Britain and vice versa, why some exist in Japan and not in Europe, and why others are peculiar to a whole variety of countries and societies. Some sports, such as soccer, also have worldwide appeal. Sport develops as an expression of aspects or attributes of communities. These links must exist if sport is to have any meaning for players and audiences. Sport and culture cannot be separated and sport is structured by culture.

A good example of the links between culture and sport can be found in the United States through the idea of the **American dream.** Achievement, success and material and social advancement have all been characterised as crucial aspects of the American dream. In turn, it also has strong links to Western lifestyles and capitalism. For the individual, it basically states that with hard work the rewards will be forthcoming in terms of material comforts, status and fulfilment. For some people who access this dream, power and influence can also be consequences. This dream has come to characterise many views of the United States and has proved a great attraction for millions of immigrants over the years. Regardless of how accurately it describes the country, it has come to be a significant aspect of the dominant cultural idioms of U.S. society.

The theme of the American dream is also expressed through sport. Nixon and Frey (1996) believe that the themes of this creed—character building, discipline, competitiveness, physical and mental fitness and **patriotism**—are imagined to be integral to U.S. sport. These function to legitimise sport as well as people's commitment to it regardless of whether they are true or not. Therefore, dominant American values are viewed as being so closely linked to sport that few questions are raised.

Clearly, a major theme of both the American dream and sport is the idea of winning. However, an overemphasis on winning can distort effort, undermine participation, create space for corruption and cheating, and construct a social avenue that, in effect, is only open to the very few. Therefore, there is a limited space to access this dream. Why can't everyone make similar headway and what functions does such a cultural environment serve? Although some people are winners some of the time, very few win anything of popular note. These questions gain further importance when we consider the commercialisation of modern sport and the omnipresence of media sport.

An obsession with winning in American sport may be reflective of the materialistic drive of the American dream. Eitzen and Sage (1993) conclude that there is an important sociological point to be made concerning this. They believe that 'competitiveness and striving to win are not natural or universal in human societies. They are behaviours shaped by cultural learning and influenced by social structures'. In other words, sport is a site for cultural expression.

Summary

Space and time are unceasing themes in our lives. We inhabit space and we constantly see ourselves in relation to the time of day, the year, and our age. These contribute to our sense of self as well as where and when we are located. Sport shows how space and time are socially determined constructs; spaces are set apart for sporting activities to take place, in terms of both time and the physical space required for its occurrence.

These concepts are not constructed in isolation, and groups, communities or societies generally agree to what they should mean. The place of sport in nations, states and societies has been important for thousands of years. From the times of ancient Greece and Rome until the present day, sport plays a role in how individuals, communities, societies and countries have constructed their identities as well as how they have projected these beyond their immediate times and spaces. The example of boxing in Cuba reflects the capacity of sport to help shape images of a society as well as become the vehicle for identity and ideology.

Sport has served to provide different things in diverse times. Although always retaining characteristics such as entertainment, competition and art forms, these have carried with them different meanings over the course of history. Where sport might once have served as a symbol of power in Roman times, it now serves more as a vehicle of power and influence, especially as conducted through the modern media.

The interaction with cultural forms like the media has become a meaningful symbol of sport in modern times. It both symbolises and reflects the place of sport in our globalised world, while it also shows how the power of commercialism and consumption have deeply influenced popular pastimes to the point that our conceptions of time and space have changed accordingly. It is often wondered if the impact of the commercialisation of sport has corrupted some of the games people have supported for generations. The influence of capital seems to have deeply affected many of the world's cultures and our answers may or may not be decided by moral or cultural perspectives. The idea of the American dream, and its hegemony within American cultural forms, economics and politics, suggests that even if you disagree with the direction elite sports are sometimes accused of taking, it should be recognised that modern sport has a significant relationship with television. Today, sport can be accessed 24 hours a day, while there is virtually nowhere in the world that a sports event cannot be transmitted from.

Our views of place and space can be partly shaped by the evolution of modern sport. This may be a First World perspective and is culturally specific, but sports events in the locality are no longer required for us to participate. This can be achieved because place and space are increasingly compressed by changing travel and media links and the capacity for commercial concerns to bridge previously immense hinterlands. Globalisation has changed many of the spaces we inhabit and where we inhabit them in relation to others. Place has also been affected, as migratory sportspeople travel for fame and fortune and in the process raise questions about community, loyalties and identities that have traditionally been involved in or invoked by sport.

Key Terms and Concepts

American dream	natural/inevitable
ancient sport	patriotism
capitalism	place
culture	power
dependency	soccer
football	socialism
function	space
lifestyles	televised sport
modern sport	time

Review Questions

1. Outline the different ways in which Rojek (1989) considers life has been divided into different spaces.
2. Explain Rojek's notion of natural and inevitable in relation to sport.
3. Critically discuss the notion of power.
4. Discuss the extent to which soccer in Britain might be viewed as contested terrain.
5. Identify and critically evaluate the ways in which advocates of different ideologies might have used sport as a contested arena.
6. To what extent did sport in Cuba during the 1970s challenge the ideology of capitalist sport forms?

7. In what ways does media coverage mediate sporting spaces?
8. Discuss how sport has contributed to the notion of the American dream.
9. Explain the difference between socialist forms of sport and capitalist forms of sport.
10. Outline three different notions of time, place and space that may be derived from within a sporting context.

Projects

1. Identify five different countries and regions and write a short report explaining the significance of indigenous games and sports.
2. Interview at least 10 home supporters attending the football code that is popular in your town, and ask them to comment on the importance of the stadium, or team, to the sense of local identity and place.
3. Identify and analyse the coverage of sport in any early-20th-century archive and compare this with any contemporary sporting archive. Use the set of documents as a basis for discussing how sport has changed over time.
4. Conduct a search of the Internet for information on the importance of sport to cities and critically evaluate the claims made.
5. Gather information from as many sources as you can on the emergence of athletics in Kenya. Use the notions of place, space and time to form a short report on the developments in Kenyan athletics.
6. Write to and/or interview selected personnel within your local authority / county board and ask them about the importance of sport to the board's sense of image and identity.

SPORT, CIVIC AND ETHNIC PASSIONS

© Bongarts Photography/SportsChrome USA

Objectives

After completing this chapter, you should be able to

- understand the relationship between ethnicity and sport,
- explain the ways in which sport reproduces civic identities,
- discuss the ways in which identity is reproduced through sport,
- consider how sport reflects and reproduces symbols and meanings,
- evaluate the notion of imagined communities in sport, and
- use case study material to explain civic and ethnic sporting identities.

The term **civic** refers to human relationships with a city, town or municipality. The geography of a city, the buildings that make up a town or the people who comprise a municipal community: all of these help constitute what we refer to as *civic*. Other aspects of civic can include the amount of finance generated, the degree and quality of public transport and the feelings that **citizens** have for the area described in physical terms. The latter point, in terms of **passion,** expression and **identity,** is important for this chapter.

Civic identity has developed in conjunction with urbanisation. Since the 19th century, when people's rural living patterns began to fragment, new loyalties developed that have entailed a sense of investment in their evolving urban experiences. Civic identity, then, can also be viewed as a construction that brings together otherwise disparate peoples by design or accident. This can be seen in the evolution of a common sense of belonging and pride in towns and **cities** during the 19th and 20th centuries, or it can be witnessed through the efforts of authorities to engender a positive image of their locality. Likewise, some political parties in recent years have been attracted to the idea of creating a civic nationalism based on adherence and loyalty to the state and the people who comprise it rather than one based on an **ethnic** typology.

Ethnicity might be considered in terms of any group that is defined or set off by **culture,** religion, national origin or some combination of these categories, which results in a common social psychological referent. Schermerhorn (1970) defines an ethnic group as

> a collectivity within a larger society having real or putative common ancestry: memories of a shared historical past, and a cultural focus on one or more symbolic elements defined as the epitome of their peoplehood. Examples of such symbolic elements are: kinship patterns, physical contiguity (as in localism or sectionalism),

religious affiliation, language or dialect forms, tribal affiliation, nationality, phenotypical features, or any combination of these.

Greely and McCready (1974) argue that an ethnic group is a 'collective based on presumed common origin' with a conspicuous trait that marks them out or even puts them at odds with the indigenous population in the country of settlement. Likewise, in nation-states that seem to be in frequent contestation over loyalties, ideologies and what constitutes a country's borders as well as the meanings attached to them, some ethnic groups will dispute the dominant ideas of culture and identity.

From this brief survey of what constitutes civic and ethnic identities, students of sport will immediately recognise that these social factors contain a rich reservoir for providing passion in sport. As a symbol of the **imagined community,** sport can be considered one of the most significant expressions and manifestations of identity today.

Case Study: The Gaelic Athletic Association and Ethnic Identity

For hundreds of years, Ireland has been a land where its people's identities have often been located in the context of its relationship with its colonising neighbour, Britain. Wars and conflict have characterised much of this relationship and, as a result, many of the identities constructed in Ireland have been expressed within a context of a perceived struggle to expel British influences and hegemony. These struggles have also witnessed manifestations through sport. Over the course of the 16th and 17th centuries, Catholic Ireland was colonised by thousands of Protestant Scots and English as part of a strategy to bring the island under the control of the British Crown. This control progressed through avenues of politics, economy and religious and cultural developments.

Cronin (1998) notes that sporting developments in Ireland have more to do with British influences than many Irish histories give credit. Nevertheless, it is also true that the evolution of the **Gaelic Athletic Association** (GAA) since 1884 can be viewed as a response to British hegemony and the exclusion of many working-class and poor Irish from sporting pursuits. This sporting opposition manifested itself against the perceived intrusion of British sports like cricket, rugby and soccer at the expense of native pastimes.

The GAA was set up to preserve and promote native Irish pursuits. Although the organisation wasn't explicitly political, national, nationalist and ethnic ideals have been vital to the GAA's development and significance. During the first decades of its existence, many members were political activists as well as cultural and sporting activists. The GAA also helped define Irish ethnic identity in the sense that it provided a focus and an expressive outlet for non-British markers and symbols. This was crucial at a time when those who recognised themselves as 'the Irish people' perceived that an ancient nation was losing its identity to the hegemonic influences of the British Empire.

Today in Ireland, the political, economic, social and cultural environments are very different from the first decades of the GAA. However, in the north of the country, perceived by Irish-nationalist minded people as remaining under the hegemony of British control, the ethnic dimension of the GAA remains important. In Northern Ireland, two ethnic groups are seen as competing over the essence of the state's identity and the resources and recognition that correspond. Sport is often viewed as an important marker of ethnicity. For example, some Protestants participate in rugby and cricket and, by so doing, seek to retain their historical sense of Britishness. In contrast, Catholics, many of whom are members of the GAA, see Gaelic sports such as hurling and Gaelic Football as intrinsic to their identity. Such practices are replicated throughout much of Northern Ireland.

Sporting Passions

It is difficult to know how many sports could survive the generations without their ability to stir an innumerable number of passions. Witness schoolchildren running round a track, jumping in a sack or carrying an egg on a spoon. Parents and guardians often look as though life itself depends on their representative winning or doing well. The tears of defeat and the joy of winning are evidence of people's passion for sport. The crowds that flock to or watch on television the Super Bowl, the World Cup and the Olympics show that at the highest levels, sport can excite some of the greatest passions characterising humanity. Countries, states and other entities, communities as well as nations, all have characteristics of thought and action—these display what is meaningful to them. Religion, politics, economy, class, cultural practices and beliefs all have a role to play in sport. The influence of the media, and the capacity for human beings to aspire to becoming or imagine themselves as sports personalities, reflect the efforts and dedication that people can contribute to sport. All of these involve passion.

Passion involves enthusiasm, hate, love, anger, intensity, affection, fanaticism, partiality, spirit, hunger and desire. All of these can be witnessed in sport. They can be controlled and positive or they can be misplaced and negative. Passion has helped sustain sport into the 21st century. It is the main factor in the creation of atmosphere at sporting occasions. It can be a source of friendship or a basis for the creation of enemies. It can be both of these simultaneously. It helps provide the very lifeblood of sporting dedication and involvement. Without passion, the cultural, political and social dimensions of sport would all disappear. Indeed, ethnic and civic identities would have no part to play in the sporting world. Without passion, sport would be limited to exercise and aesthetic delight and would have little meaning beyond these. In other words, there would be little if any need to write or read this kind of book if passion were absent from sport.

Sport and the Imagined Community

'The sky-blue shirt was proof of the existence of the nation: Uruguay was not a mistake. Football pulled this little country out of the shadows of universal anonymity.' (Giulianotti 2000)

Eric Hobsbawm, historian and social commentator, made a similar statement regarding his recognition of sport as a site for the construction, expression and imagining of national identity. Hobsbawm observed that the identity of a nation of millions 'seems more real as a team of eleven named people' (1990). Commentators such as Benedict Anderson (1991) have debated questions of imagined communities, stressing that human identity is a social construct. This means that little is inevitable concerning identity except that it is imagined in the context of time, circumstances and environment. These notions prove useful to our consideration of the civic and ethnic identities involved in sport.

Notions of imagined communities are myths, and the contradictions of the myths are lived through the description and language of the imagined community. Members of such communities, even the smallest ones, will never know most of the other citizens, meet them, or even hear of them, yet in the minds of each lives the image of their communion. They are connected though never acquainted. This is not to mean that they are false. But it does mean that communities are distinguished by the style in which they are imagined.

Communication and community construction develop through the depth and range of symbols or practices that unite, effectively forming alliances. Usually, this originates with religion, ethnicity and civic or national identity. Originating from common features, this in turn leads to a sense of place, of belonging, or of difference vis-à-vis a constructed 'other'. One of the ways that this can become pointed, can unite, can be articulated, even manifest, is through sport. Sport has become one of the greatest indicators and symbols of the imagined community.

Sport has the capacity to acquire extra-political, cultural, religious, national, ethnic and civic characteristics. At a basic level these can be expressed through emblems, flags, supporter songs, t-shirts and music. These are means of social communication. At a more sophisticated level, sport can become a significant symbol of how a people sees itself and how it wishes to be viewed by others. For many years, Soviet propagandists sought to use sport to project a united, healthy and positive image of the Soviet Union. However, as has been the case with many states, the fall of the Soviet Union revealed that this was a social construction imposed on the imaginations of many Western observers as well as on many of the state's own people. The truth was somewhat different.

The idea of the imagined community allows us to begin to understand the construction of human togetherness. Whether this is within nations, cities, towns, or within religions, languages or cultures is not important. The essential point is that all communities are socially constructed using these as the basis and legitimacy for their making. They do not remain secret and, indeed, seemingly require to be expressed in some form. Sport is one of the main forms of expression for the imagined communities.

Debating Point: What Are the Negative Features Linking Passion to Sport?

The elements that contribute to sport being viewed as a site for human passion are similar to how we might describe fans' attachment to sport. It could be argued that with such an investment, it might be possible that sport can actually be a diversion from other things that are more fundamental to human life. Sport can be seen to sap the thoughts and energies of people to an extent that it serves only those who retain economic, social, political and ideological **power** in society. Again an example might lie with the former Soviet Union where repression and suffering were masked, as citizens believed the contrivances of the state machine. This was an existence where the state's ideology was a substitute for original thinking, an opiate of the people, and where as one worker explained, 'all we could do was chat over a beer, and we were far more interested in sport' (BBC 1997). Connecting soccer to politics, Scottish National Party member Jim Sillars, implied a similar link when he criticised the Scottish international team's followers as being 'ninety-minute patriots'. Clearly, Sillars believed that such passion for Scotland on the soccer front should have been translated into something similar as far as politics was concerned.

Although competition through sport has a number of positive attributes, such as the gains made from participation and the actual effort involved, passion as a desire for better performances and winning can also lead to problems in sport. Vince Lombardi, the legendary Green Bay Packers football coach, has been famously quoted as saying that 'winning isn't everything, it's the only thing.' His counterpart in British soccer, former Liverpool manager Bill Shankly, also said that soccer was more important than questions of life and death. If these people are being truthful and not simply exhibiting hyperbole through positive enthusiasm and passion for their sport, where might such an attitude lead?

This win-at-all-costs attitude might be a contributing factor to the escalation of salaries in the most popular sports. Violence might occur on the field as well as off as players and spectators invest deeply in the passionate side of sport. Likewise, athletes' use of banned substances might arise out of the pressures instigated by financial and media backers as well as the desire to be the best. However, in light of sport's temporary and fluctuating nature, passion seems a necessary part of sports participation, spectating and involvement. Many lives might lack a degree of quality if sport was absent. After all, sport is culture and for many people it is culture that helps gives meaning to life.

Sport and Ethnic Identities

Individual and collective identities are not exclusively defined by the nation-state or even nationalism. Ethnicity and ethnic identities can be just as important, and sport provides an arena for their observation. The linking of ethnicity and sport also allows us to study societies that contain groups of people with varying origins and determine how these distinctions are managed. Parkes (1996) discusses Azoy's references to the significance of *buzkashi* tournaments, a highly dramatized equestrian game in Northern Afghanistan. There, the minority Uzbeks 'exploit these tournaments as one means to wrest a distinctive identity, to convey their own regional aspirations of rugged autonomy from the alien hegemony of Pashtun officials in the capital, Kabul'. Thus, ethnic identity is forged within this context.

Soccer has traditionally been the most popular spectator and competitive participant sport in Scotland, and has thus helped to forge ethnic identity. Towards the end of the 19th century, with approximately half a million first- and second-generation Irish in the west of the country, this community gave birth to Celtic Football Club in Glasgow. For many Irish Catholics and their offspring, Celtic has provided a successful symbol, emblem and focus for an immigrant group that has often perceived itself as the victim of **racism, prejudice** and sectarianism in the host society. Despite these perceptions and the ethno-religious competitiveness of the game, historically, the existence and presence of Celtic has also allowed this community to integrate as participants in an important arena of Scottish life (Bradley 1996).

McPherson, Curtis and Loy (1989) argue that in the United States, connections between sport and ethnicity often follow the patterns of immigration during the period in question. So, apart from Anglo-Saxons, most of the early American football players were German, Irish or Jewish, to be followed by eastern and southern Europeans who immigrated in the late 1800s and early 1900s. Like boxing, once dominated by the Irish, many of those who now dominate football are African Americans. As far as Hispanics in the United States are concerned, little attention has been given to their development within sport. Native Americans have experienced their own struggles, and the use of names like Washington Redskins and Atlanta Braves for sports teams has, for Coakley, served 'to perpetuate **stereotypes** that have contributed to the powerlessness, poverty, unemployment, alcoholism, and dependency of many native peoples in the United States' (1998).

Spain holds an example of one of Europe's ongoing ethnic problems. Amid the complexity of Spanish history and society exist a number of ethnic identities based significantly on a strong sense of anti-centralist regionalism. In the Catalan region of Spain, Barcelona Football Club has traditionally been a vehicle for the display of Catalan symbols that contest Spanishness in favour of a more meaningful regional ethnic identity. Likewise, in the northern part of the country, Athletic Bilbao has become the quintessential Basque team, virtually being viewed as the region's national representatives. Soccer in Spain is but one example of sport providing a site for the expression of ethnic identities.

Race and Sport

In recent decades, the term *ethnic* has become a more precise word to use regarding people of varying origins. However, the term *race* also has its uses when discussing prejudice and discrimination. Though most social scientists now accept that there is little meaning or sense to the word *race*, its application as *racism* affords us an understanding of the problems many people face in sport and elsewhere. Many of the wealthiest black people in Britain and the United States are sportspeople. Tiger Woods (golf), Lennox Lewis (boxing), Linford Christie (athletics) and Michael Jordan (basketball) are only a handful of sports stars in Britain and the United States who became multimillionaires during the 1990s because of, amongst other factors, their sporting prowess. Does this mean that sport, unlike other areas of British and American life, has become fully accessible to black ethnic minorities? Although black people are plentiful in athletics, American football, basketball, boxing and soccer, survey findings show that they are underrepresented in other sporting pursuits, such as golf, gymnastics, tennis, swimming and snooker. Being non-white in some societies, indeed the most powerful societies, seems to make a difference to black advancement in sport.

A persistent factor in U.S. and British history has been the stratification of whites and blacks and the lack of social, economic and political opportunities for many blacks. Among other things, this has resulted in a lack of corresponding power and influence. This we call racism: where perceived racial differences cause attitudinal prejudice and behavioural discrimination. Although racism goes beyond the black/white binary (it can be against Asians, Hispanics, Jews, the Irish, etc.), questions relating to black/white relations regularly offer the clearest distinctions and examples of the problems some sections of society have in dealing with human differences.

➤ The success of some blacks in a few sports obscures the prejudice and discrimination faced by those in black communities. Black advancement in sport has often been characterised by periods of entry to a sport and of becoming noticeable to the public. As a result, whites often cohere to tighten the exclusive mechanisms and barriers and black promotion is halted (as in the case of early-20th-century horse riding and jockeys in the United States). Historically, blacks have often made headway in sports that are considered deficient because of the lack of equipment required or their sometimes aggressive nature. These sports often dominate in poor black neighbourhoods because they are more accessible to poorer sections of the population, of which blacks form a disproportionate number.

However, not only is sport a site where **racial discrimination** and prejudice can become manifest and reproduced, it is a site where it can also be challenged. The notion of black dominance in some sports as a result of innate biological differences is frequently disputed and confronted by cultural and sociological explanations. Where a biological explanation might argue that blacks can't play certain football positions, don't become champion skiers and don't seem to be very good surfers, other factors are used to challenge these 'common sense' notions. In terms of the previous examples, white prejudice, very few blacks in Switzerland and differences in social class are some of the reasons given to extend observations beyond the highly simplistic, culturally-bound and often racially-inclined ones that proliferate. As the previous section argues, notions of ethnicity and other socially and culturally constructed identities are far better ideas to utilise if we want to understand distinctions and differences in sporting achievements. A simple black/white analysis is simply that.

Debating Point:
Is Sport Symptomatic of Society?

The preceding sections have shown how sport can be symptomatic of many of the activities of the wider society. However, there are important differences to be found within this symptomatic thesis. Two of the most significant points of this thesis are that sport reflects society and that sport reinforces patterns and processes in society. The first idea is explained by the notion that we can find in sport the same **values,** beliefs and norms that exist elsewhere in society. With regard to the second idea, sport offers us a vehicle to discover that the **inequalities** we can find in the larger society are frequently reproduced in sport. Both of these tend towards the impression of sport maintaining the status quo.

❧ Sport in the United States is symptomatic of many features of the wider society. Themes involved in the American dream, success, individualism and general achievement orientation, are all replicated in sport. Sport is viewed as a means to live out the American dream via ideas of competitiveness, discipline, character building and even patriotism. Therefore, sport in the United States has become an important part of American culture and is intrinsically linked with American values that in turn are closely related to the American dream. Likewise, the hooligan behaviour that has characterised parts of English soccer since the late 1960s is viewed by some commentators as symptomatic of a social and moral degeneracy within English society. After rioting by hundreds of English soccer hooligans at the European Soccer Championships in Holland and Belgium in the summer of 2000, one newspaper columnist wrote

> Other countries are not like this. As a matter of fact, young Britons of both sexes are the most drunken, drug-taking, promiscuous, criminal, pregnant, fattest and least-educated people in Europe. The French call us 'Les F_ _ _-Offs' because they cannot believe how much as a nation, we routinely use foul language. (*Daily Mail* 19 June 2000, 10)

Whether the author of the piece was using sound social scientific evidence to give credence to his claims that 'Forty Years of Liberalism have bred a generation of shameless, selfish louts who have earned England a deserved reputation of being the pariahs of Europe' is open to question. Nonetheless, much of the media reflected similar opinions from a variety of sources and the idea prevailed that what was going on amongst the English soccer supporters during this and other occasions was indeed symptomatic of events within society. Williams agrees that 'the "Rule Britannia" brigade also speak more deeply of our national culture and the place of football in it' (1986).

The difficulties that non-whites have experienced in the former South Africa with regard to acceptance into 'white only' sports was symptomatic of the legacy of the apartheid era. Similarly, the exclusion of non-whites from some sports and sports clubs in the United States, the difficulties experienced by Australian Aborigines in breaking down sporting barriers, the small numbers of women involved in numerous

sports, the politicising of the Olympic Games,
sections of society to sports for the masses as op
sports, and the infusion of economic considera
sport are all examples of how sport makes a st;
the wider society. It can be argued that the
between sport and culture, sport and nationalis
sport and the media, sport and religion, spc_
politics, sport and race, sport and community, etc., reflect the fact that
sport is partly symptomatic of society.

Sport and Identity

Identity is an important concept in the social sciences. A concept of
identity helps us understand the social world we construct. The term
identity should not be seen as a rigid one: one that absolutely categorises
people into one group or the other. It is used to identify common
attributes or beliefs that mark out a group of people as having something
quite significant in common with one another and, equally, as being
different from others. As well as the physical and psychological significance of sport, sport functions as a provider and resource for an array of
identities. Much of the previous discussion echoes the investment that
human beings put into sport. A significant amount of this investment is
linked with some of the chief identities found within the human experience; ethnic, civic, national, regional, religious and cultural.

Group- and self-esteem can be gained through sporting participation and achievement. At an individual level, the identity one can gain
through sport has the capacity to provide income, passage, fame and
even fortune. In whatever shape or form, sport that is organised with a
goal—winning, participation, good health, sociability, improvement,
representation or resistance—involves identity. Identity lies at the heart
of human fascination with sport, its modern development and its
continued appeal.

The creation or appropriation of certain sports as vehicles for
identity is symbolic of sport's importance for many people. Human
beings seem to feel a need to display togetherness as well as difference
and distinction. Nations, communities and groups all attempt to reinforce their identities. This is most obviously achieved through symbols,
beliefs, perceptions, systems and widely held associations. The representation of identity through sport often seems just as important. In
obvious but nonetheless sensational and dramatic fashion, the exhibiting of national symbols, music and talents at events like the Olympics
and the World Cup reflects how sport is a means to achieve this.

Identity in sport can symbolise common ground or become a mani-
festation of difference. Sport provides an environment for people to

together and constitute or further contribute to the idea of a
community, especially regional, national, ethnic and civic. The Olympic
Games during the 1980s, which included boycotts of countries within
the influence of the United States and the former USSR, show how
profound differences can be detrimental to an event and sport itself.
Sport demonstrates how people see themselves as well as how others
view them. It is a potential environment for the construction and display
of identity. Sport also constitutes a medium for group and self-analysis
as well as an opportunity to view whatever constitutes 'the other'. Sport
can represent or identify the existence, presence, origin, authority,
possession, loyalty, glory, beliefs, objectives and status of an imagined
community.

Summary

The symbols involved in sport—national flags, ethnic and regional
emblems, songs and anthems chanted, as well as the finance invested in
it —are all evidence of the concretisation of identity within the sporting
arena. As one of the biggest industries in the world today, sport enhances
its position as a cultural indicator. Sport both attracts and creates an
array of positive and negative passions and identities. Togetherness
might be viewed in the concert of nations and peoples involved in major
international tournaments and the ability of sport to create social
occasions. The negative can be seen in English soccer hooligans' intolerance of other people's cultures or the use of drugs in sport as a means of
striving to be the best. Discussions of imagined communities should not
imply that the identities that arise from these are false. These communities, national, ethnic, regional and civic, are all real for those who
constitute a part of them. Sport provides a very real setting for the
expression of these identities. Herein lies one of the main reasons for the
importance of sport in today's global existence.

Some underlying themes of this work reflect on the importance of
sport to society and sport's connections with a variety of social features,
as well as an understanding of sport itself. The capacity of a person, a
community, a nation or a group of any of these to become dejected or
elated amidst sporting failure or success is symbolic of how sport
becomes a vehicle for ostensibly non-sporting passions. Since such
things become more visible and more concrete in the sporting arena, it
might be argued that sport allows us to analyse society more precisely.
The discussion of the place of race in sport offers us a chance for social
exploration. It also demonstrates that sport can reflect many aspects of
society. Two of the many identities and passions that have developed in
sport are civic and ethnic. Pride and a sense of place based on town or

city, or on one's region, country of origin, family or community history, provide many reasons for participation in sport. In turn, these also sustain the emotional involvement and passion that has become synonymous with sport.

Key Terms and Concepts

cities	inequalities
citizens	passion
civic	power
community	prejudice
culture	racial discrimination
ethnicity	racism
Gaelic Athletic Association	stereotypes
identity	values
imagined community	

Review Questions

1. What does the term *imagined community* mean?
2. Evaluate four different ways in which sport contributes to a sense of ethnic identity.
3. Discuss the notion that sport helps to produce a sense of civic engagement and citizenship.
4. Describe the specific context of one ethnic sport of your choice. What main features stand out?
5. Critically analyse the form of ethnic identity associated with the Gaelic Athletic Association.
6. Explain the significance of the *buzkashi* tournaments in Northern Afghanistan.
7. What values are associated with sport and the American dream?
8. Argue for and against the notion that sport is an integral part of society.
9. Coakley has argued that names such as the Washington Redskins help to reproduce negative stereotypes associated with poverty and unemployment. Argue for and against this notion.
10. What is the relationship between civic identity, sport and urbanism?

Projects

1. Within a sport of your choice, hold a series of four focus group interviews with sports fans and spectators. How do they explain the content and meaning of the passion aroused by sport?

2. Identify one ethnic sports club/organisation of your choice. Examine the rules/constitution or club charter and note the specific references to ethnicity. What does this tell you about the group's sense of identity and the role that sport plays in this regard?

3. Interview 10 sports leaders within your local community and ask them how sport helps to produce a sense of civic engagement or citizenship. Critically evaluate such views.

4. Conduct an Internet search for information about a sports club that claims to have a specific ethnic identity—such as Irish, Scottish, Hispanic or Italian. Critically evaluate the evidence gained with reference to published research findings.

5. Use ethnographic methods of enquiry to collect data in relation to flags, songs and chants at a local sports event. What does the evidence tell you about ethnic or other identity politics?

6. Identify five policy documents on sport in the lives of ethnic minority communities. Develop 10 policy statements aimed at combating racism in sport.

CHAPTER
9

SPORT IN THE
MAKING OF NATIONS

Objectives

After completing this chapter, you should be able to

- understand the relationship between sport and nationalism;
- develop a critique of the contemporary thinking about sport and nationalism;
- explain at least four different approaches to nationalism;
- consider the extent to which global sporting spectacles promote nationalism and national identity;
- describe some of the key mechanisms through which sport promotes nationalism and national identity; and
- understand the difference between peripheral and centre nationalisms and the importance of sport within these different contexts.

With very few exceptions, all states are faced with the problem of managing a sense of **national identity.** At the heart of this pressure is the desire for the state and its peoples to establish a sense of national unity within an ever-changing world. The adoption of national flags, anthems, currencies, foods and policies, representation at world summits, and the extent to which sporting organisations continue to seek national affiliation to international sporting organisations can all be used to substantiate the thesis that states use various mechanisms to consolidate a sense of **territoriality.** These practices also foster a sense of belonging amongst a state's peoples, a sense of relative autonomy from globalisation or a sense of values or citizenship. In many cases these mechanisms might be mythical, but whether they are real or not they, in part, owe an allegiance to national cultures or identities. It is in this latter sense that one might talk of the American dream or Scottish socialism or the Irish Nationalist cause during the early part of the 20th century.

Many political leaders, often from nationalist parties, have commented on the inherent integrationist properties associated with national sporting performances. Studies of sport and domestic government policies, sport and international relations and sport and political ideologies are now quite common and have contributed to our understanding of the relationship between sport and government. The idea that sport and sporting achievements contribute to a nation's greatness and transcend internal strife and social deference is but one argument that has been dressed up in a number of guises. In the 1960s, the then Labour Prime Minister, Harold Wilson, made great political mileage out of England's victory in the 1966 World Cup. Throughout the 1970s,

Julius Nyerere of Tanzania often remarked that in developing nations, sport helped bridge the gap between national and global recognition. Immanuel Wallerstein suggested that African citizens could feel affection for the victorious athlete and the nation, although this affection might not have existed in the first instance given the social and ethnic divisions within African nation-states (Jarvie 1993). The process necessary to develop this affection depended on athletes accepting the politics of the nation and working with the party structures. During the 1980s, a key element of African National Congress (ANC) policy in South Africa was 'One Can Not Play Normal Sport in an Abnormal Society'. By the 1990s, President Mandela argued that sport had become part of the new glue that held the nation together. This was exemplified by South Africa's victory in the 1995 Rugby World Cup, a victory viewed as being symbolic of a new post-apartheid era.

General discussions of **nationalism** are often problematic because of the slipperiness of the term. At different times and places, different contrasts or sets of social relations seem more relevant to the situation at hand. In academic writing, the implications of specific comparisons, contrasts and distinctions used to define nationalism are, like different viewpoints on its origins, rarely value-free. Nationalism can at times be seen to be positive in relation to narrow local attachments or feudal loyalties while at the same time being viewed as a negative social force in relation to ideologies of civic community. It can seem positive in the context of combating forms of imperialism and yet negative in relation to other supranational phenomena such as humanity or international class solidarity. The issue of the values associated with nationalism depends on what one is comparing it against and, as such, the specifics of any situation will prove to have a greater explanatory potential than broad generalisations.

Case Study: Catalans and Basques Attempt to Go It Alone in World Sport

For many years, the Basque and Catalan regions of Spain have campaigned for their own national soccer sides as a stepping stone to political independence from Spain. The precedent lay in the fact that Great Britain was/is allowed to enter four teams, England, Scotland, Wales and Northern Ireland, in world soccer tournaments. By tradition, support for Spanish selection in the regional soccer teams is not favoured, and so when Catalonia began playing an annual soccer match against international opposition in 1997, the desire for a separate soccer team became much more tangible. At the end of 1999, the Basque region followed the Catalan example. This case study is illustrative of the relationship between soccer and regional and national identity in late-20th-century Spain.

In August 1999 it was announced that Spain was facing fragmentation into a number of sporting regions under a proposal brought forward by the government of Catalonia to introduce national sports teams (*Scotsman* 8 August 1999, 5). Josep Guardiola, then captain of the Barcelona football team and a Spanish international midfielder, stated that he would be amongst those who would be willing to swap the shirt of Spain for the shirt of Catalonia. Fuelled by a general resurgence in regional pride, the Catalans hired Jean-Louis Dupont, the lawyer who fought and won the case of footballer Jean-Marc Bosman in the European courts, to persuade the world sporting authorities to recognise their sporting independence. The bill passed by the Catalan regional parliament allowed Catalonia to compete in the international arena as a separate region.

Neither the Catalans nor the Basques have acted on the Dupont report as yet, but victory over one of the qualifying teams for the Euro 2000 football championships, and one of Africa's leading football nations, has further fuelled the desire of the region to be recognised as a nation in football terms. Two matches contested in Spain during December 1999 and January 2000 may yet have far-reaching implications for European international football. National sides from Catalonia and the Basque region of Spain took on and beat Yugoslavia and Nigeria respectively (*Sunday Herald* 9 January 2000, 7). Catalonia's match with Yugoslavia two days before Christmas attracted more than 43 000 spectators to Barcelona's Olympic Stadium. A few days later, a Basque side made up almost entirely of players from Athletic Bilbao and Real Sociedad defeated Nigeria 5–1. Since the unification of the Spanish principality into a single nation more than 500 years ago, these two regions have retained a strong sense of collective identity. Both areas fiercely preserve their language and customs and both see football as an ideal vehicle through which to press their nationalist sentiments.

The Conservative Spanish government of Prime Minister Jose Maria Aznar accused the Catalans of passing legislation that would create national sporting teams for Catalonia but ruin Spanish chances of winning any international sporting titles. The Spanish sports minister added that it was unthinkable that a Spanish team would be forced to compete against a Catalan or Basque team in international competition. The Catalan Nationalist Party countered that there was no reason why such a breakup of Spanish sport should not occur given that international sporting federations, such as FIFA, allow Great Britain to enter separate English, Irish, Scottish and Welsh teams in soccer's World Cup. Juan Antonio Samaranch, then President of the International Olympic Committee, himself a Catalan, declared his opposition to the creation of a separate Catalan Olympic team.

Nationalism, Sport and the Making of Nations

In many respects the original nation-state has been undermined by a number of fundamental shifts since at least the 1950s. The expansion of transnational organisations and a more complex international division of labour have certainly circumscribed the capacity of nation-states to totally control their own economies. The increasing globalisation of culture, including sport, has undoubtedly meant that the relationship between culture and the nation-state has become much more complex. Multiculturalism and hybridity are embedded within nearly every state, and any claim that the state has to a single culture or a single identity or a single form of nationalism becomes almost impossible to sustain.

Yet the example cited above classically illustrates how peripheral forms of nationalism (Catalonia) interact with more powerful **centre nationalism** (Spain). Centre nationalisms, be they Spanish, French, Canadian, American or British, have unwittingly helped to reinforce **peripheral nationalisms**—Catalonian, Basque, Scottish, Quebecois, Breton—in at least two senses. In the first sense, changing world conditions apply to everyone and one of the consequences of contemporary global changes is that simply reasserting centre nationalism does not have the same force that it once had. In the second sense, centre nationalisms have often helped to reinforce peripheral nationalisms simply by defining what peripheral nationalism is not. So, for example, the choice of the national anthem that is sung before many major sporting internationals in Great Britain is in many respects informative about the state of respective senses of Englishness, Scottishness, Irishness and Welshness. What is clear is that the national anthem of Great Britain, "God Save the Queen", is owned by none of the respective countries that play in these matches. These are all historically shifting relations and the context of any sporting international has to be closely observed in comparison to previous historical periods.

Nationalism itself is often viewed as a doctrine of political legitimacy that is subjected to diverse uses and interpretations by different groups, localities and peoples often seeking radically different objectives. It is sometimes associated with xenophobia and **racism** and on other occasions it refers to movements that defend the rights of oppressed peoples. There is no common agreement about how to define nationalism; however, it remains one of the most potent ideologies of the 21st century. As this chapter illustrates, sport is at times associated with some or all of the usual suspects or variables of nationhood, such as distinct ethnic groups, the symbolism of a land mass with a common culture, a shared self-image, or a people or peoples with a common history. Sport in both substantive and theoretical terms has been associated with the core building blocks of nationalist doctrines such as nationalism, **nationhood, national consciousness,** racism and national identity. Yet, the paradox of nationalism, in both the 20th and 21st centuries, is similar to that created by other forms of identity politics. By letting us know who we are, its construction from both the past and the present complicates our capacity to live in the present. In his discussion of the role of nationalism in understanding contemporary society, Low (2000) offers the following five points by way of summary:

1. Nationalism legitimates, or justifies, the existence and activities of modern territorial states on the basis of a range of characteristics that are conventionally shared by, and specific to, their inhabitants.

2. Theorists of nationalism have focused both on the relationships of nationalism to modern states and on the historical transformations that have made national identity possible.

3. Grand historical theories of the origins of nationalism have been less important in recent years than more partial accounts of the relationships of nationalism with other identities and ideologies in particular situations.

4. Nationalism is strongly associated with the legitimation of violence. This makes continued critical analysis imperative, especially in a context where nationalism is often misleadingly suggested to be obsolete.

5. The relationship between nationalism and democracy is ambiguous. Nationalism's persistence is connected with the difficulties democracy encounters when it has to cope with unavoidable questions about history and the future.

Not all of the above issues have been represented in the substantive or theoretical analysis of sport, but there is a vast literature on the role that sport has played in nation building (Hargreaves 2000; Houlihan 1997; Jarvie and Walker 1994; Jarvie 1999; Nauright 1997). There is no rule of social development that says that every nation must also be a nation-state or that nationhood perishes without statehood. Generally speaking, the literature on the place of sport in the making of nations has tended to be synonymous with modern nation-states. In other words, the nation-state has fused the political and the cultural together. The classical aspiration of nationalism has been that stateless nations would ultimately achieve the goal of political independence. This has been the claim of numerous nationalist movements such as the African National Congress party during the apartheid era or the Irish Nationalist Movement during the 1920s.

The need for reconciliation and nation building is common in countries emerging from a period of conflict. This is particularly the case in those nations, such as South Africa, that have experienced apartheid and where colonial rule and Western political-styled ideologies have often tempered national boundaries of religion, kinship and class. In newly transformed nations, sport often becomes a vehicle for **integration** and a catalyst for nation building. Those who have commented on the relationship between sport, nationalism and culture have tended to rely on a number of themes invariably altered to suit particular contexts or events. At a general level, a number of arguments might be mentioned:

- Sport is inherently conservative and helps to consolidate official or centre nationalism, **patriotism** and racism.
- Sport has some inherent property that makes it a possible instrument of **national unity and integration.**
- Sport provides a safety valve or outlet of emotional energy for frustrated peoples or nations.
- Sport has contributed to unique political struggles, some of which have been closely connected to nationalist politics and popular nationalist struggles.
- Sport is often involved in the process of nationalism as a natural reaction to dependency and uneven development.
- Sport contributes to a quest for identity, whether it be through **nostalgia, mythology, invented traditions,** flags, anthems and ceremonies or on a local or national scale.
- Sport helps to reinforce national consciousness and cultural nationalism.

Cronin (1999) offers a more extensive typology of the actual links between sport and nationalism. The nationalism that is connected to sport may be constructed by many different forces, be manifested within and between different types of nationalism, be real and imagined, be a creative or reflective force, be both positive and negative, transient and temporary, multifaceted and multilayered and be evolutionary in its format. Drawing on a number of specific examples, Cronin goes on to ask a number of pertinent questions concerning the ways in which sport is inextricably linked to the forces of nationalism: Is sport being appropriated by countries in the search for a new national identity? How did the relationship between sport and nationalism develop? Why is this relationship so important in contemporary society and what should we do with it or about it? Cronin is clear that, although it is increasingly difficult to sustain the argument that a single sport represents any nation, certain nation-specific games such as Gaelic games, American football, Aussie-rules football, or pelota have all thrived and continue to play a central part within various national cultures. To use one Swedish example quoted in Cronin (1999), it is suggested that

Nothing awakens Swedish national feeling so easily and strongly (at least among men) as sporting success. Glorious history, royalty, a splendid army, democracy and the welfare system, ancient ideals and traditions, Volvo and other great companies—none of these things can measure up to sport in providing bonds of national solidarity or in creating collective consciousness of one's country.

Nations, Nationalism and Identities

There are many different concepts of nations, nationalism and identities, and even the cursory discussion above illustrates that different types of national communities and identities exist in different areas of the world. To reduce the terms to some form of rational universalism simplifies the concepts and the reality of sport in society. Writers such as Seymour (2000) have suggested that nationalism is too complex for the conceptual tools we have to explain it. Nonetheless, we will briefly explain several recurring ideas about nations, only some of which have permeated the sports literature.

It may be that changing world conditions are about to shake any historical skeletons and unhappy national complexes that have often furnished the wardrobe of national identity. Whatever the nation in question, the quest for identity inevitably involves questions of representation, nostalgia, mythology and tradition. Many nations themselves are fabrications or constructions, many states are not nations and indeed many nations are not states. Modern states have often required an explicit sense of loyalty and identification that has at times been mobilised with certain symbols, icons, hymns and prayers. Hobsbawm (1990) suggests that mass and middle-class sport from 1870 to 1914 combined the invention of political and social traditions in the United Kingdom by providing a medium for national identification and factitious notions of community. Sport, along with other mass-producing traditions, became a social force of cohesion for a newly emerging middle class at that time.

Much research into sport and national identity has invoked the notion of an imagined community or invented sporting traditions that symbolise the nation. One of the enduring ideals of major national sporting occasions is the notion that an imagined community of people across the country come together in support of the nation. Yet this ideal fails to acknowledge that, for citizens to identify with the nation, a uniform national consciousness needs to exist. As the work of Bradley (2000) suggests, sports fans have many different political voting patterns and to suggest that these are forgotten at the match is simply wild nostalgia. Sporting internationals might be one of many ways in which the state may attempt to manage identity, but in reality these identities are never homogenous and are quite often forgotten shortly after the sporting event is finished.

One of the central ethical claims of nationalism, the right of nations to self-determination, is often universally interpreted to mean the right to independence. Yet there are numerous situations in which this is not the case. Take, for example, Great Britain, in which the various nations that constitute the United Kingdom (England, Northern Ireland, Scotland and Wales) are bound by a federal arrangement to an ancien regime, namely, the British state. England as of yet has no parliament, while Wales and Scotland have devolved powers. All four social formations compete separately in global football and rugby, and yet as the United Kingdom at the Olympic Games. In relation to the ethical claim of nationalism and the right to self-determination, the normative concept of nationalism is rarely considered. It is often assumed that proponents of nationalism want their own state, but what kind of state this will be is often forgotten. It is as if the notion of self-determination is the ethical end in itself. States perform different functions and are often judged by how they perform them, but rarely are states questioned as to what they represent. Perhaps in a more supranational world the normative claims of any future nationalism might be evaluated before the right to self-determination is granted.

A potential weakness in thinking of the nation as a place is that it becomes fixed in content, time and space. This view fails to acknowledge the nation or the territory as a process that is neither fixed nor immutable. Territorial expansion or contraction is but one of many ways in which the nation as a place changes over time, but the idea of what the nation is or which sports represent the nation also changes in relation to the social, cultural and political contexts. The point that we wish to establish here is that while different sporting occasions and different sporting heroes and heroines may all help to keep alive ideas of what a certain nation is, many of these experiences have at their core different notions of what the nation is, was or should be. The content, timing and symbolism of sport and nationalism in Ireland today is entirely different from what it was in the 1920s because Ireland itself as a process is different today from what it was in the 1920s. Thus geographic place and time are just part of the transcendent or changing idea of the nation as it moves through history.

Similarly, the content, timing and symbolism of sport, nationalisms and identities in present-day South Africa and during apartheid are completely different, but both sets of experiences are part of the process of South African sport and South Africa. In this sense it might be suggested that there is no one essential nation, only a number of different South Africas that embrace different territorial rings. South African athletes such as Nelson Mandela, Zola Budd, Hassan Howa, Sam Ramsamy, Jasmat Dhiraj, Basil d'Olivera, Justin Fortune and Hanse Cronje all expressed an idea of belonging to a South African nation or solid community moving up or down history. They were all embroiled at different times in the process of forging out what it meant to be a South African. Again, the specific understanding of the relationship between sport and nationalism needs to be analysed in terms of time and place.

Debating Point: Should FIFA Bestow Nationhood Upon Emerging Nations?

The acceptance of membership into the Fédération Internationale de Football Association (FIFA) is often viewed by many emerging nations as recognition of sovereignty and a legitimation of nationhood. In July 1998, Palestine became a full member of FIFA, the governing body of world football. During March 2000, Palestine competed for the first time against other Asian nations in the Asian Cup. The importance of the competition was not lost on the players. 'This means the presence of the Palestinian people: that we have our own national team despite all the challenges we are facing. The team is our national ambassador to the rest of the world' (*Guardian* 29 March 2000, 4).

For the Palestinian national football squad, the Asian Cup was more than a contest—it was the first foray by *intifada* exiles into international sport. The national football team also represented the coming together of a number of identities and factions that constituted the Palestinian *diaspora*. Some were from the former refugee camps that existed in Gaza after 1948. Some of the players witnessed relatives being jailed during the intifada, the uprising against the Israeli occupation that began in 1987 and led to the beginnings of a peace process in 1993. Indeed, for Palestinians it might be argued that football has a much greater political significance than it has in other FIFA member countries. During the Palestine/Israel conflicts, football clubs in Palestine were often the organisational centres for youths that harassed Israeli border patrols. The leading national party of Yasser Arafat, the Palestinian leader, supported the top Gaza football team. If at the time Palestinians did not have a state, they now have a football team that is recognised at world level as a national team. During the late 1990s, the Palestinian minister of sport suggested that football could provide a focus for Palestinian youth, and yet this football recognition of Palestinian statehood, however symbolic, remains highly controversial with hard-core Israeli nationalists and Hamas, the party of Islamic fundamentalism.

Nationalism: What Is It?

In recent years, much of the difficulty with the study of nations and nationalism has been finding agreed definitions of the concepts. The issue of **ethnic** and **civic nationalism** has permeated many discussions of sport (Bairner 1999). Much of the debate has centred on distinctions between civic or territorial forms of nationalism and ethnic or cultural forms of nationalism. The former is often closely associated with citizenship and territory while the latter is often associated with ties of blood. As McCrone (1998) alludes to in his discussion of the two forms of nationalism, citizenship was based on a community of descent or along bloodlines—while one American sociologist has argued that in France citizenship came to be defined in terms of the territorial community, in contrast to Germany, where the unitary state did not emerge until 1870.

A significant problem with notions of ethnic and civic nationalism is that they are used to describe certain types of abstract social relationships. However, the level of abstraction or meaning is not as crucial as their underlying relationship to reality. Ethnic forms of nationalism cannot be freely chosen. They imply, for example, that you are a Hutu, a Croat, a Catalan, a Basque, a Scot, a Welsh or English person, or you are not. You cannot opt out because within this framework ethnicity is conveyed at birth. Yet within the ever-changing 21st century, multiplicities of identity are the norm. When the English Conservative politician, Norman Tebbit, sought to apply his racist cricket test—if you live in England, you should support the national English cricket team, even if it is playing against your country of origin—he failed to acknowledge this very point. Furthermore, this distinction between absolutist civic and ethnic nationalism can be criticised on a number of grounds, not the least of which is the forms of racism embedded within either definition of nationalism. In both cases it might be suggested that it is impossible to keep blood and soil apart, and despite modern attempts at ethnic cleansing between territories such as Croatia and Serbia, or ethnic groups such as Hutus and Tamils in Tanzania and Ethiopia, how in practice can such forms of nationalism be absolute in the early 21st century? People have many complex allegiances and it might be suggested that both ethnic nationalist absolutism and civic state absolutism are untenable in a postnationalist world. Both diminish active personal choice and hence are fundamentally illiberal and, in the modern world, unworkable.

The debate about civic and ethnic forms of nationalism is often embedded within a broader debate about the origins of nations. This is a view that is often described as primordial or modernist. One of the most useful recent typologies of nationalism can be found in the work of Cronin (1999), who has outlined four approaches to the historical origins of nationalism. Cronin used these as a basis for developing the following typology, conscious of the fact that all typologies are ideal and lack a degree of reality congruence about them.

Essentially, primordialists champion the view that nationalism is a product of ethnicity that can be rooted in history and the land. Modernists, on the other hand, argue that nationalism is a product of the modern age. Cronin (1999) states that while modernists 'accept that nationalists may seek to justify themselves by using historical artefacts, traditions and other identity forming tools … nationalism itself is a direct product of the transformations that took place alongside the destruction of feudal society'. Thus the formation of nationalism is specifically tied to a particular historical epoch. The approach of statists is that nationalism itself, more than anything else, is associated with the idea of the state, and the state uses sport to manage forms of identity and allegiance. Finally, Cronin asserts there are political mythologists who locate the ideology of nationalism within the imagined or mythical symbols of national representation. The objective of this form of nationalism is to suggest that nations share a sense of community. Cronin's typology highlights a much broader analysis of sport in the making of nations than simply that of civic or ethnic nationalism or the role of sport in the imagining of the nation.

Debating Point: Do Global Sporting Events Promote Nationalism?

Supporters of the notion that global sporting events promote national-ism tend not to question the relationship between global sporting culture and patriotism. National affiliations are important to the popu-lar and economic success of global sporting events. The appeal of the soccer World Cup, the World Athletics Championships and the Olympic Games is driven by media moguls, corporate sponsors and an international sports public. All of these groups are enthralled by a nation versus nation confrontation. If global sports events were to take away the nation versus nation format, viewing figures and sponsorship would be affected. The sponsors and the public would be much less interested and the resources needed to stage large international sporting events would be reduced.

Alternatively, those who argue that globalisation has transcended mid-20th-century forms of nationalism might argue that sport is a unique activity that evokes passions capable of transcending the cul-tural politics of nations. Arguably, sport is the world's only truly global language. The staging of global sporting events is evidence of a more embracing world in search of a common identity, common comfort, common family, which could ultimately lead to global sporting events that resist national affiliation, break down nationalist tensions between nations and provide a language that mediates political conflict. The sporting events themselves would then take precedence over the ath-letic accomplishments of individuals, teams and nations. Ultimately, the elimination of national flags, national anthems and parading of national teams would reduce political tensions between nations. The changing composition of national sporting teams is more cosmopolitan than in previous decades, and supporters are more likely to associate themselves with a range of identities than any one nation so defined in simple territorial terms.

The Future of Nationalism Through Sport

Nationalism has often been disconnected too quickly from other forms of identity politics. Furthermore, it has often been suggested that nationalism is becoming obsolete as a result of globalisation. This seems doubtful, and on those occasions when the perceived global imagined community comes into view—the millennium, concerts to raise money for world hunger or AIDS victims, the Olympic Games, the World Cup, the World Athletics Championships, the Gulf War or Princess Diana's funeral—they are but occasional and rarely total global events. This is entirely different from saying that there has been an increased rate or occurrence of globalisation or global sport over the past 20 years.

In their analysis of the changing relationships between globalisation, governance and the nation-state, Hirst and Thompson (1999) argue that the role of the nation-state remains pivotal in terms of international governance. While nation-states may no longer be viewed as absolute governing powers able to impose outcomes on all dimensions of policy, they nonetheless remain a locus of power, perhaps at the local level, that remains influential because of their relationship to both territory and populations. Populations remain territorial and subject to the citizenship of a nation-state, not in the sense that they are all-powerful, but because they still have a central role to police the borders of a territory. To the extent that they are legitimately democratic, they remain representative of the citizens within the border territories.

Therefore, in at least four immediate ways, the relationship between sport and nationalism is likely to be maintained in the present. First, in a sovereign sense the nature of the nation-state may change but the existence of sports teams representing territorially defined nations or regions aspiring to be nations is likely to continue. Second, nationalist-oriented governments or organisations such as the African Nationalist Congress or the Palestinian liberation movement or forms of national sovereignty such as Great Britain (however fragile the Union may be) are likely to promote distinctive sporting policies. Third, distinctive nationalist sporting organisations such as the Gaelic Athletic Association will continue to provide a national focus for traditional national sports. Finally, whether sporting or otherwise, an international society as an association of states cannot totally rely on supranational bodies to make and enforce laws, since these require states to accept legal and constitutional limitations both within and between nation states. In this sense, the nation-state or new forms of sovereignty involving national factions remain central to any proposed international economy, society or culture. Sport will continue to contribute to all of these.

Summary

The word *nation* might be used to describe a human community that has acquired national consciousness, since it is clear that national consciousness is different from other forms of collective consciousness. But to what extent has sport contributed to the internalising of this ideology? There is no agreed definition of any of the aforementioned concepts. The most common assertions have evoked the notions of civic and ethnic nationalism or the extent to which globalisation has evoked diminishing and contrasting forms of sporting patriotism or nationalism. Only some of these have been associated with political nationalism. A number of interconnected concluding points might be made.

First, let us consider the issue of globalisation and its relationship to sport and the nation-state (cf. chapter 1). It has been suggested that if one accepts the notion that nation-states are no longer viewed as absolute governing powers but are simply one class of powers, then sport is reflected in the changing system of world power that operates from global to local levels. Nonetheless, nation-states as organising social formations remain a centrality because of their relationship to territory and populations. Sport has not been at the forefront of global change but neither has it been dormant or unaffected by changing boundaries and territories. Second, at the level of epistemology it has been suggested that all the analytic concepts that describe certain types of social relationships—nationalism, nation-state, nationhood, national identities, and national consciousness—are abstractions. What is crucial is their underlying relationship to the reality from which they are abstracted. Finally, no nation-state or national sports federation has the power to protect its citizens against global change. Yet, the advance of globalisation does not make the state redundant, and many would argue that it makes the state more necessary as a guarantor of civil and human rights, since to date no stronger medium has been found. Sport, too, can make a small contribution to the struggle for civil rights and social capital.

Key Terms and Concepts

centre nationalism

civic nationalism

cultural nationalism

ethnic nationalism

human rights

invented traditions

mythology	nostalgia
national consciousness	patriotism
national identity	peripheral nationalism
nationalism	political nationalism
national unity and integration	racism
nationhood	territoriality

Review Questions

1. Describe the ways in which sport reproduces nationalism and national identity.
2. Provide two examples of the specific ways in which sport promotes nationalism.
3. Discuss the differences between civic and ethnic nationalism.
4. Why should sport be important to new or emerging nations?
5. Evaluate the arguments for and against national flags and anthems being used at global sporting events.
6. Describe four different approaches to nationalism.
7. Explain the differences between cultural and political nationalism using sporting examples to illustrate your answer.
8. In the 21st century, to what extent can we sustain the argument that national sports exist today?
9. Evaluate the argument that sport is conservative and therefore closely associated with ethnic and racist behaviour.
10. Evaluate the argument that sports fans at national sporting events are simply being patriotic as opposed to nationalist.

Projects

1. Videotape the opening ceremony of a major sporting occasion. Write a short report on the different ways in which the opening ceremony reproduced representations of national identity.
2. Examine the nations represented at the last four Olympic Games, or any World Cup event, as a basis for substantiating how the sporting world has changed over the past 16 years.
3. Carry out an Internet search for information relating to national sporting organisations in any country of your choice. Explain the role of these organisations, and critically evaluate whether they are nationalist in the political or cultural sense of the term.
4. Examine the nationalist policies of four national parties of your choice that have used sport as a vehicle for promoting nationalism and nationhood. Write a short report, describing and contrasting the four case studies you have chosen.

5. Identify the selection and eligibility procedures for five different national sports teams and describe how these sports define eligibility in national terms.

6. Examine the content of five different popular songs sung at national sporting occasions as a basis for reporting on the ways in which such occasions are used to promote national pride and patriotism.

CHAPTER
10

SPORTING
SUBCULTURES

© Bongarts Photography/SportsChrome USA

Objectives

At the end of this chapter, you should be able to

- compare different theoretical understandings of the term *culture*;
- explain the ways in which sport reproduces meaning for at least three different subcultures;
- understand the difference between culture and subculture;
- discuss the notion of alternative sporting traditions and how they resist mainstream sporting culture;
- discuss the relationship between peripheral and mainstream sporting cultures; and
- critically evaluate the relationship between sport and hegemony.

The origins of the word **culture** lie in its use to describe growth or development, initially applied to crops and animals. It was subsequently used to suggest improvement of the mind and of society. In retrospect, it seems inevitable that the ideas behind the concept of culture would afterwards be used to describe and compare peoples and societies.

To understand the idea of culture, it is important to recognise that people who have been influential in shaping societies have traditionally been able to determine what constitutes culture. These individuals and groups have been important to the development of cultures that dominate, while also owning or using the means to disseminate culture itself. Culture can therefore encapsulate notions of knowledge and power. We can also recognise that from these developments has arisen a contestation over the **meaning** of culture.

Gramsci's (1971) concepts of **hegemony** in cultural theory and their relationship to sport can help determine what constitutes culture and who decides what is and what is not culture. Because competition over culture, sport, **power** and resources lies at the heart of these questions, such concepts also have a contribution to make in our understanding of sporting **subcultures.**

Jarvie and Maguire (1994) consider hegemony a useful analytical tool for sport studies. Like Clarke and Critcher (1985), they believe that the concept compresses a range of significant ideas relating to the development of **cultural domination** and discord. It has helped make clear that culture has no one explanation and that the term and the process of making culture are both contested arenas. The idea of hegemony has enabled scholars to open up the field of popular culture to a more extensive study and, in particular, it has 'highlighted the relation-ship between power and culture and a rejection of reductionist thinking in whatever manner it appeared' (Jarvie and Maguire 1994).

With some understanding that culture does not develop neutrally but is shaped usually by people with particular interests and aims, we might also recognise the great mass of people who have often been seen to be largely uncultured. If something is viewed as popular or common, it has frequently been the case that these social features, including those relating to sport, have not been viewed as 'real' culture. Therefore, questions of social class, race, economy and gender have also become markers of culture.

Terms such as *mass* and *popular* are additionally important to our understanding of culture, as well as what is subcultural and why a subculture develops. They are also important to our appreciation of the practical nature of the contestation over culture. However, with 19th- and 20th-century changes in politics, education, work, leisure patterns and politics, ideas about culture and access to a variety of cultural practices and experiences have also undergone **transformation.**

For some people, the communication and economic revolutions of recent decades have corresponded to the debasement of culture. This means that the authenticity and civilising functions of traditional cul-tures are being replaced by a mass or popular culture used only for amusement or diversion. In this light, popular culture can often be viewed as shallow, vulgar, undiscriminating, overly hedonistic, exces-sively violent and intellectually undemanding. Within such percep-tions, sport is often viewed as not being a valuable or worthy part of authentic or worthwhile culture. For Gruneau and Whitson (1993), 'spectator sports in particular, have been denigrated as activities too closely tied to popular tastes, too centred on the body rather than the mind, too rooted in local passions, and too closely connected to the sensuous worlds of drink and gambling'. They believe that 'What gets defined as "culture" in western societies, and how it is defined, have always been matters of negotiation and struggle between powerful and less powerful groups, often with differing ways of life'.

The premise in this chapter is that culture is viewed broadly as the multifaceted meanings, beliefs and ways of living that personify any society. Culture can be viewed as the way people live and make sense of their lives. Memory, institutions, beliefs, attitudes, activities, language, music and food all contribute to form what we know as culture. Culture itself can be found locally, nationally and globally, and in terms of language, religion, colour of skin and a variety of other ways. In another sense, it can constitute what comes to define us collectively and what defines those different from us.

Modern sport is significant as a central dimension of popular experience and collective memory. Sport plays an important role in the broader constitution of social and cultural life. However, we should also recognise that the composition or expression of a cultural derivation can also be important in any assessment of overall sporting culture. Using sport, this chapter will focus on what is often termed *subcultural*.

Subcultures are parts, fragments or derivations of common or more recognisable cultures adopted by particular sections of a society. They are ultimately related in some way to aspects of the greater, more dominant culture, but often they can be set up as some sort of response or opposition, certainly at variance, to the principal or prevailing culture. Generally, subcultures are less shared by the greater number of people than are the more common cultures.

So, subcultures are embedded in society but are usually reflective of a sense of **difference.** Classic subcultures in Britain during the 1960s and 1970s have been witnessed in such things as mod, skinhead or punk ways of dressing, attitudes to music, interests and sometimes shared values. Generally, such variations can be viewed as nonconformist. This is often typified by difference with something most people accept and share, or it can be of a confrontational nature. Sometimes these differences can also be blurred amid the experience of nonconformity.

In relation to sports transmission to millions through the media, and in terms of its comprising significant aspects of many people's cultural and recreational activities, sport is often considered to be part of mass as well as popular culture. If sport is culture, then, as with other cultural practices, it also has the capacity to be viewed in its subcultural forms.

Case Study: Soccer Hooliganism As Subculture

The origins of the term *hooligan* are uncertain, though it seems to derive from mid-19th-century Britain. Although often used with regard to wanton and gratuitous violence and destruction, **hooliganism** is frequently used to describe antisocial behaviour on match days on the part of soccer club followers. Contrary to some views, such violence has a long history and can be traced back as far as the 19th century and the early years of the development of the sport.

Because of its widespread significance in playing and spectating terms, football can broadly be described in the language of popular or mass culture. As well as many millions playing, spectating at sports stadiums has been one of the most significant features of the growth in football culture during the 20th century. As a **cultural product,** football has also spawned numerous football-related industries, developments and subcultural practices.

In Britain, football hooliganism is concerned with social **identity,** participatory and aggressive behaviour as well as, among other things, the politics of public order and control. Spectator violence and hooliganism at football matches became significant enough to be discussed at the government level in the late 1960s. By the 1970s, disorder involving supporters around the country, but significantly amongst Manchester United, Chelsea, Derby County, Millwall and Glasgow Rangers fans, served as references for policy decisions. In the 1980s and 1990s, football hooliganism on the part of some clubs' supporters, as well as on the part of the England international team's following, brought notoriety on football in England.

A number of explanations for the prevalence of hooliganism have evolved. Much of the media and a number of politicians frequently focus on excessive alcohol consumption, violence on the playing field, unemployment, affluence and permissiveness. Some of these have indirect influences on soccer hooliganism, but connections can also be overstated at the expense of other reasons. For example, the decrying of unemployment as a cause of football hooliganism is often overestimated. Unemployment was high during the 1930s, but the incidence of match-related violence was at an all-time low during this period. In addition, unemployment was at its lowest level when periodically fluctuating football hooliganism began in Britain in the 1960s.

Some of the most incisive explanations for football hooliganism come from Eric Dunning (1999). Using the figurational paradigm advocated by Norbert Elias, Dunning believes that the majority of football hooligans originate with the working classes, that is, mainly from the ranks of manual workers with low levels of formal education. Dunning also believes that many of the factors involved in working-class lifestyles have a role to play in the norms of aggressive masculinity that in itself seems to be a basic tenet of football hooliganism.

Authors such as Armstrong (1998) argue that football hooliganism cannot really be explained. It can only be described and evaluated. Giulianotti's work (1994) looks at a new type of hooligan to emerge since the 1980s based on the less coloured and ornamental stereotype of a typical football hooligan. His research focuses on the experience of the 'casuals' in Scotland, who do not wear traditional club colours but wear designer clothes to disguise themselves from the police and distinguish themselves from other supporters. During the 1980s and 1990s, they were involved in orchestrated violence against similar groups of supporters from other clubs and have been the main perpetrators of football hooliganism in Scotland in recent decades.

Soccer hooliganism is embedded in the wider cultural phenomenon of football spectating and football itself. It is subcultural because it is not a dominating feature of football and neither is it intrinsic to the sport. Its understanding is to be found in the characteristics of the particular society in which it occurs. Football matches do not take place in a social vacuum and are woven into the fabric of a society's cultural identities and activities. Likewise, football hooliganism is a subcultural aspect of football fandom.

Sport As a Social and Cultural Product

For those who consider the idea that culture should only be equated with the high arts, such as opera, sculpting and ballet, sport is often viewed as a mass or popular social product that constitutes little by way of culture. Others argue that sport is a social and cultural product and that sporting pursuits and activities have real meaning for individuals, for communities and for society generally. This outlook also assumes that these same groups of people construct sport in a way that is both expressive and reflective of their cultural beliefs, practices, attitudes and identities. As a social and cultural product, sport is frequently a focus for community and an opportunity for people to come together to emphasise their similarities and differences.

Hoberman (1984) states that sport has no intrinsic value structure, but is a ready-made and flexible vehicle through which ideological associations can be reinforced. In this view, sport becomes a carrier of cultural symbols and metaphors. For example, as a social and cultural product, American football informs us about certain features of American life. Racism in the United States, **capitalism** as the dominant economic ethos, the American dream and even eating habits are among matters expressed through and reflected in American football that elevate this 'mere sport' into something that can be seen as culturally significant. Despite the vast range of cultures and subcultures that exist in the United States, American football partly reflects the cultural constitution of U.S. society.

It seems inevitable that the sports adopted by people in a society say something about them. So, when white males in the United States develop and sustain baseball, the racial and gender dominance inherent in the sport will almost certainly be a reflection of aspects of the country at large. The development of soccer in Britain in the 19th century informs us of much of the working-class nature of British society at that time and for many decades thereafter. 'In Japan, professional baseball reflects the traditional pattern of strong group loyalty in that society. As a result, the practice of trading players and firing managers is quite different from North America' (McPherson, Curtis, and Loy 1989). Sport is a social and cultural product, and through sport we can begin to understand societies, nations and communities. It is bound to society and its manifestations are determined by the contours of a society's cultural features.

Socialisation and Sport

Socialisation is important to our sense of self, our **identities** and our participation with others in society. 'Socialisation is a process of learning how to accept and conform to cultural and social constraints embedded in social norms and roles' (Nixon and Frey 1996). Socialisation is continually renegotiated and reinterpreted and is a process that lasts from cradle to grave.

One example of the socialisation process emerges through sport. Most people do not have an opportunity to pursue any sport they want. Gender, social class, age, culture, geography, ethnicity, religion and access to facilities determine socialisation processes involved in sport. Amongst those who play golf in Scotland, the higher social classes are overrepresented while the lower income and lower status groups are grossly underrepresented. Likewise, European soccer is male dominated while keep-fit and gymnastics are frequently viewed as sports and leisure pursuits mainly participated in by women. These observations might also conclude that such statistics emerge largely because of socio-sporting processes in the respective societies.

Family, school, community and voluntary associations are all vital in the socialisation process. Studies show that many African American sportspeople in the United States will be encouraged and directed to play particular sports and even to play certain roles within those sports. The result is that although blacks seem to dominate in some sports, they are underrepresented in others. Other negative consequences result from this socialisation process. Sailes (1998) shows that although many African Americans are encouraged into sports in the United States, it often results in failure, as many do not succeed in becoming dedicated athletes. This means that black academic achievement suffers and life chances are subsequently restricted and reduced.

A different example of the socialisation process in sport might be witnessed in the case of a young male brought up in the southern part of Wales, where his family and many similar families in the local community have been involved in the local rugby scene for several generations. Such dominating local features will potentially affect the social experiences and identities of many inhabitants in the area. Family and locality as well as, in the case of Wales, the power of the media to portray rugby as especially meaningful to Welsh people, will in many cases determine the sporting cultural pursuits of many young men in the area. Such a course of events and influences can be viewed as constituting an impassioned socialisation process.

Socialisation also takes place inside sport to the point that expectations and practices become culturally determined. This might be most evident in the ethos of how particular sports are played or even in the unwritten rules involved in spectating. Where a sturdy shoulder charge might be greeted with applause in a game of Gaelic football, the same contact will often be viewed as a foul in Association football or soccer. In Latin countries, spitting is not uncommon in soccer, while the same practice is viewed as uncivilised and vulgar in countries like Britain. Where mass singing takes place at many football grounds in Europe, such crowd behaviour is uncommon in boxing, athletics and cycling. Although sporting cultures are constantly evolving, expectations mean that established practices are usually adhered to and often only change slowly.

The value of sport in socialising young people into the acceptable norms of a society has long been recognised. In countries like Britain and the United States, deprived areas, as opposed to more affluent ones, have frequently turned out boxing enthusiasts and champions, so much so that boxing champions from both societies have almost entirely been drawn from the working classes. These sporting winners have often been the victims of a multitude of social deprivations and have responded to these by being attracted to local boxing gyms, where trainers offer their time and expertise partly as a way to encourage youngsters to escape from their detrimental circumstances. Boxing can teach dedication, self-respect, achievement and a degree of community representation in a way frequently not open to a kid whose other social influences offer few of these perceived positive forces and experiences. In socialising people into sport, 'it has been argued that there are psychological, behavioural, and attitudinal outcomes derived from involvement in competitive sport programs' (McPherson, Curtis, and Loy 1989).

Being socialised into and through sport is a common cultural experience. A person, particularly a child, is often affected by a variety of social and psychological influences that lead to sporting involvement. Within these socialising processes, there are a vast number of factors that will help determine choice amidst the sports available and the level to which a participant might, if good enough, take up their chosen activity. The functions of the media, advertising and role models all have a part to play in the sporting socialisation process. In addition, beliefs, attitudes and the character-forming effects of sporting involvement all help constitute socialisation. Sport is culture and culture is a social product.

Debating Point:
Are Sporting Subcultures Important?

Sport holds a central role in the popular cultures of many countries. The dominance of football in Britain, baseball in the United States, sumo wrestling in Japan, boxing in Cuba and Australian Rules football in Australia all reflect the pre-eminent positions of these sports in their respective societies. Many of these sports also have a global significance that goes beyond national boundaries. Nevertheless, what might be considered sporting subcultures are also important in many societies and to any assessment of sport cultures.

As a sporting subculture, football hooliganism can offer us an opportunity to understand features of working-class life that might be otherwise arduous to observe. Studies of football hooliganism can elicit explanations for a wide range of social changes, from a decline in traditional working-class habits to a rise in social alienation induced by the advance of materialism and consumerism. In other words, sport can reflect features of the wider society.

A reflection on sporting subcultures can inform us of aspects of a society not considered mainstream or popular. As such they are often more difficult to penetrate by way of social analysis. Further, such consideration allows us to look at groups of people who express opposition to the wider norms of society. For example, it can be argued that at a national level, many English football hooligans view their parent culture of British and English identity as being eroded by other ethnic, cultural and ideological forces imported into the country. **Cultural resistance** to this perception has partly evolved by way of hooligans' behaviour abroad as a deviant subculture. To an extent, this behaviour has aimed in a crude fashion to put the 'Great' back in Britain and show that, at least within the perceptions of those involved, the English/ British are prepared and willing to put up a fight to regain lost prestige. For those who suffer at the hands of hooligans, such mindless and wanton violence and destruction should be dealt with by hard-hitting policing methods, regardless of sociological explanations that attempt to explain some of the rationale behind this problem.

In a more positive sense, sporting subcultures also offer people an opportunity for companionship and commonality amidst perceived conformity. The development of a sporting subculture can help non-conformist or alternative-minded individuals to express themselves in less stereotypical fashion and to link up with other like-minded individuals. Within this new social formation can evolve a sense of identity, a source of status recognition and even a significant contributing factor to lifestyle.

Apart from **mainstream sports,** subcultural sports can be viewed as important in at least two ways. They can be seen as significant in that they are a reflection of the wider society rather than some of its specific aspects. Therefore, they offer a greater and wider picture of the dynamics of any given society. In addition, sporting subcultures allow people an opportunity to express themselves in different sporting formats and contexts other than via the dominant and hegemonic features and ideas concerning sport. This is also important for any society that aspires to recognition and celebration of its varying strands and influences and, thus, to a more accurate reflection of its social diversity.

Sporting Journeys of Difference and Distinction

Sport is reflective of a number of features of any given society. It is a locale for numerous positive social inferences and it simultaneously provides a site for the manufacturing of difference, **distinction,** resistance and conflict. Sport has long been rooted in these realities, as well as in the more negative aspects of inequality and division.

In relation to culture, Gramsci (1971) believes that hegemony takes the form of a disproportionate influence and even dominance in terms of ideas, **cultural forms,** politics and finance. It is a social construction based on perceived functional abilities, resources, power and status. For Jarvie and Maguire (1994), choice is also affected by these social constructions and social structures, and these reflect our possession and deployment of varying degrees and combinations of economic, cultural and symbolic capital. Society is the context in which many of these social constructions become manifest. As well as being a reflection of society, sport can be a site for producing and transforming the expectations, practices and norms that make up any given culture. People continually shape and form sport to adhere to their own ideas and intentions. Sport is an agent of cultural production and, although choice is largely a socialised process, in the field of subcultures choice is less predictable than might be viewed as the norm.

Critical theories of sport attempt to make sense of the complex and constantly changing relationships within groups as well as between them. This is partly determined by these groups' varying amounts of power and resources. Sport has the potential to become a site for articulating individuals' and groups' interpretations of the world and, indeed, how they would like to shape that world. Sport not only reflects society, it also contributes to the creation of society.

Therefore, sport is also a means to oppose the hegemony or conformity that often corresponds with sports activity and participation. Complying with society's sporting expectations can be viewed as being subjected to a sports hegemony that is overly manufactured, controlled and limited in choice. For those who perceive this undue influence and hegemony, sport also creates an opportunity to challenge, to be different and to reshape cultural activities in a way that speaks less about conformity and more about genuine creativity and expression.

Subcultural and Peripheral Activities

Gramsci's (1971) theory of hegemony offers us much in terms of sporting analysis. However, there are other ways to look at the dominance of sports by individuals, groups and communities, as well as by influential people and institutions in the media, finance and politics. Jarvie and Maguire (1994) suggest that we can add to our understanding of these areas of sport by utilising history and empirical data. Both authors support the notion that sport should be seen more in terms of local, regional and national cultures rather than simply proposing a false dualism such as global and local. Both opine that we should look more at the 'cultural politics of location'. Such methodology enhances our scope for understanding the development of sporting subcultures in particular.

Some of the clearest examples of the development of subcultural activities within sport revolve around youth. Traditionally, young people have perceived themselves to be involved, even to be the determining influence, in the construction of clothes, music, magazines, hairstyles, dance, and the like. Of course, this is much less true than many young people imagine, and the young are often the first victims of omnipotent advertising and an assortment of commercialisation strategies. Nonetheless, when a significant number of young people adopt variations in style, we often consider this to be the evolution of a youth subculture. These can frequently demise almost as quickly as they emerge and are often simply expressions of fashion rather than subculture with substance. However, these sites of independence or freedom offer youth an opportunity for group and self-expression.

Certain leisure activities also capture these developments through the expression of **alternative sports.** These might be called marginal, peripheral or subcultural in that they are not mainstream. Such sports are usually enjoyed by fewer people than those shared by a larger, possibly more homogeneous, social grouping. Often these alternative sports are characterised by a lack of competition and organisation as well as the subsequent ranking of individuals. In addition, these sports rarely attract commercial sponsorship or media coverage. In subcultural sports, participants frequently direct the course of events themselves without regard for any formal authority.

In sport, but also beyond sporting confines, subcultural sporting activists often possess differing value systems from those considered dominant or hegemonic in mainstream society. They tend to use equipment and clothing specifically engineered for their pursuits and frequently engage in a distinctive language related to their activity. Subcultural sporting pursuits attract those who see themselves as different from the mainstream, while they also become agents for the development of **distinctiveness.**

Examples of sports (not all of them restricted to youth) considered to be subcultural or alternative are motocross, bodybuilding, snowboarding, skateboarding, karate, rock climbing and parachuting. One study of motocross in the United States in the early 1970s showed that almost all participants originated from the working class (Martin and Berry 1993). The racers of the club under study determined everything concerning the sport including the lease and construction of a dirt track. The authors of this research believe that motocross played a unique and dominant role in the social lives and identities of its participants.

When a sport is considered alternative or subcultural, this should not be considered synonymous with its being pursued by only a small number of people. Weight training is frequently considered a subcultural activity but is participated in by an estimated 85 million Americans, though only a small fraction ever enter competitions. Such large-scale involvement, as well as subsequent media attention and organised competitions, also means that questions are raised whether sports like bodybuilding should be classed as subcultural.

Beal (1995) writes of her skateboarding experiences in the United States. One of the characteristics she notes is the skateboarders' lack of awareness of formal standards in the sport. Accordingly, there are no universal criteria by which skateboarders are judged. There also exists a common desire for self-definition amongst skateboarders, including individuality, creativity and self-expression. Although these can be found in other sports, Beal opines that these qualities are enhanced through subcultural or alternative sports, ensuring that the individual needs of participating sportspeople are met. Her conclusions on skateboarding have relevance for numerous subcultural sports. Such activities can challenge the participants' mental and physical limits and allow them to socialise with like-minded people. These relatively unorganised activities without the boundaries of formal sport enable subcultural sporting activists to develop their own goals and styles that satisfy their needs and desires.

Debating Point: Are Subcultural Developments Responses to Cultural Domination?

Although sport can be reflective of dominant social forms and identities, it can also serve as an avenue for resistance to dominant forms within the wider culture. Sporting subcultures can become responses to a problem, they can arise as a result of conflict or distance evolved through a given social situation, and they can emerge from people sharing an aspect of culture and coming together to express difference from the dominant cultural forms.

If we consider Beal's work on skateboarding (1995), she proposes the possibility of subcultural sport being used as a form of popular culture that resists capitalist social relations, although she also notes that contradictions and accommodations often limit and affect the nature of this resistance. If popular cultural activities, including sport, reproduce dominant cultural norms and values, then they also have the potential to become sites of resistance to cultural domination. If dominant sport forms can reproduce racism, social inequalities and the patriarchy of capitalist relations, then sport can offer resistance to the norms and values created by such dominance.

Eichberg (1984) views 'Olympism' as a social pattern whereby local and national sports have been subjected to Westernisation as a form of colonialism. So, the 'swifter, higher, stronger' motto of the Games has marginalised the sporting values and achievements otherwise esteemed in differing cultures. However, linking with the idea of subcultural production, Eichberg also believes that a response to this Western dominance will arise in the form of more alternative sporting pursuits and activities. Regardless of such optimism or unproved theorising, the point is made that sport can be viewed as a site for resistance through the success or evolution of subcultural and other cultural developments.

Gramsci's concept of hegemony refers to the capacity of dominant groups not only to impose their ideas on subordinate others, but also to create the active consent of these others in contributing to and even maintaining their subordinate status. The important point for sport is that this hegemony creates limits of what is perceived as acceptable and possible, thus reinforcing the dominant group's agenda and place in the social hierarchy under the guise of freedom and choice. Limitations are imposed on sport by way of these dominant values, norms, regulations and attitudes. As these might be challenged in a revolutionary, reformist or even nonconformist way within civil society, they can also be challenged within the confines of sport.

In the development of subcultural leisure activities, activists resist certain features of hegemonic sports, as well as of society itself. Where sports are significantly influenced by the impact of capital, national or global sporting dominance is often the result. However, competition, elitism, bureaucracy and specialisation are also governing features of modern hegemonic sports. Any kind of social resistance is frequently required to work within the confines created by hegemonic forces within society, and therefore resistance is almost inherently limited in that it is partly shaped by what it is responding to.

Subcultural sports that become sites of resistance to mainstream sports are ritualistic in nature and are areas of negotiation between what dominates and what is dominated. This is one of the main differences with spontaneous divergence. Skateboarding was oppositional to corporate bureaucratic forms of sport and, as a consequence, corporate bureaucratic social relations. In a similar sense to Eichberg's (1984) thoughts on resisting Olympian ideas from omnipotent and dominating sports, skateboarding helped create alternative norms and relations that focused on the participants themselves and open participation rather than elite competition. Skateboarding was shared by youths that had no interest in elite standards or winning. In addition, the skateboarders themselves were viewed as the experts and were not subject to pressures imposed by outside rule makers and commentators. The nature of skateboarding was conjured up by the participants, who determined what tricks to do and how long to skateboard.

Like any social activity, space, time and social conditions alter the nature of subcultural activities. Subcultural sporting resistance can be exhausted by mainstream sporting developments or they can be absorbed into mainstream sports, thus losing their label of subcultural.

The Transformation From Subcultural to Cultural

Subcultural sporting responses to hegemonic sporting dominance do not necessarily lead to any substantial change in what is being resisted. Indeed, often a symbolic display of resistance is all that is achieved. Within the subcultural form, there are often contradictions that threaten the resistance strategy. For example, the study of skateboarders found that sexist attitudes against females and occasional racist attitudes amongst a small faction of participants reproduced negative aspects of the wider society. This raises the possibility that the **transformative** benefits of resistance can, for example, be limited to being against certain aspects of capitalism, while arguably replicating some of the negative features of the wider capitalist society. Rather than some ideological or conscious development in relation to resisting hegemonic sporting influences, it is likely that such developments are frequently about people who are more interested in the creation and maintenance of self-governing activity rather than having any real influence on wider social relations. Nonetheless, the importance of these subcultural sporting pursuits is that a degree of power is attained or reclaimed. To an extent, participants are empowered to act in their own best interests, even temporarily.

One of the most obvious threats to subcultural sports, and one that has the potential to make them mainstream—and therefore more cultural than subcultural—is the influx of new participants. This increases the chances of competition evolving, of clothing and equipment being less relaxed or, ironically, more tightly controlled, of other behaviours developing and, ultimately, of the redefinition of the meaning of the subcultural sport itself.

Klein's work (1993) on bodybuilding shows how a subcultural sport can be incorporated into the wider culture. In this case, incorporation grew from the sport's need for wider acceptance. Although bodybuilding did not set out to fundamentally change any aspect of society, outside perceptions of the vanity involved in bodybuilding, in addition to sexual suspicions cast on its practitioners, meant that it had to gain wider acceptance to restrict negative labelling and to survive. It thus acquired features involved in the wider culture, like competition and an infusion of finance. In the process, bodybuilding lost its subcultural identity and became largely mainstream.

Many subcultural sports have eventually been incorporated into mainstream cultural sporting activities. Skateboarding and bodybuilding are two examples, while a host of others, among them surfing and snowboarding, can provide further illustrations. Broadly, for many people, **peripheral sports** frequently come to accept formal competition arrangements, the measurement of achievement practices and the involvement of authority figures such as judges. Such sports also become institutionalised through the process whereby people accept more formal structures and regulations.

Alternative sports have also been transformed into mainstream activities via the involvement of commercial enterprises. This is especially conspicuous with the evolution of surfing as linked to changing lifestyles in the post–World War II period. Booth argues that consumer capitalism during the 20th century created the social space for the development of surfing as a hedonistic pastime or subculture. However, the escapism and nonconformity involved in surfing eventually gave way to codification, competitions and, ultimately, by the 1960s and 1970s, prizes, money and sponsorship on the part of global brands. For Booth, in the 1990s 'surfing joined international soccer and the Olympic Games as Coca-Cola's third global sport'. The politics involved in the evolution of surfing to this level 'illuminates the complex interaction between social, cultural, and economic interests which determine sporting forms' (1995).

In the 1990s, the commercialisation of subcultural sports like snowboarding and skateboarding, and their alignment with products such as the sports drink Lucozade, shows how alternative sports can become part of the mainstream fitness industry. Through such processes, subcultural sports lose their uniqueness and become mainstream.

Summary

Sport and culture cannot be separated. Likewise, subcultural activity and subcultural sports are inextricably linked to the culture of any given society. Sport is both reflective and expressive of society, as are subcultural sporting activities. Many subcultural sports offer an informative means of analysis into the rest of society. Some theories of sport place global and popular sports within a discourse of capitalist relationships. They are dominant and hegemonic in that they attract the most sponsorship, media coverage, spectator audiences and participants. Nonetheless, sports quite distinct from mainstream activities are alternatives that can become sites of resistance to perceived social domination, acting as outlets for difference, distinction and disagreement. However, as our references to alternative sports such as bodybuilding and surfing show, and as has been demonstrated by the inclusion of snowboarding at the Olympics, many of these subcultural sports are eventually drawn into mainstream sporting culture. A loss of independence and a measure of integration is often the outcome as a sport gradually becomes less subcultural and more cultural.

Over the last decade or more, there has been a well-documented cultural turn in social theory, with the essential argument being that culture gives everyday life meaning and significance. In this chapter we have provided a brief insight into the cultural contribution to sport. It has been suggested that the relationship between cultures and subcultures has traditionally involved the contestation of the relations of power. The objectives of this chapter have been essentially twofold. First, to understand the idea that culture, including sport in general, is universally constitutive of social relations and identity. This is essentially an epistemological argument about what is meant by the term *culture*. Second, this chapter has concerned itself with the different ways in which contemporary sports cultures have played an unprecedented role in contemporary society. This is essentially a substantive argument about the ways in which sport in different specific senses helps to constitute and reproduce social relations and identities.

Key Terms and Concepts

alternative sports	culture
capitalism	difference
cultural domination	distinction
cultural forms	hegemony
cultural product	hooliganism
cultural resistance	identity

mainstream sports	socialisation
meaning	subculture
peripheral sports	transformation

Review Questions

1. What is meant by the term *subculture*?
2. What is the difference between peripheral and mainstream sports activities?
3. Discuss the relationship between sport and socialisation.
4. Explain how the term *hegemony* helps us to understand sport.
5. Describe ways in which sporting subcultures might be viewed as a response to forces of cultural domination.
6. Discuss ways in which subcultural sports might be incorporated into the mainstream sporting culture.
7. Discuss the meaning of sport in your local community.
8. Explain some of the key criticisms of a cultural studies perspective on sport.
9. Why are alternative sports important in terms of maintaining a vibrant sports culture?
10. What is meant by the transformative capacity of sport?

Projects

1. Identify three different sporting subcultures. Use an ethnographic approach to collect data and explain the meaning of those sport subcultures you have chosen to examine.
2. Observe one of your local sports clubs over a 10-week period. Provide a short account, based on your observations, of the meaning of sport to the players and to different groups of spectators.
3. Talk to 10 sportsmen and sportswomen over the age of 60 about how sport has changed over the past 40 years or so. Write a report based on your findings.
4. Choose two peripheral sports and using ethnographic methods of enquiry write a report on how people from different subcultures experience the two sports chosen.
5. Identify the power structure within a sports organisation of your choice and comment on the mechanisms by which different groups within the organisation challenge or sustain the existing power structure.
6. Produce a critical investigative report on the different points of view expressed on any contentious sporting issue of your choice. Whose account becomes the 'official' account of the issue, and why?

CHAPTER 11

SPORT, EMOTIONS AND SOCIETIES

Objectives

After completing this chapter, you should be able to

- discuss the concept of pleasure and relate it to the experience of sport;
- explain how emotions are scripted and performed in sport;
- critically consider whether emotions are physiologically determined or socially constructed;
- discuss the main components of the quest for excitement model;
- understand the connections between sport, emotions and societies; and
- discuss whether sport pleasures reflect false needs or genuine desires.

Welcome to the pleasure dome? In any explanation of the relationship between sport, culture and society, there is always some notion of what the sport experience does for or to human **emotions** (Jarvie and Maguire 1994). For better or worse, sports events 'move us' emotionally. Sport experiences create a range of emotions that people actively seek but which may be more or less socially desirable, permissible or possible. Here we attempt to make clearer the links between sport, emotions and societies by highlighting the interplay between the psychological makeup of people, historical processes and social structures.

When people think of sport and the emotions, there is a tendency to think of the immediate participant, to focus on how the individual athlete feels. There is little probing of how emotions are collectively created and shared, and of how the sport experience involves not just the immediate participants but also a host of other groups. These groups include the athletes; the coaches and medical staff; the spectators at the actual event; television, radio and newsprint producers and consumers of the sport occasion; and the officials and administrators. All are more or less involved in the emotions experienced by any one athlete. Beyond an understanding of the scope and range of what is involved in the sport experience, it is also important to clarify what pleasure refers to and how this relates to human emotions.

The experience of sport may be more or less pleasurable. But to what does this pleasure refer? **Pleasure** is a general term that covers several dimensions: the psychological, the physical and the social. The psychological use of the term *pleasure* tends to relate it with desire and place it as the main motivator of human action. The physical connotations associated with the term relate to the senses of the body; the intensity of the experience is crucial. In examining the social dimension of pleasure, its meaning is located in its relationship to the social structure and the social practices of the people who experience it (Fiske 1987). These dimensions are interconnected with issues of power and the varying abilities of people to enjoy forms of pleasure. These categories of pleasure are not mutually exclusive: in actual experiences they shade into and overlap with each other. Let us consider the example of media sport to better grasp the complexities of pleasure.

One group of people involved in the sport experience are those who watch sports on television. Duncan and Brummett (1989) analysed television spectatorship with an emphasis on watching. The experience of pleasurable looking, they contend, is fundamental to an adult's self-concept. Viewing the spectacular images of the mass media is pleasurable because it duplicates an important stage in a child's development, the mirror stage, when a child discovers his or her own reflection in the mirror. Duncan and Brummett identified two broad categories of pleasurable looking in television spectatorship. First, **scopophilia** refers to the viewer's deriving pleasure from what is viewed. Scopophilic pleasure can be found in two broad forms: **voyeurism** and **fetishism**. Voyeurism involves illicit looking, as when one watches another without being invited or allowed to. Pleasure here stems from the secrecy involved. Fetishism occurs when the object of the look is satisfying in itself. Fetishism, then, is the pleasure of fascination directed towards a spectacle, an object of frank, even invited, viewing. The second type of pleasurable looking is **narcissism.** In this type of looking, the viewer derives pleasure from imaging him or herself in the image, by identifying with the bodies or body parts of the athletes.

These forms of pleasurable looking form part of the television spectatorship of sport. Although there may be different emphases in other forms of spectating, and different relationships between spectators and participants in the leisure experience, there will also be considerable overlap in the forms and instances of pleasure. What we must do now is to locate the issue of pleasure in a broader consideration of different conceptions of human emotions.

Debating Point: Are Embodied Emotions Physiologically Determined or Socially Constructed?

Social constructionist perspectives suggest that emotions are not simply some steady physiological state or psychological trait, they are culturally patterned and socially constructed. Let us examine the foundations of this argument. First, there is a sociogenesis, and not simply a biogenesis or psychogenesis, of emotions. When we examine grief-stricken, anxiety-ridden or joyful people, we need to locate them in their context, such as a funeral, an examination hall or a sports event. Second, aspects of people's emotions, both men's and women's, vary across societies and historical time periods. Third, both the culturally universal and the culturally relative aspects of emotions are socially stratified along, for example, class, gender, ethnic and age lines.

This emphasis on the social construction of emotions is a powerful and necessary corrective to the dominance of geneticists, ethologists and behavioural psychologists who insist that the determination of specific emotions is solely a matter of biology and physiology. The question often arises whether emotions reside in our hearts or our heads, a formulation that reflects the traditional dualistic manner in which the emotions have been understood. In physiological and psychological research, human beings are treated as isolated units with no past or present (Scheff 1983). Humans' thoughts are cut off from their feelings; their bodies are cut off both from their consciousness and from the society in which they reside. However, social constructionism also reflects dualistic thinking, focusing as it does only on the social, to the exclusion of others. For example, the probing of the self and the 'lived consciousness' has led to the neglect of the study of human beings' physiological makeup. It also leads to a focus on the subject as a single thinking mind inside a sealed container, from which she or he looks out at other subjects in the external world (Shott 1979; Denzin 1984).

Given that sports participation and spectating involve **embodied acts,** it is rather strange that the emotions have not received greater attention within the sociology of sport (Maguire 1992). A sociology of sport and embodied emotions needs to address four key areas. First, how people's biological, psychological and socio-cultural dimensions inter-weave and find expression in social (sporting) acts (Maguire 1992). In this way, a number of cherished 'natural' myths regarding sex / gender and race / ethnicity can be destroyed. Second, how embodied acts both reflect and reinforce social inequalities, be they class-, gender-, ethnicity- or disability-based (Shilling 1991). Third, how hegemonial / dominant practices focusing on peoples' bodies maintain the position of established groups while reinforcing the marginal status of outsider groups. Finally, we need studies of embodied people that explore the **hinge:** the interconnected, two-way traffic between learned and unlearned aspects of behaviour. The hinge is a way of expressing how the development of bodily habitus (socially learned dispositions that become second nature) has been, and continues to be, contoured by an interweaving of people's biological, psychological and cultural identities.

The **nature versus nurture** debate is a false dichotomy. In highlight-ing the interconnectedness of the social, psychological and biological dimensions of human existence and social life, the trap of overemphasising either the natural or the cultural can be avoided. For example, Elias (1987) shows how smiling is an unlearned sign employed by humans all over the world to signify friendly intent. And yet the learning of the more expanded system of signs and language, which is culturally specific, actually allows humans greater control over, and elaboration of, their natural repertoire. Put simply, we can now control smiling so that it is not a reaction but an intentionally deployed symbol that can convey a range of messages. The smile is also open to a more complex range of embodied interpretations. Like the smile, sport performances also become part of our second nature. So how are sport practices performed?

Performing Embodied Emotions in the Sporting Pleasure Dome

In examining the performance of embodied emotions, important clues can be gained by using a sociological perspective known as symbolic interactionism (Denzin 1985; Zurcher 1982). In this approach, meaningful behaviour emerges out of interaction with others, in turn shaping the social world of the individual. Social life is a kind of drama that individuals act out, thus, everyday interaction involves the presentation of self in the lived experiences through which the world is socially constructed. Our emotions play a significant role in the presentation of self. Emotions are socially constructed and rooted in a social situation and, as Snyder (1990) concludes, they arise out of a definition and evaluation of one's behaviour in social interaction.

A symbolic interactionist theory of emotion assumes that 'within the limits set by social norms and internal stimuli, individuals construct their emotions: and their definitions and interpretations are critical to this often emergent process' (Shott 1979). Though Shott agrees that internal states and cues are necessary for affective experience, they 'do not in themselves establish feeling, for it is the actor's definitions and interpretations that give physiological states their emotional significance or nonsignificance'. Likewise, Denzin (1985) argues that emotion is **self-feeling** and that emotionality 'arises out of inhibited, interpreted social acts in which the subject inserts self-conversations between the perception of experience and the organization of action'. Emotions are feelings that reflect the evaluations of self and others of what constitutes a desirable performance in sports events or elsewhere. That there is an emphasis on performance is not surprising, because from a symbolic interactionist perspective the expression of emotion can be considered as a dramaturgical phenomenon (Goffman 1961).

Social life, as noted, is viewed as a drama in which people act out their parts. Emotion is interpreted as role-related behaviour enacted by individuals according to their understandings of interactions in specific settings (Zurcher 1982). The advantage of this perspective is that it enables the researcher to simultaneously examine the structure of staged settings, the fixed and emergent **scripts** for emotional display, and the constructed nature of an individual's emotional experiences. The dramaturgical perspective is also helpful in teasing out the process of emotionality. Definitive stages of this process can be identified: some of the feelings expressed are anticipatory prior to performing and some are felt and expressed during and after the performance itself. What counts as appropriate feelings in anticipation of, during or after the performance are scripted by the subculture, in this case, sport. These scripts act as guides for people as they manage their emotions—for example, in the pre-match playing of national anthems or in the medal ceremonies that follow sports performances. These scripts are known as **feeling rules,** that is, emotional norms expected of a person or group of people in a given situation. People have to manage and control their emotions according to the expectations of the subculture. Consider, for example, the different demands and expectations of golf and rugby union. The degree of emotional control required of golfers is tighter than that of rugby players. The latter physically confront opponents while golfers are bound to a much greater degree by the etiquette of their sport.

This internalisation of the values of the subculture is crucial to a person in three respects. First, it provides an understanding of a desirable performance; second, it highlights the appropriate emotions based on the feeling rules; third, it emphasises the ways to manage and display emotions before, during and after the performance. Sets of emotions are co-produced and, while they are an essential part of the presentation of self, they also reflect structured events—the game and its status within the sporting calendar. Emotions are lived from the inside as well as symbolically expressed to others. Emotions, then, are an embodied experience that involves the subject's current felt attachment to their situation. This embodied experience is a moving, unfolding process that turns on itself, binding the subject into a web of emotional feelings that are both desired and not desired. Crucially, a person's body is both the vehicle for this movement forward and the structure that radiates and expresses the person's feelings. But how has this approach been applied to sport?

We can focus on American football to highlight some more general issues. Zurcher (1982), for example, focused on the orchestrating of emotions of fans, players and coaches in American college football. This begins with the arousal of expectations for an emotional experience that generates a diffuse emotional state directed into a series of discrete and identifiable emotional displays. In other words, you get 'psyched up'.

The emotional buildup of the players is carefully scripted by the coaches. This scripting occurs at the pre-match meal, during the pre-match team talk, in the warm-up period and as the players enter the playing field. But it is not just the players who experience this scripting. Zurcher (1982) describes the 'stage setters' who also contribute to the emotion management of fans. From the cues being provided by the stage setters, and from the spectators' previous experience in similar settings, they are expected to enact a range of emotions throughout the game. These emotions range from affection for fellow fans and hostility or even hatred for the opponents, compassion for the injured and pride, joy, and perhaps ecstasy, despair and anger depending on the outcome of the game. ✗

As Zurcher observes, not all the fans share or desire the same level of emotional readiness for the game. While there may be a scripting and an orchestration of the emotions, individuals vary in the degree to which they embrace scripts, enact the role of the fan and display the appropriate emotions. Nevertheless, these feeling rules do structure the experience of the subculture as a whole. The same is true for the players. The players are expected to achieve a proper mood for the game and to engage in 'emotion work'. That is, they strive to achieve emotions appropriate to the situation and the strictures of the coaches. It can be argued that similar processes are at work across leisure events.

While Zurcher focused on male team sports, Snyder focused on women's gymnastics. He concentrated on the performers' emotions, and examined the feeling rules that define 'the way gymnasts reflectively manage and control their emotions according to the expectations of the sports subculture' (Snyder 1990). For Snyder, these self-feelings also include mental preparation and concentration. In addition, he argued, gymnasts must learn to manage their feelings of nervousness and disappointment about injuries. An anxiety to perform well and to enhance one's self-identity as a gymnast falls into what Snyder terms pre-event emotions. He concluded that the process of managing emotions prior to performance 'is individually induced but is also socially promoted by other members of the team'. Work of this kind clearly demonstrates the need to pay greater attention to the construction and performance of emotion and embodied emotionality by people. The emphasis placed on dramaturgical analysis in the work of symbolic interactionists does afford the opportunity to examine both the construction and performance dimension of human emotions and the identity-forming qualities of sport. The feeling rules that Snyder highlighted with regard to women's gymnastics suggest that the predominant emotions do not always revolve around *pleasure*. The control and management of *pain* are also an integral part of the gymnastics subculture and indeed sport more generally.

Case Study: Doing Painful Embodied Sport Work

Sport experiences are not always pleasurable. Indeed, aspects of the modern sport experience can be exploitative, manipulative and dangerous to the social, psychological and physical well-being of the performer (Coakley 1992; Curry 1991; Curry and Strauss 1994; Hughes and Coakley 1991; Nixon 1996; Ryan 1995). Consider the case of gymnastics. Eleven recently retired gymnasts who had represented Great Britain at the world or Olympic level were interviewed about their experiences; attention was paid to issues of injury, diet and performance (Maguire and Roberts 1998).

Pain and injury were common with all of the gymnasts during their careers, and it was normal to feel some degree of pain on a weekly basis. Nine of the 11 gymnasts required ongoing physiotherapy for their most serious injuries. There was a common agreement amongst the gymnasts as to the definition and meaning of pain. The names that follow are all pseudonyms. Marie defined pain as something that 'hurts so much you can't carry on'. Charlotte supported this notion by saying that pain is 'when you can't do something because the pain is so severe'. What must be noted here is that the individuals who have been a part of the gymnastics subculture have experienced extremely high levels of pain. Susan described pain as 'having your leg up against your ear with the other leg on the ground and someone is pushing you and you're crying and it is hurting but you believe it is supposed to be doing you good'. In another example of the extended pain thresholds within the subject group, Charlotte described the pain she worked through before a series of Olympic trials:

> I knew I had the Olympics coming up in that year. That was the year I really knuckled under and got on with it. That was when I really worked through pain; I mean I had a stress fracture in my back, I had shin splints in my shins which I talked to . . . our Olympic doctor about and he was going to slice my shins and scrape them. He was also going to do my Achilles at the same time. So I was really training under, like, pain.

These gymnasts were aware that such high levels of pain were not normal. Sophie noted this: 'I am aware that [the pain] is not normal to the normal person but it is accepted because that is what gymnasts have to do.' Joanne stated: 'I think anyone else would look at it and think, *Oh, that is pain,* but that is just something you have to do when you are a gymnast. So you don't think of it as pain as such; you think of it as something you have to go through'. Charlotte confirmed this with reference to a personal incident:

For example, I was in Barcelona and it took me 45 minutes to be able to walk as I had an injury in my heel, and to the normal person I think after two minutes of walking they would have just sat down and put their feet up and not be able to do it. But I had to go on and keep on walking until I could walk even though I was limping and then train and compete.

To be successful in international gymnastics, gymnasts have to reach and train through a certain level of pain. As the gymnasts age and gain experience, they seem to find it more difficult to maintain such high pain thresholds. Charlotte noted that once she retired she did not participate in any sport or physical activity: 'I just can't go through the pain barrier anymore'. With age there is also an awareness of the risk of injury. Susan recounted that 'towards the end I got more frightened because you start thinking about what you're doing, you know, you start thinking that you're chucking yourself around'.

Pain and injury are not just physiological conditions that are felt within an individual. Pain and injury experiences are socially constructed. Marie explained how she 'did not like to say it was hurting as you were made to feel weedy, like you were putting it on...so sometimes you had to put up with the pain'. Charlotte also felt as though her pain was determined by others who defined what was and was not pain: 'it's your injury and you know how far you can push it.... It was like this attitude that an injury was always a fake injury, you know [the coaches] never really thought it hurt you because they can't feel the pain'. When asked why they trained and competed with pain and injuries, most replied with an answer not too dissimilar to 'you had to'. Susan said that she trained and competed when she was injured because 'You felt you had to because of the pressure from everybody else. The parents, the coaches, the peer pressure and the other gymnasts around you'. Another interviewee, Joanne, gave the following response:

> You are always going to get pain if you do gymnastics. Even, like, everyday training, I don't think there are many days when you don't have something that hurts from a pulled leg or something, so if you want to get to the top then you have to just train through them [sic] days.

It appears that gymnasts train and compete through pain and injuries for several different reasons. It may be an accumulation of pressure and expectations from influential others, and in social networks and beyond, and from the gymnasts' own perceptions that success cannot be gained without pain and injury. However, such a gain is only short term; the physical damage that can result from training and competing with pain and injuries may be long term. Susan discovered this: 'Now I am paying! I will probably have the after effects for the rest of my life'. Susan subsequently had to visit an osteopath every six weeks so that she could reduce severe back pain. Years of training have resulted in 'loose vertebrae and weak ligaments that do not support my neck'.

Despite the pain and injuries they faced, the gymnasts would do it all over again, expressing that they missed their sport. Such an approach to pain and injury may relate to over-conformity to the sport ethic, the context of social networks and the workplace in which they do their embodied emotion/work (Hughes and Coakley 1991; Nixon 1996). What is important is that these experiences had been significant in an embodied sense in their lives and have offered them excitement. How do we make sense of this?

Significant Excitement, Sport and Embodied Emotions

Elias and Dunning (1986), with the theory of **civilising processes** at the core of a model of human relations, developed a unique perspective on the relationship between sport and the emotions in their study of the sportisation of English folk pastimes. The importance of their observations lies in the fact that the early stages of the sportisation process in the 18th century set the tone for future sporting developments. In examining this early sportisation phase, Elias and Dunning concluded that these sporting forms mark attempts to prolong the emotional pleasure of victory. The mock battles of these folk games of football were symptomatic of a far-reaching change in the personality structure of human beings. This, in turn, was closely connected with specific changes in the power structure of society at large. In particular, the changing balance of power between the landed aristocracy, gentry and the rising bourgeoisie was to prove crucial. It is here that the function of sport forms becomes more evident.

One important feature of a civilising process is a marked narrowing of what is acceptable in public life. As a direct corollary of this, there is an increasing need for a social enclave in which socially approved, moderately pleasurable excitement can be aroused and expressed. A principal feature of global sport is the 'arousal of pleasurable forms of excitement' (Elias and Dunning 1986). According to Elias and Dunning, the significance of sport in relatively civilised, modern societies is based on the view that people, in growing numbers, have a socially conditioned psychological need to experience various kinds of spontaneous, elementary, unreflective yet pleasurable excitement. Therefore, the precise meaning and significance of sports activities is assessed in relation to a number of interrelated criteria. These include the degree of '**con-trolled decontrolling** of emotions'—the process by which people 'let go' in a disciplined manner; the degree to which emotions flow freely; the degree of eliciting or imitating of excitement akin to what is generated in real-life situations; the nature of the tension-balances created; and the degree to which the activity serves to counteract what Elias termed *stress tensions*. Here we are dealing with tension-balances of varying blends. The perpetual tension between routinisation and deroutinisation within activities is the principal source of sport dynamics: this 'shift to risk' is vital to the experiencing of these activities. Indeed, as societies grow more serious, the cultural centrality of leisure sport increases.

In rejecting the conventional view of work/leisure as mutually exclusive, Elias and Dunning map out what they term the **spare-time spectrum.** It is important to note that leisure activities are seen to fall into three forms: activities that are purely or mainly sociable; activities involving motility or movement; and activities that are mimetic. Mimetic activities vary considerably across the globe, both in terms of their intensity and style, but have basic common structural characteristics. They provide a make-believe setting that allows emotions to flow more easily, imitating the excitement produced by real-life situations, yet without their dangers or risks. Mimetic activities, locally constructed or globally generated, thus allow, within certain limits, for socially permitted self-centredness. Excitement is elicited by the creation of tensions: this can involve imaginary or controlled real danger, mimetic fear or pleasure, sadness or joy. The controlled decontrolling of excitement for Elias and Dunning (1986) lies at 'the heart of leisure sport'. The different moods evoked in this make-believe setting are the 'siblings' of those aroused in real-life situations. This applies whether the setting is a live theatre enactment of a Shakespearean tragedy, a computer golf game or a paint-ball 'war game'. These moods involve the experience of pleasurable excitement that is, according to Elias and Dunning, at the core of most play needs. Whereas both leisure and sports events involve pleasurable excitement, it is in sport, and especially in achievement sport, where struggles between human beings play a central part. Indeed, some global sport contests, such as the Rugby World Cup, more closely resemble real battles between hostile groups.

Other key features of this analysis of sport and the emotions deserve further consideration. The **mimetic sphere,** though creating imaginary settings, forms a distinct and integral part of social reality. It is no less real than any other part of social life. The manner in which the quest for enjoyable excitement finds expression in social institutions and customs also varies greatly over time and space. Local traditions are maintained and local meanings attached to global sport. There is no leisure activity without at least one element of the mimetic sphere—sociability, motility and mimesis—and more usually two or three elements combine with varying intensity.

In studying sport, pleasure and the emotions, Elias and Dunning focused on two interdependent questions. First, what are the characteristics of personal leisure needs in the more complex societies of our time; and second, what are the characteristics of the specific types of leisure events developed for the satisfaction of these needs? An additional question must be raised: How do global sport production and consumption processes reflect, create and/or fulfil these needs? Elias and Dunning are to be commended for providing an analysis of sport/games and of tension-balances in leisure activities more generally, avoiding the dichotomy between the micro- and macro-dimensions of emotional experience. In outlining the nature and extent of the emotional experiences involved in sport and leisure, these writers provide crucial insights into the interconnections between game dynamics, the mimetic sphere and civilising processes. However, this early work did not exhaust the debate about the gendered character of leisure practices nor the identity-formation qualities of achievement or leisure forms of sport (Dunning and Maguire, 1996; Maguire 1992).

As Dunning and Maguire (1996) argue, the quest for excitement is bound up in gender relations and the changing balance of power that contours and shapes the character of the global sport experience. Both achievement sport and leisure sport involve the quest not simply for unreflective excitement, but also for **exciting significance.** The symbolism attached to the sporting body should not be overlooked. Nor should we neglect the study of the gender order and the commodified forms of pleasure provided by global media sport. Analyses of these dimensions and questions require a multidisciplinary approach to the study of sport, the emotions and societies.

Debating Point: Are Sporting Pleasures False Needs or Genuine Desires?

In some classical Marxist accounts, sport is viewed as a form of **alienation** and spectators and consumers are viewed as cultural dupes (Brohm 1978; Hoch 1972; cf. Morgan 1994). The pleasures of popular culture are seen as the sugar-coated pill of ideological domination and control. In contrast, drawing on the work of Barthes (1975) and Bakhtin (1968), it can be argued that popular pleasures have the potential to reinforce hegemonic structures, form challenges to conventions and act as a resistance to dominant ideologies.

Duncan and Brummett, focusing on the screening of the 1988 Winter Olympic Games on U.S. television, examined three types of spectator pleasure (fetishism, voyeurism and narcissism) and the discursive, technological and social dimensions of televised sport spectating as the sources of these visual pleasures. They noted that 'sexually motivated voyeurism, while not openly encouraged by television producers, is always possible (and may be seen in camera angles and shots that are aimed at women's cleavages and buttocks)' (Duncan and Brummett 1989). Indeed, Fiske (1987) has himself noted that men faced with a set of 'macho' expectations that cannot be fulfilled in their occupations find in televised sport a highly attuned narcissistic outlet. This is a powerful critique of mediated sport and one that has been reinforced by other work (Rowe 1999; Wenner 1998). Is the picture as bleak as all this?

Barthes (1975) identified two types of pleasure produced in the reading of a text (or the watching of a film). These pleasures, *plaisir* and *jouissance,* are located not in the text itself but in its conjuncture with the reader. For Barthes, there is an 'economy' of the text where words and images in the text are exchanged for pleasure. The commodity the reader or spectator buys is not a sense of the world but rather the pleasure (*plaisir*) in the processes of representing and figuring the world. Two points need to be made here. First, human beings seek pleasure and avoid displeasure. Second, pleasure in advanced Western societies produces two forms of policing, political and psychoanalytical, that combine to channel and control the leisure of subordinate groups into ideologically acceptable forms. The history of sport highlights this very well.

Yet, for Barthes, the roots of *jouissance* lie primarily in ideological evasion. *Jouissance* involves the pleasure of the body, experienced through heightened sensualities that relate to human nature rather than culture. *Jouissance* escapes both the control of culture and meaning. It is always erotic and its peak is properly described as orgasm. This orgasm occurs at the breakdown of culture. In both elite achievement sport and leisure sport, unpredictable moments of joy or sadness can arguably engender *jouissance*. The feelings created in watching athletes produce peak performances or cope with the despair of defeat arguably involve a combination of *plaisir* and *jouissance.* That is, such occasions not only allow for the expressing of emotions and an identity that social life frequently represses (*plaisir*), but also create and sustain emotions that, because of their presence and intensity, lie outside of cultural and ideological domination.

The importance of this lies in the claim that the reader, the viewer or spectator of the sport form has some control over the production of meaning. Readers, viewers or spectators can both resist and embrace pleasures. For Barthes, popular pleasures are those that empower the subordinate. These pleasures offer political resistance, even if only momentarily and on a limited terrain. Drawing on Barthes, writers such as Fiske not only argue that popular pleasures can be resistive and subversive but that there exists a plurality of pleasures. Fiske proposed a centrifugal model allowing for a diversity of pleasures that 'suggests a line of force in active opposition to the centripetal force that attempts to centre control at the point of ideological and social unity' (1987). Pleasurable emotional experiences therefore help to preserve and legitimate the diversity within and between societies. Such an approach is far removed from the 'bread and circuses' interpretation of modern leisure forms put forward by some observers (Hoch 1972; Brohm 1978). Pleasurable experiences are not simply occasions contrived by the elite for the masses to consume; pleasure acts can be signs of resistance and counter-cultural activity.

This reinterpretation of popular pleasures also draws on the work of Bakhtin (1968), who examined the role of carnivals in society. For Bakhtin, carnivals involve the pleasures of physical excess and offensiveness. Both are bodily pleasures that stand in opposition to conventional morality, discipline and social control. The body is central to the carnival experience. **Carnival** is characterised by laughter, extremes and 'bad taste'. The body is subject to excesses, exaggeration, grotesqueness and ridicule and, for spectators, carnival involves an exaggeration of the pleasure of looking. The style of clothing and the activities surrounding the London Marathon is a good example of this. Bakhtin interprets carnivals as testimonies to the power of the 'low' to insist on their right to maintain cultural space. Carnivalesque forms celebrate a temporary liberation from the prevailing truth and established order with the suspension of all hierarchical rank, privileges, norms and prohibitions. But though it embodies creative, playful freedom, it is itself an exaggeration of play: it inverts the usual rules and turns the world upside down. Carnival is a parody of 'extracarnival life' and belongs on the borderline between art and life. Interestingly, Fiske (1987) sees carnival as standing in opposition to sport. That is, carnival celebrates the triumph of evil, unfairness and inequality; as such, it is antiestablishment. In contrast, for Fiske, sport shows a respect for rules, equality, fairness and goodness; as such, it reflects the dominant ideology by which democratic capitalism values itself.

Is this really the case? It is true to say that folk recreations are closer in some ways to the carnivalesque spirit (Maguire 1999). Yet, while these qualities did undergo significant changes in the emergence of modern sport, they did not disappear altogether. There is much in the sport experience that could be interpreted in a similar light. A little carnival is left in the spectating practices of some sport subcultures. Think, for example, of how the Afro-Caribbean celebration of cricket subverts the dominant English meaning of the game. Bakhtin's work thus assists in the general exploration of the ways in which popular sporting pleasures can evade, resist or scandalise ideology and social control. This resistance refers to the refusal to accept the social identity proposed by the dominant ideology and the social control that goes with it. Though popular pleasures are not necessarily a direct challenge to the social system, they do resist incorporation and maintain a sense of difference. As such, they allow for the potential for resistance or subversion to take place, such as the emergence of the snowboarding subculture and the development of extreme sports. But this quest to read popular pleasures as a form of resistance is seen by some as overlooking issues of political economy and the global context in which they are produced (Maguire 1999). The jury is still out on this issue.

Towards a Sociological Model of Sport and the Emotions

So how do we construct a sociological analysis of sport and embodied emotions? Let us review the various approaches to this area. Elias and Dunning provide an analysis of sport/game dynamics and tension-balances in leisure activities more generally, which avoids the dichotomy between the micro- and macro-dimensions of emotional experience. Such dichotomous thinking arguably characterises symbolic interactionist work on sport and the emotions. By virtue of the elasticity and fixity of rules, written or otherwise, quasi-autonomous networks of interdependent action emerge. In other words, these networks can only be fully understood if they are recognised as interdependent parts of a wider social structure. In teasing out the nature and extent of the emotional experiences involved, reference to the interconnections between game dynamics, the mimetic sphere and the civilising process thus becomes essential.

The functions that Elias and Dunning attribute to sport, with their emphasis on the quest for excitement and manly identity, capture only a part, albeit an important part, of the character of the leisure experience. Both achievement sport and leisure sport involve the quest for significant excitement or 'exciting significance' (Maguire 1992). In this sense, symbolic interactionist research rightly draws attention to the symbolic nature of embodied leisure experiences. To argue this perspective, however, should not blind the analysis to the existence of the 'masculine gaze' and forms of pleasure to which feminism and cultural studies draw attention. In addition, while Elias and Dunning (1986) note that sport and art forms share the same mimetic function in producing an enjoyable and controlled decontrolling of emotions, they distinguish between them through the character of sport as a battle resembling real battles fought between rival groups. The quest is for battles enacted playfully in a contrived context that can produce enjoyable battle excitement with a minimum of injuries to the human participants. Compared with the arts, the scope for the exercise of the imagination involved appears to be of a rather restricted and heavily rule-bound kind.

The symbolic interactionist perspective, therefore, rightly forces the researcher to confront the issue of the social construction and presentation of emotions. Emotions are seen to involve interwoven cognitive and affective dimensions. As such, an understanding of how various emotional vocabularies are used, and how some aspects of emotions are culturally relative and others culturally universal, is important. Our ability to describe feelings varies between cultures and may be more sophisticated than the actual physiological processes involved. Although Elias and Dunning (1986) are correct to point to differences within and between mimetic events, in doing so they appear to have underplayed the fact that identity formation in sport also involves the quest for self-realisation, the presentation of embodied emotions and emotion management (Denzin 1984; Rail 1990).

Symbolic interactionist research, however, falls short when examining the self-realisation dimension of the identity-forming qualities of sport, largely ignoring other dimensions that cultural studies, feminism and figurational sociology correctly highlight. For example, the historical and comparative structures on which social acts rest are overlooked. Furthermore, such research is more concerned with 'micro-worlds' than, following the leads of Elias and Dunning, Fiske and Bakhtin, teasing out how specific patterns of interaction are interwoven with other sets of interdependencies. As a consequence, such research fails to grasp that self-realisation is achieved in the company of 'others'. Furthermore, the quest for this self-realisation is indicative of the main long-term features of sports/leisure relations—namely, commodification, individuation, privatisation and pacification (Rojek 1985). In emphasising the ability of the person to subvert the text of a book in a pleasurable manner, Barthes' work may also overlook these broader societal trends.

For Fiske (1987), the emphasis in **consumer culture** on body maintenance and appearance is an important part of these broader societal trends. Identifying two basic embodied categories within consumer culture, the 'inner' and the 'outer' body, Featherstone argues that the 'prime purpose of the maintenance of the inner body becomes the enhancement of the appearance of the outer body' (Featherstone 1983). The implications of this observation for the study of sport and the emotions are considerable. It suggests, for example, that activities in the spare-time spectrum, and thereby the fitness industry, involving body maintenance and mimetic events may not solely be devoted to a controlled decontrolling of emotions. Rather, they are also bound up with contouring and shaping one's appearance in relation to the images derived from hegemonic forms of masculinity and consumer capitalism. What we may be witnessing is a shift to 'emotion leisure display' in which the 'performing self' plays a crucial part.

Clearly, recognition of bodily appearance also has implications for the study of the forms of emotion management enacted in sports / leisure lifestyles. The staging of emotions thus involves not only the creation of tension-balances, in which a pleasurable controlled decontrolling of emotions takes place, it also reflects the concomitant need to enhance appearance and thus maintain one's status within the mainstream of patriarchal societies and consumer culture. But the images of consumer culture do not merely serve to stimulate false needs fostered within the individual. As Elias and Dunning observe with regard to their study of sport, leisure and the emotions, such needs are genuine. What must be grasped in any future research agenda, however, is that the mimetic activities that allow the expression and fulfilment of such emotional needs are, in early-21st-century Western societies, bound up in consumer culture. Informed by the approaches outlined here, we need to examine how contemporary sporting tastes and desires are created and sustained and how they relate to genuine embodied emotional needs and desires (Bourdieu 1984). Only then will researchers be better placed to evaluate people's welcome to the sporting pleasure dome.

Summary

This chapter has sought to highlight several key issues. First, attention has been directed to how emotions are socially constructed and are patterned along cultural lines. Second, it has been emphasised that an understanding of emotions is crucial in explaining the experience of sport. Third, consideration has to be given to a range of different approaches that seek to explain the interconnectedness between sport, the emotions and societies. These approaches provide insights that help make sense of the experiences of participants and spectators alike. Finally, this chapter has sought to link ideas of pleasure, carnival, consumer culture and the emotions to an understanding of sport in modern societies.

Key Terms and Concepts

alienation	controlled decontrolling
carnival	embodied acts
civilising processes	emotions
consumer culture	exciting significance

feeling rules	*plaisir*
fetishism	pleasure
hinge	scopophilia
jouissance	scripts
mimetic sphere	self-feeling
narcissism	spare-time spectrum
nature versus nurture	voyeurism

Review Questions

1. Critically examine the idea that emotions are simply physiological states.
2. In what ways might an understanding of the concept of pleasure help make sense of the modern sport experience?
3. Discuss, in detail, the debate concerning whether emotions are physiologically determined or socially constructed.
4. In what ways might it be argued that sports spectating and participation are embodied acts?
5. How might an understanding of the concepts of self-feeling, scripts and feeling rules help explain sporting emotions?
6. Critically examine how pain is integral to the emotional experience of some sports subcultures.
7. Discuss, in detail, the concepts of significant excitement, spare-time spectrum and the mimetic sphere and apply them to a sport subculture of your choice.
8. In what ways might sport be said to involve a controlled decontrolling of the emotions?
9. Are sporting pleasures a reflection of the false needs or genuine desires expressed in and through consumer culture?
10. Explain how the concept of carnival is useful in making sense of modern sport spectacles.

Projects

1. Videotape a sports programme. Using qualitative content analysis, examine how the emotions on display are framed and represented.
2. Observe a university sports event. Taking field notes, record key moments and individuals. Interview a sample of players and ask them what emotions they experienced during the game.
3. Choose a sports team event that you are familiar with. Interview a sample of spectators for each team and ask them what they witnessed and experienced. Compare and contrast their accounts.
4. Attend both a women's and a men's event involving the same sport. Compare and contrast the emotions on display by the players involved. How would you explain the differences and similarities observed?

5. Using either newspaper or television coverage of a 'brutal body contact' sport event in which several injuries occur, critically examine how these emotional experiences are reported by the media and explained by the participants. How would you make sense of what you have found?

6. Using the concept of spare-time spectrum, interview a sample of students and allocate the tasks, chores and activities they are involved in to the various categories described. How would you explain these patterns?

CHAPTER
12

SPORT, GENDER AND SOCIAL RELATIONS

© Sport, The Library

Objectives

After completing this chapter, you should be able to

- define and discuss the concepts of sex and gender;
- identify and evaluate the networks of power that characterise gender relations in sport;
- understand the historical development of sport as a 'male preserve';
- discuss the ways in which sport is a site for the construction of feminine and masculine identities;
- critically analyse the claim that sport is a site for the reinforcement of traditional gender ideals; and
- evaluate the extent to which sport provides opportunities for people to challenge and change traditional gender relations.

The study of **gender relations** has become increasingly popular over the past two decades within the sociology of sport. When sociologists speak of gender relations, they are primarily concerned with the socio-cultural differences between females and males that are produced, reproduced and challenged in specific social contexts. The notion of **gender** is distinct from that of **sex,** even though the two are often used synonymously in everyday language and thought. Sex refers to the biological and physical differences between women and men.

It is important to distinguish between the concepts of gender and sex because not all of the differences between females and males are biological. Some differences, and often they are ones based on the biological, have become more important than others in justifying established attitudes about and inequalities between men and women. Different theories connected to gender have been used and developed as sociologists of sport try to understand the relationships between gender, power, sport, societies and culture. Several important issues are explored in the literature concerning both women and men in relation to sport and equality of opportunity, participation rates and patterns, coaching and administration, ideas and beliefs about femininity, masculinity and sexuality and the development of the superiority of males and maleness. These studies have led several authors to speak of sport as a 'male preserve' (Dunning 1986, 1999; Theberge 1985).

Here, some of the key issues concerning gender relations in sport are addressed. Broadly speaking, the aims of the chapter are threefold. First, it explores the processes through which sports have, for the most part, been constructed by males and for males (Kidd 1987). Second, it maps out the ways in which sport reflects and reinforces traditional gender relations. Third, it explores the nature and extent of some of the challenges and changes that can be made to established ideas of gender by people involved in sport.

Sport As Male, Manly and Masculine

Several authors give detailed and insightful accounts of the ways in which modern sport has, over time, been created around the assumptions, values and ideologies of males, maleness and masculinity (Dunning 1986; Hargreaves 1994; Kidd 1987; Maguire 1986; Messner and Sabo 1990). The extant literature concerning the development of modern sport forms reveals complex histories with key historical moments that have had an impact on the gendered nature of sports. It is widely noted that the Victorian period in Britain gave rise to sports characterised by organised structures and standardised rules (Dunning and Sheard 1979; Hargreaves 1994). In relation to issues of gender, sports were created around the beliefs and values of middle- and upper-class males. It was in institutions such as public schools, universities, churches and private clubs that sport came to represent all that was manly at this time. Those (men) who were key decision makers within education, business, the military and recreational settings encouraged men's participation in sport as a way of developing physical skill and strength, mental acumen, a gentlemanly demeanour and a sense of fair play. Playing and being good at games such as rugby and cricket or track and field events symbolised masculinity. Sport became what Messner (1987) described as a **masculinity-validating experience.**

It should be emphasised that the development of sport along male lines occurred within the context of wider social structures and gender relations. Rapidly increasing industrialisation at the end of the 18th and beginning of the 19th centuries gave rise to, amongst many other factors, distinct divisions of labour between women and men. Women, who generally managed the household and took on the day-to-day responsibilities of raising children, were significantly dependent on men, who tended to be the major breadwinners. The prestige, status and superiority afforded to men in society became marked at this time. 'Real men' were defined by physical strength and intellectual superiority, qualities celebrated in sport. Women were assigned roles associated with their reproductive capacity and assumed suitability for passive activities in the home. Established ideals of femininity, that is, passivity, frailty, emotionality, gentleness and dependence, were in stark opposition to the strenuous tasks required for playing sport. There was a strong belief that these male and female traits were innate, biological and somehow fixed. Hence, the marginalisation of women and dominance of men in sport came to be viewed as the natural order of things (Hargreaves 1994).

Biological differences between women and men have been central to arguments that favour the exclusion and/or limited inclusion of women in sport. Men have repeatedly been claimed to be larger and more powerful than women and, hence, naturally suited to and superior at sport. It was commonly argued, often by powerful men in institutions such as the medical professions, education and government, that women's ability to bear children would be damaged if they participated in strenuous activity. In any case, being physical was not appropriate for a (middle-class) 'lady'. So, ladies tended not to participate in sports and games. The actions and sentiments of prominent men, and to an extent some women, further perpetuated the taken-for-granted messages about women's inferior status both on and off the sportsfield.

Broadly speaking, there has been a long-term development towards what is commonly termed a **patriarchal** society. This is one in which males dominate over females and where established codes of masculinity are naturalised, taken for granted and reflected in everyday practices, including sports and games. Whilst it is not the case that all men are dominant over all women in society, the structures and ideologies of sports were, and in varying degrees remain, centred on the belief that women are and should be subordinate to men. Coakley (1998) refers to this idea as **gender logic,** which, it can be argued, is one of the most enduring examples of gendered inequality even in today's sports settings. As Paul Willis (1994) states, 'there is a massive feeling in our society that a woman has no business flexing her muscle'.

Established notions of **gender roles** and particularly of masculinity and femininity are not static. Gender relations shift with the passage of time and are contoured by the structures and belief systems of wider social life and specific sports settings that are themselves marked by processes of change. Established codes of gender exist at the same time as emergent and residual ones. In addition, the issue of gender is not one that solely concerns the plight of women. Indeed, it is important not to think of women and men as homogenous, undifferentiated groups or that all men oppress all women. It seems more useful to furthering an understanding of the complexities of gender relations if we are aware that some men are more powerful and influential than some women and, indeed, other men, and that some women are empowered at the expense of some other women and some men. Put simply, at any moment in history and in specific sport contexts, there are competing masculinities and **femininities** (Messner and Sabo 1990; Willis 1994). Both women and men can experience the constraining and enabling features of the sport experience. The sections that follow explore some of the ways in which contemporary sport provides a site for the reinforcement of and resistance to traditional gendered practices and beliefs.

Debating Point: Does Sport Reflect and Reinforce Traditional Gender Relations?

Sociologists of sport explain that gender is continually created and re-created during an individual's lifetime and across the generations through long-term processes of **socialisation** (Coakley 1998; Dunning 1999; Hargreaves 1994; Lorber 1994). Human beings learn appropriate ways of being male and female in and through an array of interactions with people in their families, peer groups, educational settings, work environments and exposure to media images. This learning process occurs from birth through childhood and adolescence and throughout adult life. Research has shown that child-rearing and educational practices are significant in the development of internalised and enduring dispositions of masculinity and femininity (Scraton 1992; Sharpe 1994). From an early age, boys tend to be encouraged to be overtly physical, whereas girls' physicality is more restricted in terms of space and place. Girls are often raised to be relatively quiet and passive.

Physical education practices are a good example of the ways in which traditional gender roles and ideas are reinforced. Gender divisions are reflected in the formal physical education curricula of many schools, where girls and boys participate in gender-appropriate sports and are taught separately and in accordance with traditional ideas about what girls and boys should and shouldn't do in relation to physical activity. Girls engage in activities that encourage less strenuous degrees of physicality, in restricted space that avoids bodily contact, whereas boys are encouraged to be aggressive, dominating and physically competitive. Children can often be seen to adopt these segregationist practices in more informal settings such as the playground, where boys play more vigorous games and take up more space and girls tend to be relegated to the sidelines where they play more passive games. Figure skating and gymnastics, netball in Britain and softball in the United States tend to be thought of as girls' sports. Rugby, soccer, American football and ice-hockey are sports that boys and men play.

In her observations of space, place and gender, Doreen Massey (1994) emphasises that 'spaces and places, and our sense of them are gendered through and through'. Soccer, American football and rugby pitches and weight training rooms are predominantly male places. When women do 'invade' these sports spaces, the reactions to and attitudes about their involvement is often dismissive or derogatory, and this serves to put women firmly in their subordinate place. This **gendered space** reinforces traditional ideas about women, men and gender-appropriate physical activity. Hargreaves (1994) and Young (1990) also make the point that socio-cultural ideals and practices have an impact on the physical/biological development of boys and girls. If boys are more physically active, it is not unreasonable to expect them to have a greater degree of muscular development, physiological capability and motor co-ordination as they mature into adulthood. Not only do experiences of physical activity in childhood affect what we assume as gender-appropriate, they also influence what we are physically able to do. Since the markers of achievement in sport are male/masculine and based on men's achievements, it has been continually difficult for women to realise their own achievement goals. 'Swifter, higher and stronger' sporting records have been achieved by men. If women are constantly compared against these records, they can never match up. It would appear, then, that sport does reflect and reinforce traditional gender relations.

Shaping Up to Genderhood

When women do participate in sports, their performances are often labelled as inferior and described in rather derogatory terms. When someone has thrown, run, jumped or played badly, he or she has performed 'like a girl' (Coakley 1998; Sharpe 1994). This reinforces the notion that men are physically and naturally superior to women. Of course, there are women who enjoy the opportunity to be aggressive and dominant in sport and are comfortable with the development of a muscular body. Yet, the appearance of power and strength and the display of aggression by women in sport do not fit in with established ideals of femininity. These women are often treated with suspicion. Their sexuality is called into question and they can be labelled as 'tomboys', 'butches' or 'dykes'. So great is the fear of masculinisation that the International Olympic Committee (IOC) still enforces a sex chromatin test for women as a way of verifying their sex (Ferguson-Smith and Ferris 1991).

The separation of the sexes in the context of physical activity continues in voluntary adult sports such as in British universities, recreational teams and private clubs. As Coakley (1998) notes, private golf clubs epitomise a resistance to equal opportunity along gender lines (as well as class and ethnic lines). Women are often excluded from taking out membership, voting on club policies, gaining access to some bars, restaurants and car-parking areas and playing at popular/peak times. In the health club setting, activities are also structured along gendered lines. In gyms and fitness centres, it is more usual for men to build muscular, strong bodies in the gym whilst women dominate the dance studio, where they sculpt slim, lithe, feminine bodies in exercise classes such as aerobics (Maguire and Mansfield 1998; Mansfield and Maguire 1999).

According to Biskup and Pfister (1999), one of the dominant ways in which children and adolescents are oriented towards traditional **gender identities** and hierarchies is via role models and idols. Popular celebrity figures from movies, music and sport symbolise and maintain established ideals of gendered action, emotion and appearance. For these authors, sporting role models and idols tend to be men who are, in the main, revered by boys. Male sports stars represent ideals of masculine strength, aggression and dedication, and these are the qualities that boys strive for. Their findings revealed that boys wanted to be like their favourite sportsmen not only in relation to performance but also appearance. In addition, famous and visible sportspeople were not held up as role models for girls, who would rather that male sports stars were their boyfriends. The authors conclude that in and through a variety of sports experiences girls often come to embody traditional gender roles that focus on the idea that women's lives should be contoured by **heterosexuality,** marriage and child-rearing. Boys' experiences in sport teach them that strength, power, skill and mental and physical toughness are qualities that make 'a man out of you'.

The dominant ideal of masculinity that is most often represented in sport is one that can be limiting and restrictive to some men as well as women. It is rare that opportunities are available for men to participate, without prejudice, in sports that are not based on established 'macho' values of aggression and domination. Indeed, boys and men who are not good at sports or who do not participate often have their masculinity called into question and can be labelled as 'gay', 'puffs' or 'queers'. Not only is it appropriate for women to be heterosexually feminine, so too is it the norm for men to be heterosexually masculine. Curry (1991) makes some insightful comments on this issue in his research on how men talk and behave in the locker room (changing room) environment. He notes that the men he studied often talked about sex (with women) and treated women as sexual objects. He concludes that this type of behaviour can encourage rape cultures and an extreme intolerance of **homosexuality (homophobia).** It is assumed that only 'real men' play sports and that homosexual sportsmen are an exception or non-existent in sporting environments. Sport has developed as a preserve of established masculinity, and homophobic attitudes and practices help to maintain the structures and ideologies of sport that define it as a bastion of traditional male privilege, power and prestige (Messner and Sabo 1990). Homophobic behaviour and language in sport not only marginalise gay men, but, as Fusco (1998) notes, also operate to 'silence lesbians'. The message in sport is that it is wrong to be gay and that sports are not the place for lesbians or gay men. It should be added that in societies where the cultural norm is heterosexuality, deviation in any form, be it homosexuality, bisexuality or any other sexual expression, is a threat to the established order. In her research about the experiences of lesbian sportswomen, Fusco highlights that an emphasis on heterosexuality perpetuates the myth that something is wrong with **lesbianism** and that women should look and behave in traditionally feminine ways. Being a lesbian is most commonly seen as a threat in sporting environments because it challenges the norms of heterosexuality that are assumed to be an inextricable part of the established masculine ideology. Discrimination, ostracism and the silencing of lesbian athletes are based on the established belief that heterosexuality is 'natural and right' (Fusco 1998).

Sport, Images and Gender Identities

In an increasingly image-conscious society, there is a tendency for people and especially women to be preoccupied with bodily appearance. It seems impossible to escape the message that the female body beautiful is slim and toned. It should be recognised that there are many competing and ambiguous body images that maintain the dominance of (hetero)sexually attractive female bodies. The body beautiful is not just represented by the waif-like models of fashion. Several images, particularly ones from elite sports, such as Anna Kournikova (tennis) and Gabrielle Reese (beach volleyball) can be identified as symbolic of feminine beauty, success, discipline and control. Yet, the sporting performance of these women is often marginalised at the expense of the sexual image. Whilst it was noted previously that there are many images of femininity, contemporary beauty is characterised, to a large extent and arguably on a global scale, by the lean, toned, fit and healthy sports images that are presented to us. These bodies signify success and (hetero)sexual attractiveness.

In a recent campaign to raise money for the Wheelchair Sports Worldwide foundation, TAG Heuer have brought together some of the world's most famous and fittest sports performers to be photographed in fashion clothing and model poses (Blanchard 2000). The elite performers in these photographs are both men and women. Yet the images portrayed in the men's attire reflect masculine qualities such as strength, power and aggression, and those of the women display the sexually erotic and alluring qualities associated with feminine ideals. Colin Jackson and Boris Becker are dressed in a gold body shield and chain mail tunic respectively, symbolic of the protective armour of war, battle and male aggression. Marion Jones is dressed in leather hot pants and bra, which speaks more of eroticism and sexual bondage than of athletic ability, and Monica Seles strikes a rather alluring and provocative pose in a black dress.

Professional sportswomen, like their male counterparts, are successful, dedicated and talented. It is encouraging that they too have the opportunity to reap financial rewards from commercial endorsements in the way that male sports stars can. Many successful sportswomen are empowered in this way. In the case of tennis and golf, some elite women performers receive relatively large prize winnings and receive relatively extensive media attention. Yet, it is also apparent that unless these women are clearly (hetero)sexually attractive, they are unlikely to be offered large commercial sponsorship deals or receive positive press in the media. Fusco (1998) notes that Martina Navratilova's open expression of her lesbian identity meant that she became too controversial for many sponsors, despite being a highly talented and successful tennis player. As Barrett (2000) states, 'Her endorsement income, though considerable, would undoubtedly have been higher had she not made public several lesbian relationships'. So, being athletic and lesbian seems to present multiple reasons for discrimination. Indeed, when the stratified nature of identity is considered, gender is but one dimension on which prejudice is based. Other factors that affect gender inequality include age, class, race and ethnicity, (dis)ability and sexuality. In the case of Navratilova, there seem to be multiple reasons for discriminating against her. She threatens the ideals of feminine appearance and physicality as well as threatening established beliefs about sexuality.

The path to elite professional sport status is a difficult one for any athlete. Yet institutional support for women still falls behind that of men. There is evidence of reduced financial resources and facilities for women (Coakley 1998); less media attention and marginalisation and trivialisation of women's sport by the media (Creedon 1994); and a marked inequality in the number of women in coaching, administrative and decision-making positions in sport (Hargreaves 1994; White and Brackenridge, 1985). As Coakley (1998) notes, the institutionalised marginalisation of women in sport can be seen clearly in what is 'probably the most powerful administrative body in global sports', the IOC. Figures for 1998 reveal that before 1980 there were no women on the IOC committee, and after this date the maximum number of women members was 7 as opposed to 99 men. By 2005 the IOC aims to achieve a 20 percent target for women in decision-making positions (Jennings 1996). This might well represent a move towards **gender equity**, but at a very slow rate. Without women's voices being heard and taken seriously in powerful sports institutions, it will remain difficult for women to have their interests expressed and realised.

There is still a clear inequality in the financial rewards available to women as compared to men in several professional sports. Take tennis as an example. The Grand Slam championships consist of the Australian, French and U.S. Opens, and Wimbledon. As an example of increasing equality in prize money payouts for men and women, the U.S. Open offers equal sums of $750,000 for the men's and women's singles title. Yet in every other Grand Slam tournament, the men's singles prize money is greater than the women's. Table 12.1 lists the men's and women's prize monies for the singles competitions.

Table 12.1
Prize Money for Grand Slam Tennis Championships, 1999

	Total prize money	Men's singles First prize	Women's singles First prize
Australian Open (Aus$)	11,008,700	722,000	679,000
French Open (FF—French francs)	64,825,800	4,040,000	3,840,000
The Championships Wimbledon (£—Pounds sterling)	7,595,330	455,000	409,000
U.S. Open (US$)	14,503,000	750,000	750,000

Data from Barrett 2000.

In the men's game, prize money figures are issued by the ATP tour. Earnings from official playing sources, where entry is based on merit, are listed (circuit bonuses, play-offs and team events). Davis Cup, invitation events and commercial endorsements are not included. Andre Agassi was the highest prize money winner for 1999, earning $4,269,265. In addition, 4 men earned more than $2 million for the year, 17 men earned above $1 million and 42 won over $500,000. In comparison, figures issued for the women by the Corel WTA tour revealed the following. For earnings from official tournaments, again where entry is gained on merit alone (not including Federation Cup, exhibition events and endorsement fees), Martina Hingis was the highest earner, banking $3,291,780 in 1999. In total, 4 women earned more than $2 million, 5 women secured more than $1 million and 15 earned greater than $500,000. Both male and female tennis players earn a considerable amount in prize money from their playing achievements. But overall, men still earn more in prize money than women, and more men earn more money than women on their respective tours.

Several studies have explored the structures, ideologies and experiences of women who have increasingly become involved in recreational and competitive physical activities and professional sports (Birrell and Cole 1994; Cahn 1994; Cohen 1993; Hargreaves 1994; Nelson 1994; Rail 1998). Along with this increased participation and opportunity, there has arguably been a widening acceptance of female strength, power and musculature. Nevertheless, traditional ideas about what women can and cannot do with their bodies and what they should and should not look like still contour the experiences of many women.

In their conversations with female bodybuilders, Miller and Penz (1991) highlight that women's expertise and achievements can be used as a means of colonising the male preserve. To some extent, it is reasonable to suggest that women who engage in the practice of building large muscles are rejecting conventional ideals of feminine beauty by remodelling their bodies as they choose. Nevertheless, the authors note that female bodybuilders are still conforming to traditional pressure on women to correct 'problematic' aspects of their appearance. Obel (1996) agrees that the muscled bodies of women who bodybuild challenge traditional notions of femininity. Yet at the same time, differential rules and judging criteria for women reinforce dominant notions of what it is to be feminine. In competitive events, for example, female bodybuilders should not be 'too bulky'. Judging criteria for women incorporate the notion that the size of their muscles must be balanced with displays of feminine deportment, shape and attitude. To stay within the bounds of femininity, competitive women bodybuilders wear extensive amounts of makeup, dye their hair blond and often undergo surgery for breast augmentation (St. Martin and Gavey 1996). Despite displaying heavily muscled bodies that may be resistant to feminine ideals, these women are still shaped into femininity via the rules of competitive bodybuilding.

That women have become more involved in physical activity is, in part, attributable to an increased emphasis on health and fitness during the latter half of the 20th century. Many of the practices and techniques involved in these activities emphasise the established feminine ideals of slimness, tone and (hetero)sexual attractiveness. In her work on women and aerobics, Markula (1995) argues that 'aerobicizing' women participate because they are persuaded that they can be firm, shapely, fit, sexy, strong and thin. Whilst there are many reasons that women participate in aerobics and other health and fitness activities, the main motivation is weight loss and the construction of a slender, muscularly toned body (Maguire and Mansfield 1998; Mansfield and Maguire 1999). The women who were involved in these studies revealed a dominant aspiration to be slim, which represents part of the established feminine 'look' and is associated with (hetero)sexual attractiveness, youth, health, vitality and longevity.

Debating Point: Can Sport Challenge Traditional Gender Relations?

Many of the examples already discussed provide evidence that involvement in sport can be constraining for some girls, some women and some men. Sports are organised in such a way that they can restrict participation opportunities and trivialise performances on the basis of traditional beliefs about gender and gender relations. It is also the case, however, that many people are provided with several potential opportunities to become empowered by being involved in sport in spite of traditional gendered ideology. Although there is a tendency to presume that male homosexuality is rare in sport, for example, some research has shown that there are many gay men competing in sports at recreational and elite levels. Whilst these sportsmen often fear derogatory and violent responses if they publicise their sexual orientation (Messner 1992), there are events such as the Gay Games that allow gay athletes to compete in a relatively unprejudiced environment.

Some women gain personally from their sporting achievements. They can experience feelings of independence, confidence and increased self-esteem and, as previously noted in the case of professional sport, some women gain considerable financial wealth and worldwide recognition from sporting success. The extent to which sport is oppressive and liberating for women is culturally specific and related to the political and economic conditions in which women live out their lives.

A cursory glance at the figures for female involvement might support the argument that participation rates and opportunities for women in sport have increased over the past 100 years and the rate of this escalation has been more rapid in the latter half of the 20th century. But a more in-depth analysis reveals that the continuing debate surrounding the involvement of women in sport is more complex than this. The progressive and emancipatory features of the history of women's sport is more relevant for women in countries such as the United States and Great Britain, where a focus on women's rights more broadly, and in sport specifically, has been a relatively dominant feature of social change. In countries such as Kenya, Nigeria, Ethiopia, Saudi Arabia and Algeria, the inferior status of women in sport is exaggerated by wider social factors such as poverty, famine, political instability and religion. Even in so-called developed countries, the relatively established status of women in sport is marked by inequalities between specific groups of women on the basis of race/ethnicity, age, social class, (dis)ability and political and economic dimensions. In many sports played by women in developed Western countries, for example, white, middle-class, young women tend to be advantaged by increased parental encouragement, financial security, opportunity and access.

Gender, Women's Rights and Cultural Differences

In relation to cross-cultural participation patterns, religion is a significant factor in the restriction and prohibition of female involvement in

sport. Different religious ideologies have different effects on the experiences of women in sport (Hargreaves 1994). There has been some
research on Islamic beliefs and their influence as oppressive to Muslim
women. The Muslim code of purdah has, in particular, prevented
women from being involved in sport. Amongst other things, this code
forbids the display of women's bodies to men. Participating on a public
sports stage in contemporary Western sports clothing that tends to put
female bodies on display is seen by many defenders of the Muslim faith
as threatening the gender values and gender power relations of their
culture.

This puts into context the condemnation of Algerian athlete Hassiba
Boulmerka. Her athletic achievements have been visible on a global
sports stage. They include gold medals in the 1500m at the 1991 World
Championships and 1992 Olympics. The most aggressive and threatening response to her sports participation came from the Muslim fundamentalist party, the FIS (Islamic Salvation Front/Front Islamique du
Salut) (Hargreaves 1994; Morgan 1998). Boulmerka was a target for
those wanting to strengthen the codes of Islam and reject Western ideas
about women. It is possible to argue that this is an example of an
enduring restriction on the progressive liberation of women in Muslim
societies. Yet her achievements have been widely acclaimed by some
Muslim people as a positive image for contemporary Muslim women.
As Morgan (1998) notes, Boulmerka herself emphasises the positive
experience of sport despite receiving death threats from fundamentalist
factions and being forced to live in exile. She has publicly highlighted the
potential of sport to improve health, self-esteem, control of one's life and
individual striving. She also speaks of her achievements as serving to
strengthen her sense of Algerian nationality and religious beliefs, and
they have encouraged her to spread more positive messages about the
Muslim faith than those conveyed by the extreme and often violent
behaviours of fundamentalist groups. She notes that the code of purdah
is not necessarily hostile and repressive towards women. She is keen to
blend contemporary ideas about equal rights for women with more
traditional Islamic ideology.

The success of her campaign has had some positive impact on
other female Algerian athletes. At the 2000 Olympics in Sydney,
110,000 people saw Nouria Merah-Benida win gold in the 1500m. Like
Boulmerka, Merah-Benida has publicly stated that she hopes her athletic success can enhance sporting opportunities for Arab women and in
some way improve their day-to-day experiences of life. Rather than
being subjugated by the pervasive gendered ideology of their culture,
the message of women like Boulmerka and Merah-Benida encourages
the idea that there are alternative ways of living out gendered lives that
may not necessarily fit into existing structures and ideologies.

The history of the Olympic Games is a particularly good example of the achievements, failures and battles for recognition and involvement of women in sport. Revived in 1896, the Modern Olympics have continued to resist women's involvement and were developed under the ideology of Baron Pierre de Coubertin, who believed that it was unnatural for women to play sports and that Olympic sports should provide a forum for the display of male athleticism. There has been gradual progress towards increasing involvement of women since 1896, when there were no female participants at the Games in Athens, to 3,684 female participants at Atlanta in 1996. Still, the 1996 figure falls very much short of the male participation of 7,059 (Coakley 1998).

That 197 countries are now represented at the Olympic Games demonstrates the massive global scale of this sports event. More women than ever participate and more countries send participants to the Games. Given this, it is more likely that sport will become a feature of many women's lives. As more high-performance and professional sportswomen become visible to the world, the more likely it is that other women will be inspired to take up sport and exercise for reasons of health, fitness and personal esteem. Yet there are reasons to be cautious about the positive benefits of increased participation rates and opportunities for women in sport. The fact that some women are empowered by playing sports does not necessarily mean that gender equity is certain in sport specifically or in a wider social context. It is only when personal **empowerment** is utilised to change the organisation, practices and value systems of sport that equality between the sexes can become an enduring reality.

Case Study: Women, Tennis and the Media

There is no doubt that women's tennis is a relatively high-profile mediated sport. Global events such as Wimbledon receive worldwide television and newspaper attention, and professional women tennis players are certainly in the media spotlight. There has been increasing interest in the women's game as arguments escalate over the entertainment value of the power game that dominates men's tennis versus the variety of the women's game, which is characterised by longer rallies and more varied shots and tactics. The Women's Tennis Association (WTA), founded in 1973, has been at the centre of the development of a game that has become a global commercial enterprise. This has been done through the organisation and administration of the Grand Prix circuit, raising the profile of the game, supporting the needs of the players and, in particular, securing higher prize monies.

There are many key players who have contributed to this situation via their involvement in the organisation of professional tennis, and/or their achievements as players. One of the most influential people in the historical development of women's tennis is Billie Jean King. The first sportswoman to win $100,000 (Hargreaves 1994), she has 39 Grand Slam titles to her name. Billie Jean King has always fought for the rights of women in tennis and recognition for the game. She was one of the founders of the women's professional tour in 1970 and continues to be involved in the organisation and administration of the U.S. women's team (Barrett 2000). Other professional players have made their mark on the women's game. For example, Martina Navratilova, whose career prize money was $20,283,727 when she retired in 1995, has won a total of 56 Grand Slam titles and Steffi Graf is the only player, male or female, to have won all four of the world major titles four times (Barrett 2000). These professional women players have been relatively empowered, in several ways, by their involvement in tennis. They have become recognised and respected for their athletic talent and have amassed great wealth from prize monies and endorsement fees.

Increasingly, media attention is afforded to those professional women tennis players who look sexy. For some, there is an overemphasis on the way women players look that far outweighs the way that they play (Henderson 2000). The argument here is that beauty, charisma and sexual attractiveness are threatening to usurp performance. Looking good is a highly sought after commodity for sponsors of the game and for the media. Many of today's young women professional players epitomise youth, health and sex appeal. Who cares if they can play tennis? The media often seem to see their performances as incidental to their looks and this is a powerful message expressed by a powerful institution.

Not only does the media provide us with information about sport, it shapes the way we think about sport and sportspeople. Traditional beliefs and values about gender are commonly presented in mediated sport and are messages that often go unquestioned by readers, listeners and viewers. Rather, they reinforce the 'common-sense' notion that women are inferior to men in sport and if women are to receive positive media attention from sports journalists and large financial benefits from commercial sponsorship and advertising contracts, they must look (hetero)sexually attractive. What we read, hear and see in the context of media sport is framed by established images of femininity and mascu-linity (Creedon 1994). In tennis, as in many other high-profile commer-cial sports, those women players who embody the ideals of feminine beauty dominate newspapers and magazines and benefit from the most lucrative endorsements. These images reflect, reinforce and maintain the idea that, for women, being physically attractive and sexually appealing is far more important than athletic success.

One of the most popular women professional tennis players, for sportswriters, photographers and sponsors at least, is Anna Kournikova.

At the beginning of 2000 she was ranked 12th in the world. In 1999, Kournikova earned $748,424 from playing tennis (Barrett 2000). But she earned approximately $10 million from sponsorship and advertising. Her ability to command such high endorsement fees is for the most part due to the way she looks rather than how she plays. Her media image focuses on aspects of beauty, sex and scandal. These images have become central to much media commentary about women's tennis in recent years. Most column inches and headline news in many (British) newspapers have been more concerned with Kournikova's alleged relationships with professional ice-hockey players Sergei Fedorov and Pavel Bure, her body appearance and clothing, and the trials, tribulations and tantrums of her private life than her tennis ability and achievements. Stories that emphasise appearance, male partners, family and weaknesses are commonly told about elite sportswomen and they serve to trivialise women's sport performance as well as maintain traditional gendered ideology.

Summary

Since the early 19th century, modern sport has been (re-)created within a variety of specific and changing social conditions and beliefs about the nature and characteristics of both men and women. Socialisation processes in and through sport and in the wider social context teach people not only about gender-appropriate sports and behaviour but also about gendered ways of shaping and using the body. As Lorber (1994) explains, a system of gender-appropriate action is constructed via human interaction and becomes part of the order of social life.

The term *gendered ideology* refers to established ideas, beliefs and values about gender. When this ideology is institutionalised and maintained in the rituals and practices of everyday life and popular physical activities and professional sports, it becomes part of our taken-for-granted world and is often accepted without question. But as noted previously, the prevailing 'gender order' (Messner and Sabo 1990) already outlined should be thought of as a dynamic set of processes that can and do change through time and space. Whilst the term **patriarchy** has been used here, and in many other texts, to define a male-dominated society or particular social context, it does not capture the multifaceted nature of male/masculine domination specifically or **gender power networks** more broadly. In addition, the concept of patriarchy does not embrace the fact that both women and men have resisted and negotiated traditional notions of gender and established gender power hierarchies in sport and society. Opposition to traditional gender relations, by both women and men, is evident in many physical activities and sports. These challenges and changes demonstrate that sport is a site of contested gender ideology.

Key Terms and Concepts

empowerment	heterosexuality
femininities	homophobia
gendered space	homosexuality
gender equity	lesbianism
gender identities	masculinity-validating experience
gender logic	patriarchy
gender power networks	sex/gender
gender relations	socialisation
gender roles	

Review Questions

1. Discuss the concepts of sex and gender as they relate to sport.
2. Examine the contention that sport has developed as a 'male preserve'.
3. In what ways did the historical development of sport reinforce gender stereotypes?
4. Discuss the ways in which physical education has traditionally contributed to the making of femininities and masculinities.
5. Identify and explain the nature and characteristics of gender power networks in a sport of your choice.
6. Identify specific sporting spaces and places that reflect dominant gendered beliefs.
7. Evaluate the extent to which increasing opportunities and participation rates for women in sport have contributed to gender equity.
8. Critically examine the contention that sport reinforces established codes of heterosexuality.
9. Discuss the ways in which sport can be empowering for girls and women.
10. Examine the ways in which traditional values about gender are reflected in mediated sport.

Projects

1. Spend one day in a physical education department of a local school. Examine the curricula for physical education. Note the activities that are taught separately and in mixed-sex groups. Observe one physical education lesson

and take field notes regarding the nature of the activity, the interactions between the teacher and the pupils and the relationships between the pupils. What do your observations reveal about gender relations?

2. Select a sports team at your university and observe one training session, one competitive match and one social occasion. Take field notes at each stage. Make observations about the behaviour, emotions and language on display. Explain the ways in which sport contributes to the construction of gendered identities.

3. Select a sample of newspaper reports for a sports event of your choice. Conduct a content analysis and identify the type and form of language used to describe the performances of men and women. Use existing research to make sense of your findings.

4. Critically assess the presentation and marketing of an elite female sports performer. Identify her sponsors and the advertising campaigns with which she is associated. Examine the extent to which such advertising and sponsorship is based on sexual imagery.

5. Conduct an interview with one male and one female who belong to a local health/fitness club. Focus your questions on the type of activities experienced and how the use of their bodies in such activities relates to views of themselves. What do their responses reveal about gender and the body?

6. Construct a questionnaire that addresses male views about women who participate in rugby. Select a sample of male rugby players and administer the questionnaire. Analyse the results. What do your findings reveal about how female rugby players are perceived by their male counterparts?

CONCLUSION

The sport worlds that you, the reader, experience in your daily life, and which we have examined in this book, were made in the past. People—some like you, some not so—in your own society, and across different cultures and societies, contributed to the making of today's sport worlds. There is, then, both a temporal and a spatial dimension to sport worlds. Just as the shape of the sporting present was made in the past, a sporting future can be shaped in the present. Future sport worlds can be similar to today's, or they can be made anew. Such worlds can enhance the positive aspects of contemporary sport worlds, or they can reinforce, or make worse, what we already experience as negative features. The choice is ours. In making this case we are aware that power resources are unevenly distributed within and between societies. Class, gender, race/ethnicity and disability are but some of the fault lines along which sport, and other worlds, are splintered. Those students who protest against certain aspects of globalisation are not, by any stretch of the imagination, the most powerful players in the global political economy; nevertheless, specific actions, sometimes direct, *can make a difference.* Consumer boycotts, targeted media campaigns and political movements, such as the anti-Nike sweatshop movement that exists on U.S. campuses, *will* make a difference. It is important to hold out hope that we can change things—we hope this book provides you with a few key tools for doing just that.

The struggle to change what counts as possible, permissible and pleasurable in sport worlds begins with consciousness raising and knowledge accumulation. It has been our hope that this book provide the reader with insights into the issues and challenges—and the opportunities—that confront us right now. We hope that students will take up the challenge to make a difference—either in their own participation in sport worlds, or as coaches, consumers, teachers and parents. There are many obstacles to this struggle for change. The general denial and lack of discussion of the socially constructed nature of sport worlds is one such obstacle and acts as a social taboo, but so too is the idea that people cannot make a difference. Knowledge is power. If, through education, including physical education and sport science degrees, more of us demand that our sporting masters be held accountable, their decisions made transparent and their positions more democratically based, then we will be well on the way to a brighter future for sport worlds.

Let us close with these thoughts on the responsibility we share with others. Sport worlds of the past have developed into our contemporary sport worlds, just as our actions of today shape what may come tomorrow. We have a responsibility to ourselves and to others, as stewards of such a world, to share good practice, to use the sporting arena on land and sea wisely, and to cherish body cultures and traditions from across the globe. In doing so, we must develop 'green' and sustainable notions of sport worlds so that we are sustained in our experience of sport as embodied individuals, with a healthy habitus, and so that the planet, and its varied habitats, can 'breathe a sigh of relief'. We must work together towards shaping future sport worlds that are better—better for individuals, for communities and the environment. Sport worlds that balance our local needs with global interdependence: that is the challenge that faces us. That should be the new global order.

REFERENCES

Achenbach, J. 1996. Pebble Beach: The forest or the tees? *Golfweek* [Online], November 23. Available: **http://golfonline.com/news/golfweek/nov96/pebble1123.html** [October 31, 1999].

Allison, L. 1993. *The changing politics of sport.* Manchester: Manchester University Press.

———. 1996. Politics. In *Oxford concise dictionary of politics,* 388. Oxford: Oxford University Press.

Anderson, B. 1991. *Imagined communities: Reflections on the origins and spread of nationalisms.* London: Verso.

Anthony, A. 2000. White men can't run. *Observer Sport Monthly* (June):45–47.

Armstrong, G. 1998. *Football hooligans: Knowing the score.* Oxford: Berg.

Athelaide, D., and R. Snow. 1979. *Media logic.* London and California: Sage.

Bairner, A. 1999. Civic and ethnic nationalism in the Celtic vision of Irish sport. In *Sport in the making of Celtic cultures,* ed. G. Jarvie, 12–25. Leicester: Leicester University Press.

Bakhtin, M. 1968. *Rabelais and his world.* Cambridge: MIT Press.

Bale, J., and J. Maguire, eds. 1994. *The global sports arena: Athletic talent migration in an interdependent world.* London: Frank Cass.

Bale, J., and J. Sang. 1996. *Kenyan running: Movement culture, geography and global change.* London: Frank Cass.

Barnett, S. 1990. *Games and sets: The changing face of sport on television.* London: British Film Institute.

Barrett, J., ed. 2000. *World of tennis 2000: Countdown to Sydney 2000.* London: Collins Willow.

Barthes, R. 1975. *The pleasure of the text.* New York: Hill Wang.

BBC Television. 1997. The people's century. 16 February.

Beal, B. 1995. Disqualifying the official: An exploration of social resistance through the subculture of skateboarding. *Sociology of Sport Journal* 12(2):252–67.

Beck, U. 2000. *What is globalization?* Cambridge: Polity Press.

Becker, H. 1982/1984. *Art worlds.* Berkeley: University of California Press.

Bellamy, R. 1998. The evolving television sports marketplace. In *MediaSport,* ed. L. Wenner, 73–88. London: Routledge & Kegan Paul.

Berger, P. 1963/1976. *Invitation to sociology.* London: Pelican.

Birrell, S., and C. Cole, eds. 1994. *Women, sport and culture.* Champaign, Ill.: Human Kinetics.

Biskup, C., and G. Pfister. 1999. I would like to be like her/him: Are athletes role-models for boys and girls? *European Physical Education Review* 5(3):199–219.

Blanchard, T. 2000. Athletic chic. *Observer Sport Monthly* 1:30–33.

Boje, C., and H. Eichberg. 1996. *A third way of sports.* Copenhagen: Kulturministeriet.

Booth, D. 1995. Ambiguities in pleasure and discipline: The development of competitive surfing. *Journal of Sport History* 22(3):170–181.

Bourdieu, P. 1984. *Distinction: A social critique of the judgement of taste.* Cambridge: Harvard University Press.

———. 1990. *In other words: Essays towards a reflexive sociology.* Cambridge: Polity Press.

———. 1998. A reasoned utopia and economic fatalism. *New Left Review* 227:125–30.

Boyle, R., and R. Haynes. 2000. *Power play: Sport, the media and popular culture.* London: Longman.

Bradley, J.M. 1996. Facets of the Irish diaspora: 'Irishness' in 20th century Scotland. *Irish Journal of Sociology* 6:79–100.

Bradley, J.M. 2000. Imagining Scotland: Nationality, cultural identities, football and discourses of Scottishness. *Stirling Research Papers* 1:1–36.

Brohm, J.M. 1978. *Sport: A prison of measured time*. London: Ink Links.

Bromberger, C. 1994. Foreign footballers, cultural dreams and community identity in some north-western Mediterranean cities. In *The global sports arena: Athletic talent migration in an interdependent world*, eds. J. Bale and J. Maguire, 171–82. London: Frank Cass.

Cahn, S. 1994. *Coming on strong: Gender and sexuality in twentieth century women's sport*. New York: Macmillan.

Cantelon, H., and R. Gruneau. 1982. *Sport, culture and the modern state*. Toronto: Toronto University Press.

Cashmore, E. 1996. *Making sense of sports*. 2nd ed. London: Routledge & Kegan Paul.

Chamberlain, S. 1995. Golf endangers Hawai'ian ecology and culture. *Earth Island Journal* [Online], Summer. Available: **www.earthisland.org/journal/golf.html** [October 31, 1999].

Chandler, J. 1988. *Television and national sport: The United States and Britain*. Champaign: University of Illinois Press.

Chatterjee, P. 1993. Clubbing Southeast Asia: The impacts of golf course development. *Multinational Monitor* [Online], November. Available: **www.essential.org/monitor/hyper/issues/1993/11/mm1193_13.html** [September 19, 2000].

Clarke, J., and C. Critcher. 1985. *The devil makes work: Leisure in capitalist Britain*. London: Macmillan.

Clubbe, C. 1996. Threats to biodiversity. In *Global environmental issues*, eds. R. Blackmore and A. Reddish. London: Hodder & Stoughton.

Coakley, J. 1992. Burnout among adolescent athletes: A personal failure or social problem? *Sociology of Sport Journal* 9(3):271–86.

———. 1998. *Sport in society: Issues and controversies*. Boston: Irwin/McGraw-Hill.

Coalter, F. 2000. *The role of sport in re-generating deprived urban communities*. Edinburgh: Scottish Executive.

Cohen, G. 1993. Women in sport: Issues and controversies. London: Sage.

Coleman, J. 1988. Social capital in the creation of human capital. *American Journal of Sociology* 94:95–119.

Creedon, P. 1994. *Women, sport and the media*. London: Sage.

Cronin, M. 1998. The nationalist history of the Gaelic Athletic Association and the English influence on Irish sport. *International Journal of the History of Sport* 15(3):36–56.

———. 1999. *Sport and nationalism in Ireland: Gaelic games, soccer and Irish identity since 1884*. Dublin: Four Courts Press.

Curry, T. 1991. Fraternal bonding in the locker room. *Sociology of Sport Journal* 8:119–35.

Curry, T., and R. Strauss. 1994. A little pain never hurt anybody. *Sociology of Sport Journal* 11:195–208.

Davis, R., and O. Harris. 1998. Race and ethnicity in the U.S. sports media. In *MediaSport*, ed. L. Wenner, 154-169. London: Routledge & Kegan Paul.

Denzin, N. 1984. *On understanding emotion*. Washington: Jossey-Bass.

———. 1985. Emotion as lived experience. *Symbolic Interaction* 8(2):223–40.

Dezalay, Y. 1990. The big bang and the law: The internationalization and restructuration of the legal field. *Theory, Culture and Society* 7:279–94.

Duncan, M.C., and B. Brummett. 1989. Types and sources of spectating pleasure in televised sports. *Sociology of Sport Journal* 6(3):195–211.

Dunning, E. 1986. Sport as a male preserve: Notes on the social sources of masculine identity and its transformation. *Theory, Culture and Society* 3(1):79–90.

———. 1999. *Sport matters: Sociological studies of sport, violence and civilization.* London: Routledge & Kegan Paul.

Dunning, E., and J. Maguire. 1996. Aspects of sport, violence and gender relations: Some process-sociological notes. *International Review for the Sociology of Sport* 31:295–321.

Dunning, E., and K. Sheard. 1979. *Barbarians, gentlemen and players: A sociological study of the development of rugby football.* Oxford: Martin Robertson.

Edwards, P. 2000. Avoiding own goals in the sports field. *Planning* 8:12–13.

Eichberg, H. 1984. Olympic sport: Neocolonialism and alternatives. *International Review for the Sociology of Sport* 19: 97–105.

Eitzen, D.S., and G.H. Sage. 1993. *Sociology of North American sport.* 5th ed. Dubuque, Iowa: Brown & Benchmark.

Elias, N. 1939/1978. *The civilising process.* Oxford: Blackwell.

———. 1987. On human beings and their emotions: A process sociological essay. *Theory, Culture and Society* 4:339–61.

———. 1991/1994. *Mozart: Portrait of a genius.* Cambridge: Polity Press.

Elias, N., and E. Dunning. 1986. *Quest for excitement: Sport and leisure in the civilising process.* Oxford: Blackwell.

Etzioni, A. 1995. *New communitarian thinking: Persons, virtues and communities.* Charlottesville: University Press of Virginia.

Falcous, M., and J. Maguire. 1999. Sport and globalisation: NBA strategies, English basketball and local lives. Paper presented at the European Congress of Sports Science, July, Rome.

Featherstone, M. 1983. The body in consumer culture. *Theory, Culture and Society* 1(2):18–33.

———. 1991. *Consumer culture and postmodernism.* London: Sage.

———. 1995. *Undoing culture: Globalization, postmodernism and identity.* London: Sage.

Featherstone, M., S. Lash, and R. Robertson, eds. 1995. *Global modernities.* London: Sage.

Ferguson-Smith, M., and A. Ferris. 1991. Gender verification in sport: The need for change. *British Journal of Sports Medicine* 25(1):17–21.

Finbow, R. 1999. United decision is not the end of the road. *Sports Business* (May):11.

Fiske, J. 1987. *Television culture.* London: Methuen.

Forrest, R., and A. Kearns. 1999. *Joined-up places? Social cohesion and neighbourhood regeneration.* York: Joseph Rowntree Foundation.

Frazer, E. 2000. *Communitarianism in understanding contemporary society.* Edited by G. Browning, A. Halcli and F. Webster. London: Sage.

Fusco, C. 1998. Lesbians and locker rooms: The subjective experiences of lesbians in sport. In *Sport and postmodern time,* ed. G. Rail, 87–117. New York: SUNY Press.

Giddens, A. 1994. *Beyond left and right: The future of radical politics.* Cambridge: Polity Press.

Giulianotti, R. 1994. *Game without frontiers: Football, identity and modernity.* Arena: Aldershot.

———. 1994. Taking liberties: Hibs casuals and Scottish law. In *Football, violence and social identity,* eds. R. Giulianotti, N. Bonney, and M. Hepworth, 229–61. London: Routledge & Kegan Paul.

———. 2000. Built by the two Varelas: The rise and fall of football culture and national identity in Uruguay. In *Football culture: Local contests, global visions,* eds. G.P.T. Finn and R. Giulianotti, 134–154. London: Frank Cass.

Goffman, E. 1961. *Encounters.* New York: Bobbs-Merrill.

Goldlust, J. 1987. *Playing for keeps: Sport, the media and society.* London: Longman.

Goudsblom, J. 1977. *Sociology in the balance.* Oxford: Blackwell.

Gramsci, A. 1971. *Selections from prison notebooks of Antonio Gramsci.* New York: International Publishing Co.

Gratton, C., and P. Taylor. 2000. *The economics of sport.* London: E&FN Spon.

Greely, A.M., and D. McCready. 1974. Does ethnicity matter. *Ethnicity* 1(1):91–108.

Gruneau, R. 1976. Class or mass: Notes on the democratisation of Canadian amateur sport. In *Canadian sport: Sociological perspectives,* eds. R. Gruneau and J. Albinson, 108–40. Toronto, Ontario: Addison-Wesley.

———. 1989. Making spectacle: A case study in television sports production. In *MediaSports and society,* ed. L. Wenner, 134–157. London: Routledge.

Gruneau, R., and D. Whitson. 1993. *Hockey night in Canada: Sport, identities and cultural politics.* Toronto: Garamond Press.

Guttmann, A. 1978. *From ritual to record: The nature of modern sports.* New York: Columbia University Press.

———. 1994. *Games and empires: Modern sports and cultural imperialism.* New York: Columbia University Press.

Hargreaves, I. 1999. *New mutualism: In from the cold.* London: Trafford Press.

Hargreaves, J. 1986. *Sport, power and culture: A social and historical analysis of popular sports in Britain.* Cambridge: Polity Press.

———. 1994. *Sporting females: Critical issues in the history and sociology of women's sports.* London: Routledge & Kegan Paul.

———. 2000. *Freedom for Catalonia? Catalan nationalism, Spanish identity and the Barcelona Olympic Games.* Cambridge: Cambridge University Press.

Harris, J. 1998. Civil society, physical activity and the involvement of sport sociologists in the preparation of physical activity professionals. *Sociology of Sport Journal* 15:138–53.

Heinilä, K. 1970. Notes on the inter-group conflicts in international sport. In *The cross-cultural analysis of sport and games,* ed. G. Luschen, 174–82. Champaign, Ill.: Stipes.

Held, D., A. McGrew, D. Goldblatt, and J. Perraton. 1999. *Global transformations.* Stanford: Stanford University Press.

Henderson, J. 2000. Sex and the singles women. *Observer Sport Monthly* 2:18–23.

Herd, M. 1998. Marion beats the clock with big Ben's legs. *London Evening Standard,* 23 July.

Hill, J. 1999. *Nelson: Economy, politics, community.* Keele: Keele University Press.

———. 2000. Sport and social class. In *Encyclopaedia of British sport,* eds. R. Cox, G. Jarvie, and W. Vamplew, 40. Oxford: ABC-CLIO.

Hirst, P. 1994. *Associative democracy.* Cambridge: Polity Press.

Hirst, P., and G. Thompson. 1999. *Globalization in question.* Cambridge: Polity Press.

Hoberman, J. 1984. *Sport and political ideology.* London: Heinemenn.

Hobsbawm, E. 1990. *Nations and nationalism since 1780: Programme, myth, reality.* Cambridge: Cambridge University Press.

Hoch, P. 1972. *Rip off the big game: The exploitation of sport by the power elite.* New York: Doubleday.

Holt, O. 2000. Lewis crosses the pain barrier to strike gold. *London Times,* 25 September.

Horne, J., A. Tomlinson, and G. Whannel. 1999. *Understanding sport: An introduction to the sociological and cultural analysis of sport.* London: E&FN Spon.

Houlihan, B. 1997. Sport, national identity and public policy. *Nations and Nationalism* 3:113–38.

———. 2000. Politics and sport. In *The handbook of sports studies,* eds. J. Coakley and E. Dunning, 213–27. London: Sage.

Hughes, B., and J. Coakley. 1991. Positive deviance among athletes: The implications of overconformity to the sport ethic. *Sociology of Sport Journal* 8(4):307–325.

Hutton, W. 1995. *The state we're in.* London: Jonathan Cape.

Jackson, S. 1996. Lacrosse. In *Encyclopaedia of world sport,* eds. D. Levinson and K. Christensen, 219–22. Oxford: ABC-CLIO.

Jarvie, G. 1993. Sport, nationalism and cultural identity. In *The changing politics of sport,* ed. L. Allison, 58–83. Manchester: Manchester University Press.

———. 1999. *Sport in the making of Celtic cultures*. Leicester: Leicester University Press.

Jarvie, G., and J. Burnett. 2000. *Sport, Scotland and the Scots*. Edinburgh: Tuckwell Press.

Jarvie, G., and J. Maguire. 1994. *Sport and leisure in social thought*. London: Routledge & Kegan Paul.

Jarvie, G., and I. Thomson. 1999. Sport, nationalism and the Scottish parliament. *Scottish Affairs* 27:82–96.

Jarvie, G., and G. Walker. 1994. *Scottish sport in the making of the nation: Substitutes and ninety-minute patriots*. Leicester: Leicester University Press.

Jennings, A. 1996. *The new lords of the rings*. London: Pocket Books Inc.

———. 2000. *The great Olympic swindle*. London: Simon & Schuster.

Jhally, S. 1989. Cultural studies and the sports/media complex. In *Media, sport and society*, ed. L. Wenner, 70–97. London: Sage.

Jones, C. 1996. Political economy. In *Oxford concise dictionary of politics*, 389. Oxford: Oxford University Press.

Keane, J. 1988. *Civil society and the state*. London: Verso.

Kidd, B. 1987. Sports and masculinity. In *Essays by men on pleasure, power and change*, ed. M. Kaufman, 250–267. Buckingham: Open University Press.

Kidd, B., and P. Donnelly. 2000. Human rights in sport. *International Review for the Sociology of Sport* 35:131–48.

King, A.D., ed. 1991. *Culture, globalization and the world-system: Contemporary conditions for the representation of identity*. London: Macmillan.

King, S. 2000. Human rights, tax and sports justice. *SportsBusiness Journal*, 14 October.

Kinkema, K., and J. Harris. 1992. Sport and the mass media. *Exercise and Sport Sciences Reviews* 20:127–59.

Klein, A.M. 1991. *Sugarball: The American game, the Dominican dream*. New Haven, Conn.: Yale University Press.

———. 1993. Pumping iron: Crisis and contradiction in bodybuilding. In *Sport sociology: Contemporary theme*, 4th ed., eds. A. Yiannakis, T.D. McIntyre, and M.J. Melnick, 563–576. Dubuque, Iowa: Kendall/Hunt.

Korr, C.P. 1990. A different kind of success: West Ham United and the creation of tradition and community. In *Sport and the working class in modern Britain*, ed. R. Holt. Manchester: Manchester University Press.

Krieger, J. 2000. *British politics in the global age: Can social democracy survive?* Cambridge: Polity Press.

Lanfranchi, P. 1994. The migration of footballers: The case of France. In *The global sports arena: Athletic talent migration in an interdependent world*, eds. J. Bale and J. Maguire, 63–77. London: Cass.

Lash, S., and J. Urry. 1994. *Economies of signs and space*. London: Sage.

Lechner, F.J., and J. Boli. 2000. *The globalization reader*. Oxford: Blackwell.

Lindsey, E. 1997. Cashing in on the clamour for glamour. *Observer*, London, 29 June.

Lobmeyer, H., and L. Weidinger. 1992. Commercialization as a dominant factor in the American sports scene: Sources, developments, prospects. *International Review for the Sociology of Sport* 27:309–27.

Lorber, J. 1994. *Paradoxes of gender*. London: Yale University Press.

Low, M. 2000. Nationalism. In *Understanding contemporary society: Theories of the present*, eds. G. Browning, A. Halcli and F. Webster, 356–72. London: Sage.

MacLennan, G. 1995. *Pluralism*. Milton Keynes: Open University Press.

Maguire, J. 1986. Images of manliness and competing ways of living in late Victorian and Edwardian England. *British Journal of Sport History* 3(3):265–87.

————. 1988. The commercialization of English elite basketball, 1972–1988. *International Review for the Sociology of Sport* 23:305–24.

————. 1992. Towards a sociological theory of sport and the emotions: A process-sociological perspective. In *Sport and leisure in the civilising process: Critique and counter-critique*, eds. E. Dunning and C. Rojek, 96–120. London: Macmillan.

————. 1994. Preliminary observations on globalisation and the migration of sports labour. *Sociological Review* 42(3):452–80.

————. 1996. Blade runners: Canadian migrants and global ice-hockey trails. *Journal of Sport and Social Issues* 20:335–60.

————. 1999. *Global sport: Identities, societies, civilizations*. Cambridge: Polity Press.

Maguire, J., and P. Donnelly. 2000. *Sociology of sport in Vade Mecum: Directory of sport science*. 2nd ed. Berlin: International Council for Sport Science and Physical Education.

Maguire, J., and L. Mansfield. 1998. No-body's perfect: The exercise body beautiful complex. *Sociology of Sport Journal* 15(2):109–13.

Maguire, J., and R. Pearton. 2000. The impact of elite labour migration on the identification, selection and development of European soccer players. *Journal of Sports Sciences* 18:759–69.

Maguire, J., and S. Roberts. 1998. Less weight, more gain? Pain, injury and elite British female gymnastics. Paper presented at the annual British Sociological Association conference, April, Edinburgh.

Maguire, J., and D. Stead. 1996. Far pavilions? Cricket migrants, foreign sojourn and contested identities. *International Review for the Sociology of Sport* 31:1–24.

————. 1997. Border crossings: Soccer labour migration and the European union. *International Review for the Sociology of Sport* 32:59–73.

Maguire, J., and J. Tuck. 1998. Global sports and patriot games: Rugby Union and national identity in a united sporting kingdom. In *Sporting nationalism: Identity, ethnicity, immigration and assimiliation*, eds. M. Cronin and D. Mayall. 103–126. London: Frank Cass.

Mansfield, L., and J. Maguire. 1999. Active women, power relations and gendered identities: Embodied experiences of aerobics. In *Practising identities: Power and resistance*, eds. S. Roseneil and J. Seymour, 81–106. London: Macmillan.

Markula, P. 1995. Firm but shapely, fit but sexy, strong but thin: The postmodern aerobicizing female bodies. *Sociology of Sport Journal* 12:424–533.

Marquand, D. 1988. *The unprincipled society*. London: Jonathan Cape.

Martin, T.W., and K.J. Berry. 1993. Competitive sport in post-industrial society: The case of the motocross racer. In *Sport sociology: Contemporary themes*, 4th ed., eds. A. Yiannakis, T.D. McIntyre, and M.J. Melnick, 279–85. Dubuque, Iowa: Kendall/Hunt.

Massey, D. 1994. *Space, place and gender*. Cambridge: Polity Press.

McKay, J., G. Lawrence, T. Miller, and D. Rowe. 1993. Globalisation and Australian sport. *Sport Science Review* 2:10–28.

McPherson, B.D., J.E. Curtis, and J.W. Loy. 1989. *The social significance of sport*. Champaign, Ill.: Human Kinetics.

————. 1992. *Power at play: Sports and the problem of masculinity*. Boston: Beacon Press.

Messner, M., and D. Sabo. 1990. *Sport, men and the gender order: Critical feminist perspectives*. Champaign, Ill.: Human Kinetics.

Metcalfe, A. 1996. Sport and community: A case study of the mining villages of East Northumberland, 1880–1914. In *Sport and identity in the north of England*, eds. J. Hill and J. Williams, 13–40. Keele: Keele University Press.

Miller, L., and O. Penz. 1991. Talking bodies: Female body builders colonize a male preserve. *Quest* 43:148–64.

Mills, C.W. 1959. *The sociological imagination*. New York: Oxford University Press.

Mitchie, J. 1999. *New mutualism: A golden goal.* London: Trafford Press.

Moffat, A. 1999. Cut privilege out of the body politic. *New Statesman and Society* (June):35–37.

Moller, J., and J. Anderson. 1998. *Society's watchdog—Or showbiz pet?* Copenhagen: Danish Gymnastics and Sports Associations.

Morgan, W.J. 1994. *Leftist theories of sport: A critique and reconstruction.* Champaign: University of Illinois Press.

Morgan, W.J. 1998. Hassiba Boulmerka and Islamic green: International sports, cultural differences and their postmodern interpretation. In *Sport and postmodern times,* ed. G. Rail, 345–67. New York: SUNY.

Morrow, S. 2000. Mutual sport and trust: The case study of Celtic PLC. *Irish Journal of Accounting* 15:14–27.

Nauright, J. 1997. *Sport and cultural identity in South Africa.* London: Cassell.

Nelson, M. 1994. *The stronger women get, the more men love football: Sexism and the American culture of sport.* New York: Harcourt Brace Jovanovich, Inc.

Nixon, H. 1984. *Sport and the American dream.* Champaign, Ill.: Human Kinetics.

————. 1996. The relationship of friendship networks, sports experiences, and gender to expressed pain thresholds. *Sociology of Sport Journal* 13(1):78–86.

Nixon, H.L., and J.H. Frey. 1996. *Sociology of sport.* London: Wadsworth.

Obel, C. 1996. Collapsing gender in competitive body building: Researching contradictions and ambiguity in sport. *International Review for the Sociology of Sport* 31:185–201.

Olin, K., and M. Penttila. 1994. Professional sports migration to Finland during the 1980's. In *The global sports arena: Athletic talent migration in an interdependent world,* eds. J. Bale and J. Maguire, 78–98. London: Frank Cass.

Pahl, R., and L. Spencer. 1998. The politics of friendship. *Renewal* 5(3):100–07.

Parkes, P. 1996. Indigenous polo and the politics of regional identity in northern Pakistan. In *Sport, identity and ethnicity,* ed. J. Clancy, 43–67. Oxford: Berg.

Petrie, B. 1975. Sport and politics. In *Sport and social order,* eds. D. Ball and J. Loy, pp. 187–237. London: Addison-Wesley.

Plimmer, D., E. Parkinson, and K. Carlton. 1996. *The environment.* London: Cassell.

Putnam, R.D. 1995. Bowling alone: America's declining social capital. *Journal of Democracy* 6:65–78.

Rail, G. 1990. Physical contact in women's basketball: A first interpretation. *International Review for the Sociology of Sport* 25(4):269–86.

Rail, G., ed. 1998. *Sport and postmodern times.* New York: SUNY.

Richardson, J. 2000. And it's green for Australia. *Ansett Inflight Magazine* September:208–13.

Richardson, M. 1995. The myth of athletic gifts. *London Independent,* 5 September.

Robertson, R. 1992. *Globalization: Social theory and global culture.* London: Sage.

Rojek, C. 1985. *Capitalism and leisure theory.* London: Tavistock Publications.

Rojek, C. 1989. Leisure time and leisure space. In *Leisure for Leisure,* ed. C. Rojek. 191–205. London: Macmillan Press. Quoting Eileen and Stephen Yeo, Ways of Seeing: Control and leisure versus class and struggle, in Yeo, E. and Yeo, S. (eds) *Popular culture and class conflict 1590— 1914: Explorations in history of labour and leisure* (Brighton: Harvester, 1981), 136.

Roudometof, V., and R. Robertson. 1995. Globalization, world-system theory, and the comparative study of civilizations: Issues of theoretical logic in world-historical sociology. In *Civilizations and world systems,* ed. S.K. Sanderson, 273–300. Walnut Creek, Calif.: Alta Mira.

Rowe, D. 1999. *Sport, culture and the media: The unruly trinity.* Buckingham: Open University Press.

Ryan, J. 1995. *Little girls in pretty boxes.* New York: Warner Books, Inc.

Sage, G. 1990. *Power and ideology in American sport.* Champaign, Ill.: Human Kinetics.

————. 1995. Deindustrialization and the American sporting goods industry. In *Sport in the global village,* ed. R.C. Wilcox, 39–51. Morgantown, W.Va.: Fitness Information Technology.

————. 1999. Justice Do It! The Nike transnational advocacy network: Organization, collective action, and outcomes. *Sociology of Sport Journal* 16:206-235.

Sailes, G. 1998. *African Americans in sport.* New Jersey: Transaction.

Saward, J. 1997. How Bernie built his Formula One fortune. *Sports Business* (November):12.

Scheff, T. 1983. Towards integration in the social psychology of emotions. *American Review of Sociology* 9:333–54.

Schermerhorn, R.A. 1970. *Comparative ethnic relations: A framework for theory and research.* New York: Random House, Inc.

Schuller, T. 1997. Building social capital: Steps towards a learning society. *Scottish Affairs* 19:77–91.

Scraton, S. 1992. *Shaping up to womanhood: Gender and girls, physical education.* Buckingham: Open University Press.

Selman, P. 1996. *Local sustainability: Managing and planning ecologically sound places.* London: Chapman.

Seymour, M. 2000. Quebec and Canada at the crossroads: A nation within a nation. *Nations and Nationalism* 6(2):227–57.

Sharpe, S. 1994. *Just like a girl: How girls learn to be women.* London: Penguin.

Shilling, C. 1991. Educating the body: Physical capital and the production of social inequalities. *Sociology* 25(4):653–72.

Shott, S. 1979. Emotions and social life: A symbolic interactionist analysis. *American Journal of Sociology* 84:1317–334.

Simmel, G. 1978. *The philosophy of money.* Edited and translated by T. Bottomore and D. Frisby. London: Routledge & Kegan Paul.

Sklair, L. 1991. *Sociology of the global system.* London: Harvester.

Smith, M. 1991. Steeled for a greener shoot. *London Independent,* 7 January.

Snyder, E. 1990. Emotion and sport. *Sociology of Sport Journal* 7(3):254–70.

Sport England. 1998. *The value of sport.* London: Sport England.

St. Martin, L., and N. Gavey. 1996. Women's bodybuilding: feminist resistance and/or femininity's recuperation. *Body and Society* 2: 45–57.

Stead, D., and J. Maguire. 2000. Rite de passage or passage to riches?: The motivation and objectives of Nordic/Scandinavian players in English league soccer. *Journal of Sport and Social Issues* 24(1):36–60.

Stephen, A. 2000. What's in a game? Class and history. *New Statesman and Society* (June): 20–22.

Sugden, J. 1996. *Boxing and society: An international analysis.* Manchester: Manchester University Press.

Sugden, J., and A. Tomlinson. 1998. *FIFA and the contest for world football: Who rules the people's game?* Cambridge: Polity Press.

Symington, B., and J. Angel. 2000a. What is Green Games Watch 2000 (GGW2000), what are their aims, what have they done and who funds them? In *Frequently asked questions.* [Online]. Available: **www.nccnsw.org.au/member/ggw/** [July 12, 2000].

————. 2000b. Olympic green losses. In *Green Games Watch 2000 Media Release.* [Online]. Available: **www.nccnsw.org.au/member/ggw/** [August 23, 2000].

————. 2000c. What role did the environment play in helping Sydney's 1993 winning Olympic bid? In *Frequently asked questions.* [Online]. Available: **www.nccnsw.org.au/member/ggw/** [July 12, 2001].

———. 2000d. Biodiversity. In *Green issues*. [Online]. Available: **www.nccnsw.org.au/member/ggw/** [September 11, 2001].

———. 2000e. Frogs in hot water. In *News/media*. [Online]. Available: **www.nccnsw.org.au/member/ggw/** [August 3, 2000].

———. 2000f. Olympic green wins. In *News/media*. [Online]. Available: **www.nccnsw.org.au/member/ggw/** [August 18, 2000].

———. 2000g. Olympic social impacts. In *Green issues*. [Online]. Available: **www.nccnsw.org.au/member/ggw/** [August 21, 2001].

———. 2000h. Did anyone get into trouble for not following the environmental guidelines? In *Frequently asked questions*. [Online]. Available: **www.nccnsw.org.au/member/ggw/** [July 12, 2000].

———. 2000i. Was a rare type of forest cleared to build a cycling track? In *Frequently asked questions*. [Online]. Available: **www.nccnsw.org.au/member/ggw/** [July 12, 2000].

———. 2000j. No green cars at the green games. In *News/media*. [Online] Available: **www.nccnsw.org.au/member/ggw/** [September 11, 2001].

———. 2000k. PVC—The poison plastic. In *News/media*. [Online]. Available: **www.nccnsw.org.au/member/ggw/** [July 28, 2000].

———. 2000l. Green merchandising? In *Green issues*. [Online]. Available: **www.nccnsw.org.au/member/ggw/** [August 22, 2001].

———. 2000m. Olympic sponsors. In *News/media*. [Online]. Available: **www.nccnsw.org.au/member/ggw/** [August 23, 2001].

———. 2000n. ESD beyond the Olympics: Ecologically sustainable development. In *Green issues*. [Online]. Available: **www.nccnsw.org.au/member/ggw/** [September 11, 2001].

Theberge, N. 1985. Toward a feminist alternative to sport as a male preserve. *Quest* 37:193–202.

Therborn, G. 2000. Globalizations: Dimensions, historical waves, regional effects, normative governance. *International Sociology* 15(2):151–80.

Thomson, I. 1992. *Sport in Sweden*. Edinburgh: Scottish Sports Council.

Tomlinson, J. 1999. *Globalization and culture*. Cambridge: Polity Press.

Wagg, S. 1984. *The football world: A contemporary social history*. Brighton: Harvester.

Walker, G. 1994. Nancy Riach and the Motherwell swimming phenomenon. In *Scottish sport in the making of the nation*, eds. G. Jarvie and G. Walker, 170–184. Leicester: Leicester University Press.

Walker, N. 1995. More than one winning colour. *Observer*, London, 17 June.

Wallerstein, I. 1974. *The modern world system*. New York: Academic Press.

Walvin, J. 1994. *The people's game: The history of football revisited*. Edinburgh: Mainstream.

Wenner, L., ed. 1989. *Media, sport and society*. London: Sage.

Wenner, L.A., ed. 1998. *MediaSport*. London: Routledge & Kegan Paul.

Wenner, L., and W. Gantz. 1989. The audience experience of sports on television. In *Media, sport and society*, ed. L. Wenner, 241–70. London: Sage.

Whannel, G. 1992. *Fields in visions: Television sport and cultural transformation*. London: Routledge & Kegan Paul.

White, A., and Brackenridge, C. 1985. Who rules sport? Gender divisions in the power structures of British sport organisations from 1960. *International Review for the Sociology of Sport*. 20 (1,2): 95-108.

Williams, J. 1986. White riots. In *Off the ball*, eds. G. Whannel and A. Tomlinson, 5–19. London: Pluto.

Williams, R. 1997. *Racers: A portrait of Formula One*. London: Penguin.

———. 1998. In the driving seat. *Hot Air Magazine*. Virgin Atlantic (September).

Willis, P. 1994. Women in sport in ideology. In *Women, sport and culture*, eds. S. Birrell and C. Cole, 31–47. Champaign, Ill.: Human Kinetics.

Wolff, J. 1981. *The social production of art*. London: Macmillan.

———. 1991. The global and the specific: Reconciling conflicting theories of culture. In *Culture, globalization and the world-system*, ed. A.D. King, 161–73. London: Macmillan.

Yearley, S. 1992. Environmental challenges. In *Modernity and its futures: Understanding modern societies, an introduction*, ed. S. Hall, D. Held, and T. McGrew, 117–168. Cambridge: The Open University / Polity Press.

———. 1996. *Sociology, environmentalism, globalization*. London: Sage.

Young, I. 1990. Throwing like a girl and other essays in philosophy and social theory. Indianapolis: Indianapolis University Press.

Zurcher, L. 1982. The staging of emotion: A dramaturgical analysis. *Symbolic Interaction* 5:1–22.

INDEX

A

achievement sport 10
    global culture of 20
Adidas 17
adjustment 38
advertising
    and NBC Olympic rights 53
    and power of television 126
    and revenue on global scale 50
    and sponsorship of sports events/
        teams 56–57
    and televised sports 48
    virtual 65
Afghanistan 139
Africa
    national identity 149, 152
    nationalism through sport 159
aggression 141
    and soccer hooliganism 167
alcohol, and soccer hooliganism 167
alienation 192
alternative sports 173
    transformation to mainstream sports
        177
amateurism 126
American dream 128, 142, 148, 168
American football
    emotional responses to 186–187
    Green Bay Packers 105–106
    as reflection of American culture 168
    revenues 126
Americanisation 39
ancient sport
    historical changes to 122
    place in society 121
apartheid 108, 142, 149, 152
appearance 195–196
    and gender identity 208
    and women in sport 211
ascribed status 35
athletes. *See also* women
    in achievement sport 10
    cross-cultural identities of 17–18
    as dramatic performers 54
    emotional readiness for game 187
    and emotions 182
    genetics and success 19

    as heroes 126
    image and gender identity 208
    image construction 127–128
    marketing of 5
    migration of talent 19
    as part of marketing package 5
    as role models 112
    superman myth 19
    Swedish and taxes 74–78
    types of migrants 33
athlete salaries
    and employment rights 37
    gender inequality 209
    and passion in sport 139
    and televised sports 126
audience
    attracting to televised sports 53
    for major mediated sporting events 52
    and mediated sport development 49
    motivations for viewing sports 56
    skilled consumers vs. cultural dupes
        57
    television vs. live 124
autonomy 71
    from globalisation 148

B

basketball 183
    Americanisation in England 39
Basques 149
behaviour
    antisocial 166
    learned and unlearned aspects xiv, 184
biodiversity 90, 92
black athlete
    in media sport 58–59
    and racism 140
    underrepresentation in sport 169
body building 177
    and women athletes 211
body culture 7
    homogenisation of 22
    as shaped by white males 14
    sport as representative of 76
body image 61–62
Bosman ruling 36, 38
boxing in Cuba 121–122

C
capitalism 70
    and American dream 168
    and boxing in Cuba 122
    and consumerism of sport 125–126
    and development of English soccer 120
    influence on sport 73
    and subcultural sports 176
    and third way 74
carcinogenic chemicals 94
carnival 194
case studies
    Catalans and Basques 149
    Danish sport as third way 76–78
    Formula One racing 62–66
    Gaelic Athletic Association 135–136
    pain of gymnasts 188–190
    soccer hooliganism as subculture 166–
        168
    soccer in Britain 119–120
    social capital in U.S. 111
    Swedish athletes and tax system 74–78
    women tennis players 214–216
Catalans 149
centre nationalism 151, 153
cities 134
citizenship 11, 17–18. See also dual
        nationality
    and civic identity 134
    and communitarianism 100
    of migrant athletes 28
    and national identity 148
    and nationalism 157
    and social capital 110
civic associations 108
civic, definition 134
civic disengagement 111
civic engagement 101
civic nationalism 157
civic pride 103, 144
civilisational struggles 6
civilising processes 190
civil rights 160
civil society 101
    in Denmark 107–109
    and sport 107
class 76, 78
    and socialisation 169
    and sporting subculture 165
collective bargaining 36
colonial links 34
commercialisation 125
    of subcultural sports 177
commercial processes 49
    and rugby 55
communism, and third way 74

communitarianism 100
    as social theory 101–104
community 100
    imagined 102, 144
    is sport good for? 104
    and sport ownership 105–107
competition
    and ideology of participants 20–21
    between media outlets 50
    and national ideology 122
    and passion 138
    resemblance to battles 191
    world championships 11
conflict
    competition as resemblance to battles
        191
    and Gaelic Athletic Association 135–136
    in global culture 8
    and global sporting events 158
    and media-sports relationship 57
    role of sport in resolving 72
    sport as vehicle for integration 153
conformity 171
CONMEBOL 30
conservation 86
consumer culture 195
consumerism 125–126
consumption 51
control
    and development of English soccer 120
    of Formula One racing 63–64
    in media sport 54–57
    and ownership of mediated sports 52
    and race 59
controlled decontrolling of emotions 191,
        195
co-operative ventures 105–106
corporate sponsorship 38–39
corruption of sport 126–127
creativity
    and quality of performance xiii
    and sporting subculture 172
creolisation 13
Cuban boxing 121–122
cultural adjustment 38
cultural commingling 9
cultural domination 164
cultural dupes 57, 192
cultural forms 172
cultural product 166
cultural resistance 171
culture. See also subculture
    adaptation of migrant athletes 37–39
    American dream 128, 142
    and civic identity 134
    commingling of 9

and consumerism of sport in Western
    culture 125–126
cross-cultural identities of athletes 17–
    18
decline of indigenous and non-
    occidental 10
definition 165
development of global 7
of global achievement sport 20
indigenous and interpretation of sport
    12
Islamic and women athletes 15, 213
meaning of 164
and migration patterns of soccer
    players 32
national 148
and nationalism 151
nation-specific games 153
origins of the word 164
and self in time and space 119
sport as representative of 139
and sport as social product xiii
television and sport as part of 48–49
in time and space 127–129
values reflected by televised sports 53
and women's rights 212–214

D
dance xvi
debating points
    culture and subcultural development
        174–176
    embodied emotions 183–185
    FIFA and nationhood of emerging
        nations 156
    functions of sport 122–123
    gender relations 205–206
    global sports and nationalism 158–159
    importance of sporting subcultures
        170–172
    media and corruption of sport 126–127
    media sport and social values 57–58
    negative features of passion in sport
        138–139
    sport and environment 85–86
    sport and social capital 111–112
    sport and traditional gender relations
        211–212
    sport as symptom of society 141–143
    sport dependence on media 52–54
    sporting pleasure: false or genuine
        192–195
    sports and politics 70–71
democracy
    changing nature of 76
    and community ownership 105–107

in Danish sport 77, 107–108
and privilege 78–80
and social capital 109
in sports 70, 73–74
in Sweden 74
demutualised communities 105–107
Denmark sport ownership 107–109
dependency on television 125
dependent development 37, 42
de-skilling 37
difference 143–144
    and sporting subculture 172
    and subculture 166
dioxin 91
diplomatic relations 70–71
discrimination 141
    homophobia 207
    and lesbianism 209
distinction 172
distinctiveness 174
dominant cultural values 53
dominant ideologies 60
donor countries 37
dual nationality 40

E
Eastern Europe, as source of soccer talent
    35
ecological degradation 86
economics
    as dimension of global flows 5
    and environmental management 88
    influence on politics in sport 72
    as motivation for migration 32, 34–35
    and sporting subculture 165
    of sport-media relationship 52
    unemployment and soccer hooliganism
        167
embodied acts 184
embodied emotions
    and pain in gymnastics 188–190
    and quest for excitement 190–192
    in sporting pleasure dome 185–187
emotional release 153
    and Swedish sport 154
emotions 182
    as role-related behaviour 186
    source of 183–185
employment rights 36–37
empowerment 214
England
    decline of influence 21
    and elite soccer 31
    and Gaelic Athletic Association 135–136
    national identity 155
    sportisation of pastimes 10–13

English basketball 39
English soccer 144
    development 119–120
entertainment value of sport 53, 55, 123
environment
    and concepts of space, place, time 118
    impact of sport on 11
    and Olympic sponsors 91–92
    sport as threat to 85–86
    and Sydney Olympics 89
    use during leisure activities 86–87
environmental guidelines for Olympics 85
environmentalism 85
environmental management 88
epistemology 101, 160
ESPN 50
established relations 7
ethics 101
    and nationalism 155
ethnic 140
ethnic group 134–135
    and nationalism 151
ethnic identity 139–140
ethnicity
    and civic identity 134
    and development of global culture 7
    and Gaelic Athletic Association 135–
        136
    and governance of global sport 18
    in media sport 58–60
    and nationalism 157–158
    and pride 144
ethnic nationalism 157
ethnic typology 134
etiquette of sport 186
Europe
    in global sports development 11
    in international soccer labour market 30
    as source of soccer talent 35
exciting significance 192, 195
exclusion
    of athletes 142
    of black athletes 141
    and Gaelic Athletic Association 135
exclusivity
    in communities 102
    of golf club memberships 95
exploitation
    of female gymnasts 36
    in Formula One racing 64
    of Nike labourers 76
    of soccer players and migration 35
    and wages of African/East European
        soccer players 37
extreme sports xix, 15

F
fans. *See also* spectators
    emotional readiness for game 187
    and passion in sport 138
Federation Internationale de Football
        Association (FIFA) 29, 156
feeling rules 186
femininity 61–62, 203
fetishism 183
five-phase model 10
football. *See also* American football; soccer
    Catalan in Barcelona 106
    Catalans and Basques 149–150
    development of English soccer 119–120
    ethnic identity of players 139–140
foreign policy 71
Formula One racing 62–66
functions of sport 122–123

G
Gaelic Athletic Association 135–136, 159
gambling 49
Gay Games xix, 212
gemeinschaft 113
gender
    concept of 202
    and contemporary global sport order
        15–17
    double standard by Nike 17
    and global order 13–15
    and host culture 37
    masculine Western influence on sport
        12
    in media sport 60–62
    and migration patterns 28
    and power 8
    and quest for excitement 192
    rights and sport 108
    and socialisation 169
    and sporting subculture 165, 176
gendered ideology 216
gendered space 205
genderhood 206–208
gender identities 207
    and image 208
gender logic 203
gender power networks 216
gender relations 202
    debate about 205–206
    role of sport in 211–212
genetics, and athletic success xiii, 19
geographical proximity 34–35
gesellschaft 113
Global Anti-Golf Movement 92
global culture 7

global flows 5
global idiom 11
globalisation
    and conflict 8
    and evolution of modern sport 10–11
    historical development of 11
    vs. homogenisation 8
    as a process 6–7
global media sports complex 4, 50–52, 183
    marketing of soccer products 4
global sport/gender order 15
golf
    and environmental issues 92–95
    and privilege 79
governance 17–18
governing bodies
    of global sport 17–18
    and politics of sport 73
    of Swedish athletes 74
government
    control of sport 71–72
    and private ownership 107
    relationship to sports 148
    and taxation of Swedish athletes 74–78
    use of sport 73
Great Britain, national identity 155
Green Bay Packers 105–106, 138
green issues 84
    and sport 88–92
green politics 85
gymnastics
    emotional responses of athletes 187
    pain embodied work 188–190

H
habitus xiv, 14
hegemony
    in cultural theory 164
    and difference in sporting subculture
        172
    and sporting subculture 175
    of Western culture 12
heterosexuality 207
hinge xiv, 184
homogeneity/heterogeneity 22
homogenisation 8, 21
    of body cultures 22
homophobia 207
homosexuality 16, 207, 212
hooliganism 166–168
host culture 37–39
human conflict 72
human rights 108, 149, 153, 160
    labour practices 4, 17
    of women 212–214

I
identity 134
    ethnic 139–140
    in imagined communities 137, 144
    multiplicity of 157
    self in time and space 119
    and soccer hooliganism 167
    and socialisation 169
    and sport 143–144
identity politics 38
ideology
    and competition 20–21
    and competition among nations 122
    democracy as 76
    as dimension of global flows 5
    dominant 60
    gendered 216
    nationalism as 151
image 208
    of women athletes 61
    of women bodybuilders 211
imagined communities 102
    and identity 144
    and national identity 154
    and sport 137–138
    sport as symbol of 135
inclusion, in communities 102
indigenous players 42
individualism 102
    and communitarianism 101
    identity and sport 143
    and sporting subculture 174
Industrial Revolution 122
    and division of labour 203
inequalities 142
    reflection in embodied acts 184
    for women in sport 209
integration 153
interdependency chains 4
    as part of globalisation process 6
intergenerational equity 84, 89
International Olympic Committee (IOC) 8
intragenerational equity 90
invented traditions 153
Ireland
    Gaelic Athletic Association 135–136
    national identity 155
Irish Nationalism 148, 152
Iron Curtain 35
Islamic culture, and women athletes 15,
        213

J
jouissance 193
journalism 50

K
knowledgeability 57

L
labour migration 18
    definition 26
    and employment rights 36–37
    patterns 27–29
labour practices 4, 17
lead poisoning 87
legal influences
    on anti-golf movement 92
    Bosman ruling 36, 38
    Factory Act of 1850 120
    Sports Act in Finland 109
    taxation of Swedish athletes 74–78
leisurewear industry 4
lesbianism 208
    and athlete sponsorship 209
liberal individualism 101–102
lifestyle
    of athletes vs. image 128
    hegemonic 118
    influence of modern 121
local talent drain 37
    in English basketball 39–40

M
mainstream sports 171
    transformation of subcultural sports to
        176–177
majority rule 74
male preserve 202
marketing. *See also* advertising
    of athletes 5
    double standard by Nike about
        women's role 17
    of Formula One racing 62–66
    of media sport 51
    of Nike footwear 4–5, 17
    of non-Western products 21–22
    and sameness 13
    and sexual orientation of athletes 16
    of soccer products 4
    and sponsorship of sports events/
        teams 56–57
martial arts 13
Marxism 72, 101, 192
masculine influence
    on body culture 14
    on development of sport 203–204
    and functions of sport 123
    in media sport 60–62
    on soccer hooliganism 167
    on Western sport 12

masculinity 203
masculinity-validating experience 203–204
mass culture 165
mass media 48
    as profit oriented organisation 49
media. *See also* global media sports complex
    and consumerism of sport in Western
        culture 125–126
    and corruption of sport 126–127
    as dimension of global flows 5
    and global flows 5
    portrayal of women athletes 14–15
    sport dependence on 52–54
    and women tennis players 214–216
mediated sport
    and gender 60–62
    growth of 48–50
    and race/ethnic relations 58–60
    and social values 57–58
membership restrictions 79
    at golf clubs 95
mercenaries 33
merchandising 50
meritocracy 78
metaphysics 101
migrant dimension 5
migrant types 33
migration
    effect on English basketball 39–42
    of labour 18
    and labour rights 36–37
    motives for 32
    as part of globalisation process 15
    soccer-specific factors motivating 34–
        35
    of talent 19, 27
    World Cup case study 29–32
military training 123
mimetic activities 191
mimetic sphere 191
mirror stage 183
modern sport 121
    and globalisation 9–10
money. *See* athlete salaries
monocausal logic 8
monopolies
    in Formula One racing 65–66
    and media control of sport 55
motility activities 191
multicausal analysis 22
multidirectional movements 7
Murdoch, Rupert 31, 38
mutuality 101, 106
mutual sport 105–107
mythology 153

N

narcissism 183
narrative techniques 57
nation 160
National Broadcasting Company (NBC) 53
national consciousness 152, 160
national culture 7, 148
    adaptation of migrant athletes 37–39
    and boxing in Cuba 121–122
    identity and migration 37
    sport as representative of 13
national identity 38, 148, 152
    concepts of 154–156
    and imagined communities 137
national integration 153
nationalism 10, 149
    concepts of 154–156
    definition 156–158
    future through sport 159–160
    and global sporting events 158–159
nationality 28
    and attitudes toward athletes 35
    and migrant athletes 38
National Parks 87
national unity 153
nationhood 152
nation-states
    and civic identity 134
    concepts of 154–156
    emerging and FIFA membership 156
    in global culture 151
    and governance of global sport 17–18
    identity through sport 151–154
    patriotism and passion in sport 138
    place of sport in 121–122
    rank order in global sport environment 20
    success and identity 19
    and use of sports in politics 70–71
natural resources 86
    management 89
nature vs. nurture 184
networks of power 18
Nike 17
    exploitation of labourers 76
    marketing of soccer products 4–5
nomadic investors 34
nomads 33
nonconformity and subculture 166
Nordic soccer players 35
normative values 101
nostalgia 153

O

Olympic Landcare Program 90

Olympics
    Catalan team 150
    control of 12–13
    England influence on 21
    global audience 52
    independence from nation-states 8
    influence of television on 53
    marketing of athletes 5
    sexual orientation test 206
    Sydney environmental guidelines 85, 89
    television rights to 50
    women athletes in 214
    women on IOC 209
Olympism 175
ontology 101
outsider relations 7
ownership 52
    of Denmark sport 107–109
    in media sport 54–57
    of sport club by community 105–107
ozone layer 84, 92

P

pain 188–190
Palestine 156, 159
Paralympics 15
particularism 8
passion 134, 136–137, 144
    negative features in sport 138–139
pastimes, sportisation of in England 10–13
patriarchal society 203, 216
patriotism 138, 153
    and American dream 128
    and global sporting events 158
performance quality xiii–xiv
peripheral nationalism 151
peripheral sports 177
phthalates 91
physical education 205
pioneers 33
place 118
    and national identity 155
plaisir 193
pleasure 182
    and embodied emotions 185–187
    jouissance 193
    plaisir 193
pluralism 72, 73
points of departure xvi–xvii
political economy 12, 72
    as motivation for migration 32
politics
    and anti-golf movement 92
    and communitarianism 101–104

politics *(continued)*
    and governance of global sport 17–18
    and green issues 85
    and media control of sport 55
    relationship to sports 70
    sports as vehicle for 70–71
    taxation of Swedish athletes 74–78
politics of sport 71–74
pollution 84
    from chemicals on golf courses 92–93
    and communitarianism 100
    dioxin 91
    from lead 87
    from motor vehicles 85, 90–91
    and national sporting performances
        148
    pesticides 93
    phthalates 91
    polyvinyl chloride (PVC) 91
polyvinyl chloride (PVC) 91
popular culture 165
power
    balance in fifth phase of sportisation 12
    challenges to Western dominance 22
    in English basketball 41
    in Formula One racing 64
    and functions of sport 123
    and globalisation 7
    and global sports development 11
    and leisure sport center development
        88
    in media sport 54–57
    networks of 18
    and ownership of mediated sports 52
    and politics of sport 72
    of Premier League soccer clubs 31
    in sporting subculture 164, 176
power networks 6
prejudice 139
print media 56
privilege 78–80
production 51
professionalism 126

R
race 18, 144
    in media sport 58–60
    rights and sport 108
    and sport 140–141
    and sporting subculture 165
racial discrimination 141
racism 139–140
    and nationalism 151–152, 157
    in United States 168

recruitment 27
    of American basketball players to
        England 40
    of elite soccer players 31
    and migration 37
recycling 84
Reebok 17
representation 51
resource management 89
retention 27
returnees 33
ritualised aggression 60
rugby 54–57
rule modifications 54

S
salaries. *See* athlete salaries
sameness 123, 143–144
    and sporting subculture 171
scopophilia 183
Scotland
    soccer 139
    socialism and national identity 148
scripts 186
seasonal migration patterns 28
second nature xiv
sectarianism 139
self-determinism 155
self-esteem 110
    and sport 143
self-expression 173–174
self-feeling 185
self-image
    and consumer culture 195
    and gender identity 208
    and nationalism 151
    and socialisation 169
settlers 33
sex, concept of 202
sexual orientation 207
    and body culture 14–15
    and marketing of sports 16
    testing for 206
Sierra Club 86
skateboarding 174–176
skilled consumers 57
soccer
    and English society image 142
    and ethnic identity 139
    FIFA and nationhood of emerging
        nations 156
    hooliganism 166–168
    hooliganism as subculture 171
    impact of migrant players 42

product marketing 4
regional divisions in Spain 149–150
television audience 125
World Cup migration case study 29–32
sociable activities 191
social capital 100, 109–111, 160
in Denmark sport 108
sport role in promoting 111–112
social class. *See* class
social communication 137
social constructionist perspectives 183
social distinctions 78–79
social inclusion 100
social inequalities 184
socialisation and sport 169–170
gender relations 205–206
socialism, and boxing in Cuba 121–122
social nature of sport 168
social values. *See* values
social welfare 71
society, sport as reflection of 141–143
sociogenesis 183
sociological model of sport 195–197
sociology of sport xviii–xix
solidarity 108
South Africa 149, 155
Soviet Union 138
space 118
and culture 127–129
gendered 205
and national identity 155
and televised sports 123–125
Spain
ethnic identity of athletes 140
regional divisions 149–150
spare-time spectrum 191
spatial divisions 118
spectacles 53–54
spectators
and pleasure 183, 192–193
soccer hooliganism as subculture 166–168
sponsorship 53, 56–57, 126
effect on subcultural sports 177
and gender identity 209
of Olympics and environmental issues 91
sport
as collective activity xv–xviii
contribution to community 104
dependence on media 52–54
evolution of modern version 10–11
as global idiom 11
historical changes to 122

masculine Western influence on 12
relationship with media 48
social contribution of 103
as social product xiii–xv
as spectacle 53–54
sporting culture
and global sporting events 158
and socialisation 170
sporting press 49
sporting subculture 164
and difference 172
importance of 170–172
pain in gymnastics 188–190
and peripheral activities 173–174
as response to cultural domination 175
sportisation 10–13
of English pastimes 190
sports industry 96
sports migration. *See* migration
sports worlds xix–xx
stakeholder model 106
statehood 152
status 78
stereotypes 58–59, 140
stress tensions 191
subculture
definition 166
and emotional response 186
importance in sports 170–172
and peripheral activities 173–174
as response to cultural domination 174–176
soccer hooliganism 166–168
in sports 164
transformation to cultural 176–177
superman myth 19
sustainability 87
sustainable development 84, 85, 90
and golf 95
and Olympic sites 89
and sport 86–88
Sweden
emotional release of sport 154
taxation of athletes 74–78
symbolic interactionism 185
symbols, of national identity 154
symbols of sport 144
and social communication 137

T
talent pipeline 27
of European soccer players 31
and local talent drain 37
taxes 74–78

technology
    as dimension of global flows 5
    and globalisation 7
    and mediated sport representation 51
    and televised sports 49
television
    and advertising 48
    advertising power 126
    benefits to sport 55–56
    and decline in social capital 111
    influence on sport 53
    and popularity of sport 124–125
    ratings 56
    and sport in time and space 123–125
    ways of representing sport 57
tennis
    athlete salaries 209–210
    portrayal of women athletes 61
    women players 214–216
tension-balances 191, 195
territoriality 148
third way 74
    Danish sport example 76–78
time 118
    and culture 127–129
    and national identity 155
    and televised sports 123–125
transformation 165
    of subcultural to cultural 176–177
transfrontier responsibility 84
transitory migration patterns 28
trust 109
typology of sports migration 32

U
UEFA 29
underdevelopment 30, 37
    effect of migrant players on 42
    of indigenous talent 38
unionisation 36
    and protection of indigenous workers
        38
United States, decline of social capital 111
universalism 8
urban communities
    and civic identity 134
    regeneration through sport 103, 108

V
values
    and global flows 5
    and media sport 57–58

normative and communitarianism 101
    and politics of sport 72
    reflected by televised sports 53
    and sport as reflection of society 142
    and sporting subculture 173
    of subculture and emotional response
        186
    traditional Islamic and women athletes
        15
violence 139
    in ancient sport 122
    and soccer hooliganism 166–168
virtual advertising 65
visual techniques 57
voluntarism, in Denmark sport 107
voyeurism 183, 193

W
wages, and employment rights 37
water consumption on golf courses 94
Western culture 165
    challenges to dominance 22
    control of global sport culture 20
    and control of Olympic Games 12–13
    cultural idioms in U.S. society 128
    and homogenised body culture 7
    influence of other cultures on 21
    influence on global sports development
        11
    role of television 124
    and self in time and space 119
Western hegemony 12
winning
    at all costs 138–139
    and American dream 128–129
    in global sports environment 18–21
    and passion 136
women
    as challenge to masculine hegemony 12
    development of sports for 13–14
    double standard by Nike regarding 17
    and gender logic 203
    marginalisation in sport 209
    portrayal in media sport 16, 60–62
    problems unique to 15
    sport performance 206
World Cup case study 29–32

X
xenophobia 151

ABOUT THE AUTHORS

Joseph A. Maguire, PhD, is a professor of sociology of sport at Loughborough University in the United Kingdom. He has more than 20 years of experience in the field and is the current president of the International Sociology of Sport Association. Dr. Maguire has published extensively on the subject of sociology of sport and lectures frequently on the topic around the world. He is the sole author of *Global Sport: Identities, Societies and Civilizations*, co-author of *Sport and Leisure in Social Thought* and a co-editor of both *The Sports Process* and *The Global Sports Arena*.

Grant Jarvie, PhD, is a professor of sport studies at the University of Stirling in Scotland. He previously held established research chairs and was appointed the first professor of sport studies in Scotland in 1997. Professor Jarvie also served as president of the British Society of Sports History. Well published in the field of sociology of sport, he most recently authored *Sport, Scotland and the Scots* and *Sport in the Making of Celtic Cultures*. He co-authored *Sport and Leisure in Social Thought* and is joint editor of the recent *Encyclopedia of British Sport*.

Louise Mansfield is a senior lecturer in the final stages of completing her PhD in sociology of sport at Loughborough University in the United Kingdom. She has been published in the *Sociology of Sport Journal* and the *JAI Series Research in the Sociology of Sport*. She has also authored book chapters on women's sport, exercise and gender relations. She serves on the editorial board of the *Sociology of Sport Journal*. Additionally, she served as chair for a presentation session at the 2000 Pre-Olympic Scientific Congress. Mansfield is a member of the British Sociological Association, the North American Society for the Sociology of Sport and the International Sociology of Sport Association.

Joseph M. Bradley, PhD, is a lecturer in sport studies at the University of Stirling in Scotland. His interests lie in sport's relationship with ethnicity, identity, race, religion and politics. Dr. Bradley is widely published in the sport studies field. His publications include *Ethnic and Religious Identity in Modern Scotland: Culture, Politics and Football*, and *Sport, Culture, Politics and Scottish Society: Irish Immigrants and the Gaelic Athletic Association*.